WISCONSIN

ON-THE-ROAD HISTORIES

WISCONSIN

Mark D. Van Ells

Interlink Books

*To my family and friends in
Wisconsin, whose hospitality
helped make this book possible.*

First published in 2009 by

INTERLINK BOOKS
An imprint of
Interlink Publishing Group, Inc.
46 Crosby Street, Northampton,
Massachusetts 01060
www.interlinkbooks.com

**Library of Congress Cataloging-in-
Publication Data**
Van Ells, Mark D. (Mark David),
1962–
Wisconsin / by Mark Van Ells.
—1st American ed.
    p. cm.—(On-the-road histories)
Includes bibliographical references.
ISBN-13: 978-1-56656-673-5
(pbk. : alk. paper)
ISBN-10: 1-56656-673-8
(pbk. : alk. paper)
1. Wisconsin—History. 2.
Wisconsin—Description and travel.
I. Title.
F581.V36 2007
977.5—dc22
2006031036

Printed and bound in Korea

Snowy Milwaukee street © Red

CONTENTS

Preface

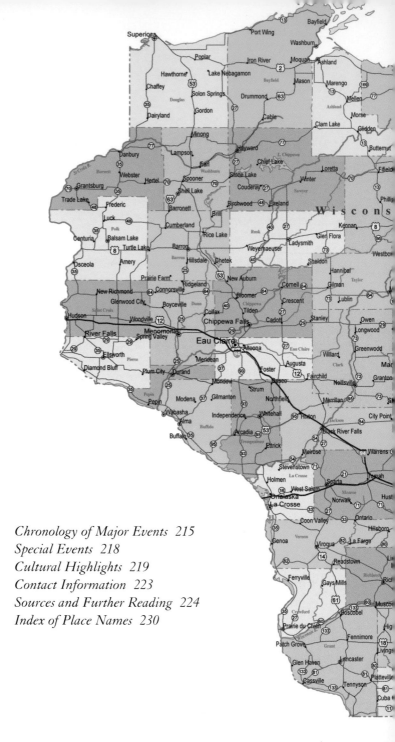

★ **State Capital**
◉ County Seat
● **Cities 500,000+**
● Cities 100,000-499,999
● Cities 50,000-99,999
● Cities 10,000-49,999
● Cities 0-9,999

‑‑‑ State Boundaries
‑‑‑ County Boundaries

Preface

Mention Wisconsin, and what comes to mind? Those funny cheddar cheese hats? Bitter winter cold? The Green Bay Packers? For many, Wisconsin is just another one of those amorphous "fly-over states" lying somewhere between the Appalachians and the Rockies. Wisconsin-born novelist Edna Ferber once described the image of her home state as being "little more than a snowy waste sprinkled with pines, Indian tepees, small inland lakes and Milwaukee German breweries, all lying somewhere in that wilderness north of Chicago." Years ago I mentioned to someone that I was born and raised in Wisconsin. "Oh, yeah, I've heard of it," he said. Then pausing for a moment, somewhat embarrassed, he asked, "What state is that in?"

Wisconsin is situated between the Great Lakes and the Mississippi River in the middle of the Midwest. It has a land area of 54,314 square miles, ranking it 26th out of the 50 states in physical size. Its population of 5,509,026 people (2004 census estimate) ranks 20th among the states. But in many ways Wisconsin is an extraordinary place. Its gently rolling hills and pastoral settings offer a countryside as beautiful as any in the world. Its cool deep woods and clear blue lakes are a paradise for outdoor enthusiasts. Wisconsin also has an interesting and illustrious history. Admitted to the Union in 1848, the Badger State recently celebrated its sesquicentennial, but the state's history goes back much further than just 150 years. Its written history goes back nearly 400 years, and human beings have inhabited the land for roughly 12,000 years. It has been home to many different cultures, all of whom have left their mark on Wisconsin life today. The Badger State has sometimes stood at the very center of national events, and produced men and women of international fame and importance.

One can read about Wisconsin's history in books, but its past can also be read on the land and in the faces of its people. Whether exploring a rustic rural road or hurtling down an urban expressway, travelers to Wisconsin pass through time as well as place. Most people do so unwittingly, but if travelers seek out the connections between the past and the world around them, their experience will be all the more meaningful and memorable. For a few tanks of gas and some modest admission fees, travelers can explore a few thousand years of history within the borders of a medium-sized state in the heartland of the United States. The experience can be interesting, rewarding, emotional, and even entertaining.

Prehistoric Wisconsin

Visitors to Wisconsin are often surprised at the variety of landscapes within the state. "I had never been to Wisconsin," wrote John Steinbeck in his classic *Travels with Charley*. "I must have considered it one big level cow pasture." But Steinbeck was pleasantly surprised as he drove into southern Wisconsin one October day in 1960:

> I never saw a country that changed so rapidly, and because I had not expected it everything I saw brought a delight. The air was rich with butter-colored sunlight, not fuzzy but crisp and clear so that every frost-gay was set off, the rising hills were not compounded, but alone and separate. It was a magic day. The land dripped with richness, the fat cows and pigs gleaming against the green, and, in smaller holdings, corn standing in little tents as corn should, and pumpkins all about.

In his glowing description of the Wisconsin countryside, Steinbeck illuminates the driving force behind all of Wisconsin's history: the land. People did not just wander into the region randomly, but were attracted by the opportunities the land offered—its rich glacial soils for farming, its abundant wildlife for fur or food, its variety of natural resources, and its geographic advantages at the center of the North American landmass. Such was the case even before recorded history. Prehistoric man was drawn to Wisconsin by the numerous possibilities of its primeval landscape.

Wisconsin's forests, prairies, hills, and lakes provide more than just a stage for the drama of the state's history. That drama is intimately connected to the land itself.

LAND AND LANDSCAPE

Geologically, Wisconsin can be divided into two primary zones. The bedrock of the northern third of the state is part of a larger geological formation known as the Canadian Shield, a horseshoe-shaped region that extends from Labrador to northwestern Canada and forms the core of the North American continent. The formation dips into the northern United States, and includes the Adirondacks in New York as well as the northern Great Lakes region. The rocks of the Canadian Shield were formed during the Precambrian geologic era, and consist primarily of igneous and metamorphic rocks such as granite, basalt, and quartzite. Some of the oldest surface rocks in the world are found on the Canadian Shield. Some rocks in northern Wisconsin were formed approximately two billion years ago during the mid-Precambrian period.

About 1.1 billion years ago, a huge volcanic rift formed in the heart of the North American continent, creating a vast depression in the bedrock now occupied by Lake Superior—by surface area, the largest freshwater lake in the world. The bedrock of northern Wisconsin contains numerous minerals of use to humans, such as iron ore, copper, and zinc. Gold and silver have also been found in small quantities. Though worn down by eons of erosion and glaciation, the landscape of northern Wisconsin is generally more hilly and of higher elevation than the rest of the state. The headwaters of many of the state's most important rivers, such as the Wolf, Black, Chippewa, and Wisconsin, originate on the Canadian Shield. Rapids and waterfalls are common as these rivers flow off the shield and onto lower and younger bedrock formations to the south, as indicated by city names such as Wisconsin Rapids or Chippewa Falls. Ancient igneous and metamorphic bedrock formations are sometimes found south of the Canadian Shield. The Baraboo Range in Sauk and Columbia Counties, for example, is an island of quartzite surrounded by the younger sedimentary rocks of southern Wisconsin.

The Canadian Shield was once located much closer to the equator. Warm, shallow seas on the edge of the continent frequently covered most of what is now southern and western Wisconsin. Over millions of years, layers of sediment washed off the Canadian Shield, built up off the coasts, and hardened. Sedimentary rocks in Wisconsin are stratified, with sandstone composing the lowest layers, and limestone—an admixture of sea sediments and the fossilized remains of ancient coral reefs—closer to the top. A ridge of dolomite—a particularly sturdy form of limestone—runs across eastern Wisconsin from the Illinois border to Door County before submerging into Lake Michigan. Wisconsin's dolomite ridge is part of a much larger formation known as the Niagara Escarpment, over which Niagara Falls on the New York–Ontario border flows. Over time, present-day Wisconsin drifted northward and rose above sea level, and limestone and sandstone deposits eroded away. This erosion was uneven; in some areas hard limestone remained atop the sandstone, in others limestone washed away to expose sandstone. Sandstone bluffs are common in much of central Wisconsin. Travelers along Interstate 90 will note many such bluffs in the area of Camp Douglas in Juneau County. The Wisconsin Dells, one of the most amazing and picturesque landscapes in the Midwest, are the most notable example of Wisconsin's sandstone formations.

The last major geologic event to shape Wisconsin's landscape was glaciation. During the Ice Age, glaciers crept southward from the arctic regions into portions of the present-day United States. Wisconsin has been through several periods of glaciation, the earliest occurring perhaps more than one million years ago. The most recent episode, which began about 25,000 years ago, is known as the Wisconsin Glaciation because its effects on the landscape are especially profound in the Badger State. During the Wisconsin Glaciation, most of the state was covered by six glacial lobes of varying size—Superior, Chippewa, Wisconsin Valley, Langlade, Green Bay, and Lake Michigan. In some parts of Wisconsin the ice was two miles thick. The glaciers carried with them tons of material known as *till* (a combination of earth, rock, sand, and clay) and deposited it on top of the bedrock once they melted away.

The glaciers left several distinct landforms in their wake that are clearly evident on the Wisconsin landscape today. A *moraine* is a ridge of till deposits that formed at the edges of glaciers, marking where the ice sheets stopped their advances. Moraines also formed between glacial lobes. A *drumlin* is an elongated hill created when earth and rock

were trapped between the moving glacier and the underlying terrain. Roughly 5,000 drumlins have been mapped in Wisconsin; the Wisconsin State Capitol in Madison sits atop one of them. Some of the best examples of drumlins in the world can be found near Campbellsport in Fond du Lac County. Drumlins are clearly evident to travelers on Interstate 94 between Waukesha and Madison. An *esker* is a snake-like gravel deposit formed by rivers flowing underneath a glacier. Sadly, most eskers have been dug up for gravel, and are very rare today. A *kame* is a conical hill formed when glacial till fell into the cracks and crevices of a melting glacier. *Kettle holes* are the result of ice chunks being buried in glacial till deposits. When the ice melted, it created a depression in the land in which a lake or pond formed. Many of the lakes in northern Wisconsin, so vital to the tourist industry of that region today, are kettle hole lakes.

Whether covered by ice or not, every part of Wisconsin was shaped by the Ice Age. Meltwaters from the glaciers flowed away from the ice margins, creating flat outwash plains. Located in the heart of Wisconsin was a large lake formed by meltwater from the great ice sheets. Many of the sandstone bluffs in central Wisconsin today were once islands in what geologists call Glacial Lake Wisconsin. The combination of outwash plains and glacial lake bed created Wisconsin's Central Plain, a region flatter and sandier than most parts of the state. Many of Wisconsin's most important river valleys, like those of the Chippewa, Black, and Wisconsin Rivers, were deepened by glacial meltwaters roaring toward the Mississippi River and on to the Gulf of Mexico. One region that was never glaciated is the so-called Driftless Area of southwestern Wisconsin. The region avoided glaciation for two reasons. First, the Lake Superior basin steered the flow of the glacial ice westward into present-day Minnesota and toward the Great Plains. At the same time, the Lake Michigan lowland channeled the flow of ice eastward. With ice flow diverted, glaciers avoided southwest Wisconsin. As a result, the topography of the Driftless Area is far more varied than that of the rest of the state. In most of Wisconsin, the glaciers leveled the hills and

The Wisconsin Dells © *Krzysztof Wiktor*

filled in the valleys, but not in the Driftless Area. The landscape of southwestern Wisconsin is characterized by long limestone ridges with deep valleys and ravines cut by millions of years of erosion. It is probable that much of Wisconsin looked like the Driftless Area before glaciation. During the Ice Age, the Driftless Area was cold, barren, and windswept. The howling winds deposited a blanket of fine soil known as *loess*—up to sixteen feet deep in some places.

By about 12,000 years ago, the glaciers started to retreat. The last glaciers left Wisconsin only about 7,000 years ago. Glacial meltwaters formed the Great Lakes, which initially flowed southward into the Mississippi River. As the glaciers disappeared, land depressed under tons of glacial ice slowly began to rise. This phenomenon, which geologists call *glacial rebound*, occasionally creates small-scale earthquakes in Wisconsin even today. As the land rose and the glaciers continued their retreat northward, the waters of the Great Lakes began to flow northeastward into the St. Lawrence River Valley of Canada instead of the Mississippi.

Located in the center of North America, Wisconsin has a continental climate characterized by cold winters and warm summers. Westerly winds from the Pacific—dried by the Rocky Mountains—dominate Wisconsin's weather. However, the Great Plains channel warm air from the Gulf of Mexico and cold air masses from the Arctic into the Badger State, giving Wisconsin its changeable climate. As a result, travelers to Wisconsin can experience a great variety of weather conditions. Wisconsin is infamous for its long, harsh winters. It is a reputation well deserved. Visiting the state on a January day, one might question whether the Ice Age ever really ended in Wisconsin. The coldest temperature ever recorded in Wisconsin was -54°F (-47.7°C) in Danbury in 1922. Winter snowfall is common, especially along the shores of the Great Lakes. Residents of the Lake Superior shoreline experience on average 140 days of snow cover every year. During the summer months, prevailing winds carry warm humid air from the Gulf of Mexico northward into Wisconsin. In southern Wisconsin, summer high temperatures average above 80° F (26.6°C), while in northern Wisconsin they average about 75°F (23.6°C). Extreme temperatures can occur, however.

The highest temperature ever recorded in the Badger State was 114°F (45.5°C) at Wisconsin Dells in 1936. When this warm air collides with cold air from the north, violent storms often occur. Lines of severe thunderstorms containing high winds, heavy rain, hail, and deadly lightning frequently rake the Badger State in spring and summer. On occasion there are tornadoes, some of which can be quite destructive. In 1984, a tornado destroyed 90 percent of the village of Barneveld in Iowa County and killed nine people. An even more devastating tornado stuck New Richmond in 1899, killing 112 and injuring 146. On average, Wisconsin experiences about 19 tornadoes a year.

Climate strongly affects the state's natural vegetation. Wisconsin is divided into distinct northern and southern vegetation regions. Between the two is a narrow zone of tension, running roughly from Eau Claire in the west to Sheboygan in the east. Before the advent of European settlement and agriculture, most of Wisconsin north of the tension zone was covered by a mixed conifer-hardwood forest. Numerous types of evergreens were found in the region, including spruce, fir, cedar, hemlock, tamarack, and various kinds of pine, including the majestic white pine. Hardwoods commonly found in northern Wisconsin forests included varieties of birch, maple, and poplar. Along the shores of Lake Superior, the boreal forest environment once predominated, characterized by balsam fir and white spruce. The region south of the tension zone consisted of hardwood forest and prairie environments. Wisconsin's southern hardwood forests included trees such as sugar maple, elm, hickory, oak, and basswood. Tall grass prairies were found in many parts of southern and western Wisconsin. Fire greatly shaped the environment of southern Wisconsin. On some prairies, stands of widely scattered, fire-resistant oak trees stood, known as oak savannas. The pre-settlement vegetation was severely altered by the arrival of Euro-American settlers in the nineteenth century; the forests and prairies of the south were carved up into farmland, and the northern woods were hacked down for lumber. Only small remnants of Wisconsin's ancient ecosystems remain.

White pines on the Menominee Reservation. A man stands next to the trees on the lefthand side of the image.

THE FIRST WISCONSINITES

Most archaeologists believe that the first human beings migrated to the New World during the last Ice Age. As the glaciers grew they consumed more and more of the planet's water. Sea level lowered and a "land bridge" opened between North America and Asia, allowing free passage between the two continents. At the time of the Ice Age, Siberia was inhabited by small bands of hunting and gathering peoples. It is believed that as game animals crossed over the land bridge from Asia into North America, the Siberian hunters followed them eastward into the New World. Over several thousand years these earliest of Americans gradually trekked southward into the interior of the continent, inhabiting lands never before seen by human beings. Sea level rose when the glaciers melted, once again separating the continents. Those people living in

Starting Points

Wisconsin is home to many excellent museums that tell the Badger State's history from cover to cover.

Wisconsin Historical Museum

30 North Carroll Street, Madison, WI 53703

(608) 264-6555

www.wisconsinhistory.org/museum/

This is the logical place to start. The State Historical Museum has a big job—tell the tale of Wisconsin's history—which it does very well. The second floor explores Wisconsin's Native Americans and contact with Europeans. The third and fourth floors discuss the state's ethnic diversity, economic development, and political innovations. The first floor is reserved for changing exhibitions.

Milwaukee Public Museum

800 West Wells Street, Milwaukee, WI 53233

(414) 278-2728

www.mpm.edu

This is one of the finest museums in the US today. Although not focused specifically on history, the museum contains many excellent exhibits on Wisconsin's past, most notably "A Tribute to Survival" about Wisconsin's Native Americans, and "The Streets of Old Milwaukee," which has remained one of the museum's most popular features since its debut in 1965.

Neville Public Museum

210 Museum Place, Green Bay, WI 54303

(920) 448-4458

www.nevillepublicmuseum.org

The museum's permanent history exhibit traces the development of Wisconsin's oldest city from the Ice Age (visitors can walk through a simulated glacier) to the present.

Wisconsin Veterans Museum

30 West Mifflin Street, Madison, WI 53703

(608) 267-1799

museum.dva.state.wi.us

This facility, located kitty-corner from the Wisconsin Historical Museum, is one of the nation's top military museums and explores the Badger State's war record from the Civil War to the Persian Gulf. In addition to its Madison location, the museum maintains satellite facilities at the Wisconsin Veterans Home in Waupaca County and at Camp Williams/Volk Field, a military base near Camp Douglas. Travelers can also check out the Wisconsin Veterans Memorial Catalog, a searchable database of monuments and memorials dedicated to Wisconsin veterans, found on the museum's website.

North America were then cut off from the rest of the world and began their own social and cultural evolution. These peoples were the ancestors of the Native Americans, whom Europeans met when they "discovered" America thousands of years later. Exactly when the first humans arrived in the Americas is not clear. Some archaeologists believe the human habitation of America began as early as 40,000 years ago; others suggest it was as recent as 15,000 years ago.

The human habitation of present-day Wisconsin began about 12,000 years ago. As the glaciers began to retreat to the north, small bands of people known to archaeologists as Paleo-Indians pressed into Wisconsin from the south or southwest, living along the margins of the glaciers. As the ice sheets crept ever northward, so did the Paleo-Indians. Very little is known about the everyday lives of these very first Wisconsinites. Wisconsin was then a vast frozen tundra, and the population density was probably very low, since the subarctic environment was unable to support a large population. Paleo-Indian archaeological sites are rare, and those that have been uncovered yield only fragmentary clues about the lives of these people. The Paleo-Indians were nomadic, traveling in small bands in search of game and gathering opportunities. Occasionally Paleo-Indian bands would congregate, probably for trade and to seek marriage outside of their small bands. Archaeologists have discovered hundreds of artifacts from one such meeting place along the banks of the Yahara River near Madison. Evidence of their hunting culture survives in the form of chipped stone spearpoints that have been unearthed across the Badger State. Many spearpoints are made of native stones, most notably Hixton silicified sandstone. Scores of stone quarries dating back 10,000 years are still visible at the Silver Mound, a protected archaeological site in Jackson County. Other Paleo-Indian spearpoints found in Wisconsin are made of stones traced to faraway places such as Indiana and the Dakotas, suggesting the existence of ancient trade links between the earliest Americans.

Wisconsin's Paleo-Indians hunted a variety of animals. Some species are familiar today but no longer found in Wisconsin, such as the caribou and the musk ox. But they also hunted many animals that are now extinct, including ancient species of bison and camel and a giant variety of beaver.

It also appears that the Paleo-Indians hunted mastodons and woolly mammoth. These creatures were hairy, cold-weather cousins of modern-day elephants, some of which stood more than ten feet tall. The remains of several ancient pachyderms have been found in the Badger State. After a severe storm passed over their farm near Boaz in Richland County in 1897, four boys discovered the bones of a mastodon protruding from an eroded stream bank. A spearpoint found with the remains suggested that humans may have killed the animal. The "Boaz mastodon" was the first pachyderm skeleton found in Wisconsin, and is presently on display at the University of Wisconsin Geology Museum in Madison. In 1964, a Kenosha County farmer named Frank Schaefer accidentally unearthed the skeleton of a woolly mammoth while digging a trench on his property. The mammoth bones contained numerous cut marks, suggesting a thorough butchering. The "Schaefer mammoth" is believed to be 12,000 years old. Mammoth remains have been found in other areas in Kenosha County, and can be viewed today in the Kenosha Public Museum. Exactly why the mammoth, mastodon, and other so-called megafauna became extinct is not known. Noting that the extinction of many species roughly coincides with the arrival of humans, some archaeologists speculate overhunting by Paleo-Indians may have led to their demise. It may be the case, however, that as the glaciers receded and the region's climate grew warmer, the great beasts may have been unable to adjust to the rapidly changing environmental conditions.

As the climate warmed, Wisconsin became home to a greater variety of flora and fauna, and Wisconsin's native peoples adapted to the changing conditions. A subtle transformation to a more complex way of life took place after 8000 BCE that archaeologists have labeled the Archaic period. Archaic societies still relied on hunting and gathering, but their economic activities became more diversified. With the megafauna extinct, hunters began to target smaller game, such as elk and deer in the hardwood forests and prairies of southern Wisconsin, and moose and caribou in pine forests of the north. Fishing grew in importance to the Archaic peoples' diet, as did plant foods such as nuts and seeds. Beginning about 3000 BCE, Archaic peoples began to utilize copper. Because copper is a relatively soft metal, they could

Must-See Sites: Ice Age National Scenic Trail

The Ice Age National Scenic Trail, a cooperative effort between the National Park Service, the Wisconsin Department of Natural Resources, and the Ice Age Park and Trail Foundation, guides visitors through the state's unique glacial landscapes. The trail resulted from the vision of Raymond Zillmer, a Milwaukee lawyer and outdoor enthusiast who campaigned vigorously to preserve the state's glacial heritage.

The Ice Age Trail is a work in progress, at present approximately 300 miles long. Once completed, it will snake more than 1,000 miles through 30 counties, following the margins of the last episode of glaciation from Door County to the Minnesota border. Along the trail, hikers can see some of the best examples of glacial formations in the world, as well as remnants of outwash plains, glacial lakes, and other glacial landforms. Highlights include:

Kettle Moraine State Forest—The Kettle Moraine is a highland that runs through eastern Wisconsin. It was the contact point between the Lake Michigan and Green Bay glacial lobes, and was formed from the deposits of a river of meltwater that flowed between the glaciers.

Devil's Lake—The lake was a segment of the Wisconsin River until glaciers closed off either end of the steep quartzite canyon through which the river flowed. Now a state park, the area illustrates the stark contrast between glaciated and non-glaciated landscapes.

Wisconsin Dells—These spectacular sandstone bluffs on the banks of the Wisconsin River were carved by water rushing from Glacial Lake Wisconsin to the Mississippi River and the sea. Several companies operate boat tours of the dells, including the "Wisconsin Ducks"—World War II amphibious vehicles modified to provide access to this unforgettable region.

Timm's Hill—Part of a terminal moraine in Taylor County, it is the highest point in Wisconsin.

Dells of the St. Croix—Powerful currents of meltwater carved a deep gorge in the hard bedrock in the St. Croix River along the Wisconsin– Minnesota border. Today part of Interstate State Park, the St. Croix dells are noted for their glacial potholes—round shafts drilled into the bedrock caused by rocks getting caught in swirling eddies along the riverbank.

The best place to begin a journey on the Ice Age Trail is at one of the Ice Age interpretive centers located in the Kettle Moraine State Forest in Sheboygan County and at Interstate State Park in Polk County.

Contact Information
Ice Age Park and Trail Foundation
207 East Buffalo Street Suite 215, Milwaukee, WI 53202-5721
(414) 278-8518
www.iceagetrail.org

Ice Age National Scenic Trail
700 Rayovac Drive, Suite 100, Madison, WI 53711
(608) 441-5610
www.nps.gov/iat

fashion it into a wide range of implements, such as knives, fishhooks, and spearpoints. The source of copper was the Keweenaw Peninsula of northern Michigan, where nearly pure veins of copper appeared at the surface. People mined the copper by heating it with fire, then cooling it rapidly, causing the rock to crack and split. It was then cold-hammered into the desired instruments. Eastern Wisconsin seems to have been the center of the "Old Copper" cultural complex that thrived in the Great Lakes region from 3000 BCE to 1200 BCE. Archaic peoples also developed distinctive burial practices. The dead were typically interred in natural knolls or flat graves. Some corpses were covered with a mineral substance known as red ochre, and many were buried with stone and copper implements, suggesting a concept of an afterlife, as well as a sense of spirituality and ceremonialism. Some graves contain more goods than others, indicating social stratification within Archaic societies. As with the Paleo-Indians, archaeological sites related to Archaic peoples are rare. Not only did the population remain small, but the water levels of the Great Lakes were far lower during much of the Archaic period than they are today. Given the tendency of Archaic peoples to live along bodies of water, it seems probable that many remnants of Archaic societies lie beneath the waves of the lakes.

Several new cultural and technological developments occurred after 500 BCE, leading to a phase archaeologists call the Woodland period. Woodland peoples began to manufacture fabrics and pottery, for example. Ceramic artifacts such as pots, bowls, and pipes often contain distinctive designs, suggesting cultural diversity among native peoples as well as a sense of artistry. Several rock paintings and carvings—depicting humans and animals—can also be found in parts of Wisconsin. Roche-A-Cri State Park in Adams County is the site of a picturesque sandstone bluff and is the only public place in the state were visitors can view Native American rock art. The Woodland period also saw the beginning of agriculture in Wisconsin, though hunting and gathering remained the predominant economic activities.

The advent of agriculture seems to have precipitated a rise in population and the increasing propensity to settle in semi-permanent villages. Such villages were small—

probably fewer than 100 people—and their inhabitants migrated between seasonal village sites. The growing population increased the competition for land and hunting grounds, which apparently stimulated conflicts between Wisconsin's Woodland peoples. Warfare appears to have been a regular feature of Woodland life. Village sites were often protected by wooden stockades. Human remains dating to the period have been found with arrow and spear points embedded in them, and some skulls bear marks that suggest scalping.

During the middle Woodland period, the peoples of present-day Wisconsin interacted with the Hopewell culture of the Ohio River Valley. Hopewell culture is known for its massive earthworks, extensive trade links, and dynamic culture. After 200 BCE, native people in Wisconsin began to bury deceased leaders in conical burial mounds in the Hopewell style. Such graves contained exotic trade goods from distant parts of North America, like seashells from the Gulf of Mexico and obsidian from the Yellowstone region of Wyoming. They also contain the distinctive works of Hopewellian artisans, including beads, finely crafted pottery, and numerous kinds of carvings, including funeral masks.

Between 800 and 1200 CE, Wisconsin's Woodland peoples constructed mounds in specific images, or effigies. The so-called effigy mound culture was unique to southern and central Wisconsin and adjacent areas of Minnesota, Iowa, and Illinois. Some effigies clearly depict animals such as birds, bear, and deer. Others are more ambiguous, and appear to be turtles, lizards, and a variety of other creatures. A few are of human figures. Frequently accompanying effigy mounds are numerous conical, oval, and elongated mounds. Most mounds contain human burials, but many do not. Effigy mounds are no higher than a few feet, and most are less than 100 feet in length. Some can be quite large, however. One bird mound in Richland County— since destroyed by farming—had a wingspan of a quarter mile. The mounds have long puzzled and fascinated all who have seen them. Unwilling to believe that Native Americans could have produced such works, early Euro-American settlers ascribed the effigy mounds—as well as nearly all Indian mounds—to such peoples as the Lost

Tribes of Israel, refugees from the lost continent of Atlantis, Hindus from South Asia, and an extinct race of giants.

Most archaeologists today believe the mounds were the sites of religious ceremonies. The effigy mounds are located in areas that seem to have had spiritual significance for their creators. They are often situated in particularly scenic locations, such as atop high ground overlooking lakes and rivers. They are also found near the sites of natural springs and food resources. According to one theory, the effigies were involved in religious rituals designed to maintain a balance in nature. Bird mounds represent the "upper world" in the cosmology of many native peoples, for example, while land animals and lizard-like "water spirits" represent the "lower world." One category might prevail at a particular mound cluster, but both are almost always present, suggesting a desire to create natural harmony. The effigies might also represent tribal clan symbols. Even today, many of Wisconsin's Native Americans consider the effigy mounds to be sacred.

Around 1000 CE, the Woodland lifeway in southern Wisconsin was giving way to a new cultural tradition known as Oneota, or Upper Mississippian. Oneota peoples lived mainly in the river valleys and lakeshores of the southern half of Wisconsin, especially in the vicinity of Lake Winnebago and along the Mississippi River. An agricultural people, the Oneota lived in larger and more permanent villages than previously seen in Wisconsin; some villages may have contained up to 90 families. These villages consisted of wooden structures in a variety of shapes, including circular, rectangular, and club-shaped buildings. Some structures were up to 10 feet wide and 30 feet long. Deep pits in the earth provided storage for food and other supplies. By about 1200, Oneota culture extended from the western shore of Lake Michigan to the Missouri River Valley in present-day Kansas and Nebraska. The origins of Oneota culture are not clear. Some speculate that Oneota peoples may have migrated into Wisconsin, most likely from the south. Others suggest they represented a cultural and technological evolution among existing Wisconsin Woodland peoples. Their relationship to the Native Americans of the historic period is also unclear. Because of similarities between Oneota artifacts and those of several tribes of historic times, many archaeologists speculate that the Oneota may be the ancestors of Siouan-speaking peoples, such as the Ho-Chunk who inhabited much of central Wisconsin at the time of European contact. Oneota culture made little headway in northern Wisconsin. The harsh climate and poor soils of that region inhibited the development of agriculture, and the Woodland lifeway persisted into the historic period.

Also emerging in Wisconsin around the year 1000 are peoples of Middle Mississippian culture, so called because of its origins in the central Mississippi River Valley around 800. It was characterized by large stockaded villages and an agricultural economy. The Mississippians also developed vast trade networks that stretched from the Appalachians to the Rockies. The largest center of Mississippian culture was Cahokia near present-day East St. Louis, Illinois. At its height, Cahokia had a population of perhaps 20,000, making it one of the largest cities in the world at the time. Some speculate that it may have been the center of the first great empire in North America, though its political structure is unknown. The city of Cahokia was dominated by stepped, flat-top earthen pyramids, reminiscent of the Maya and Aztec of Central America. One such pyramid at Cahokia covered sixteen acres. From Cahokia, Mississippian culture spread northward along major waterways.

Several Mississippian sites have been identified in Wisconsin. The largest is Aztalan, located on the Crawfish River—a tributary of the Rock River—in Jefferson County. Named by white settlers because they believed it related to the Aztecs of Mexico, the village emerged about the year 1000 and at its peak had a population of perhaps 500. The site today is Aztalan State Park, and features reconstructions of several mounds as well as the wooden stockade fence that surrounded the village. Mississippian sites have also been found in other parts of Wisconsin. A pyramid mound is located in the present-day village of Trempealeau on the Mississippi River, for example. The Trempealeau outpost was possibly established to gain access to the Hixton sandstone—found in substantial amounts at Cahokia—that was quarried nearby. For reasons still unknown, Cahokia declined after 1200. When it did, Aztalan and other Mississippian outposts in Wisconsin were abandoned.

Must-See Sites: Effigy Mounds

The effigy mound culture that emerged around the year 800 was unique to southern Wisconsin and nearby areas. According to one estimate, 80 percent of the effigy mounds that existed before Euro-American settlement have been destroyed by farming and urban development. Many examples still exist, of course, and they are one of the Badger State's unique treasures. Among the best surviving examples:

High Cliff State Park

N7630 State Park Rd., Sherwood, WI 54169
(920) 989-1106
www.dnr.state.wi.us
Located on a high bluff overlooking Lake Winnebago, the High Cliff mounds highlight the tendency of effigy-mound builders to locate their mounds in scenic locations.

Man Mound County Park

Man Mound Road, Baraboo, WI
The only surviving mound in the shape of the human figure. Though partially destroyed by road construction, most of the mound is still intact.

Mendota State Hospital Mound Group

Mendota Mental Health Institute
301 Troy Drive, Madison, WI 53704
(608) 301-1000
www.dhfs.state.wi.us/MH_Mendota/Mendota/Mendota.htm
The Mendota hospital grounds contain some the best preserved mounds in the state, including a bird effigy with a wingspan of 624 feet.

Panther Intaglio

State Highway 26, Fort Atkinson, WI
Located near downtown on the north side of the Rock River, this is the only surviving intaglio (an effigy engraved into the ground rather than built up into mound form). Intaglios are very rare. Only about a dozen were ever recorded in Wisconsin.

Wyalusing State Park

13081 State Park Lane, Bagley WI 53801
(608) 996-2261
www.dnr.state.wi.us
A high concentration of mounds located at the strategic and scenic confluence of the Wisconsin and Mississippi Rivers.

Although the effigy mound culture was centered in Wisconsin, Effigy Mounds National Monument, which boasts 31 effigy mounds and more than 100 other kinds of Indian mounds, is located in Iowa across the Mississippi River from Prairie du Chien.

For a complete list of surviving Indian mounds in Wisconsin, see Robert A. Birmingham and Leslie E. Eisenberg, Indian Mounds of Wisconsin (Madison: University of Wisconsin Press, 2000).

NATIVE PEOPLES ON THE EVE OF CONTACT

On the eve of European contact in the seventeenth century, Wisconsin was home to three Indian nations, numbering perhaps 60,000 to 70,000 people, with a fourth encroaching from the northeast. The Menominee lived in northeastern Wisconsin, ranging from the shores of Green Bay southward along the Lake Michigan shoreline as far south as present-day Milwaukee. Part of the Algonkian cultural and linguistic family, the Menominee are believed to have lived in Wisconsin for more than 5,000 years, and are probably the state's oldest continuous residents. Inhabiting much of central and southern Wisconsin was the Ho-Chunk Nation, long known to their Algonkian neighbors as the Winnebago, a term that meant "people of the stinking waters," perhaps due to the area's many marshlands. Though the lands of the Ho-Chunk did indeed contain swamps, it also held some of Wisconsin's best agricultural lands and hunting grounds. The Ho-Chunk were a Souian-speaking people, as were their relatives to the north and west, the Mdewakanton band of the Dakota, long known to Euro-Americans as the Santee Sioux. Although the Dakota are associated in the popular mind today with life on the Great Plains, in the seventeenth century many Dakota peoples lived in the woodlands of the western Great Lakes, including northwestern Wisconsin. Entering Wisconsin after 1600 was the Algonkian-speaking Ojibwe, also known as the Chippewa. According to tribal oral tradition, the Ojibwe had once lived along the Atlantic seaboard, but over the course of centuries had gradually migrated westward, reaching Wisconsin during the seventeenth century.

Although Wisconsin's native nations all had distinctive cultures, they also shared many traits. Religious beliefs and practices are one example. Native Americans believed that the world was populated with a great number of spirits. Animals had spirits, which hunters were required to honor. So did trees and plants. The sun and the moon were also considered spirits, as were natural phenomena such as thunder, lightning, and wind. Indian peoples conducted dances and other rituals to please the spirits, and carried charms and other personal items to ward off disease and injury. Offerings of tobacco were meant to invoke the intervention of spirits. There were evil spirits as well as good, including ghosts, malevolent water spirits, a giant cannibal known as a *windigo* that stalked the winter woods, and a trickster (*manabush* in Menominee) who performed both good and evil. Linking the world together was a "great spirit"—not a God in the Judeo-Christian sense but rather a life force animating the universe. Souian-speaking people referred to this great spirit as the *wakan tanka*; in Algonkian languages it was the *manitou*. The spiritual affairs of the community were the province of a shaman. Because of their great spiritual powers, shamans were often the most important and powerful members of the community. The shaman was responsible for the interpretation of dreams and the conduct of dances and various religious practices. With the arrival of Europeans, many Native Americans became Christians, either voluntarily or by force. However, many others remained faithful to traditional beliefs or blended them with Christianity. Pre-European religious beliefs still have wide currency with Wisconsin Indians today.

The political and social organization of native peoples in Wisconsin was also similar. Each nation was divided into clans, the members of which were believed to be descended from a common animal ancestor. Clans typically had a specific function within the larger group. The Menominee, for example, had 34 clans organized into five major divisions: bear (civil administration), eagle (military affairs), moose (internal security), wolf (hunting), and crane (builders). Among the Ho-Chunk, the thunderbird clan provided leadership. One's clan was determined patrilinially, and people were prohibited from marrying within their own clan. Wisconsin's Indian nations had little in the way of centralized authority. The primary job of the headmen, or chiefs, was to maintain order within the tribe. There were many different kinds of chiefs, including those responsible for civil affairs and those responsible for warfare. Indian chiefs were not kings or princes in the European fashion, but rather ruled only with the consent of tribal members. Major decisions were typically made through tribal councils after thorough deliberations. Tribes often formed alliances or joined together in confederations. Men and women had clearly defined gender roles. Men

Native American Heritage

Arvid W. Miller Memorial Library/Museum

N8510 Mo-He-Con-Nuck Road, Bowler, WI 54416
The museum of the Stockbridge-Munsee Indians chronicles the tribe's long history from the Massachusetts and New York colonial frontiers to their arrival in Wisconsin in the 1830s.

Forest County Potawatomi Historical/Cultural Center

5460 Everybody's Road, Crandon, WI 54520
(800) 960-5479
Opened in 2002, the museum covers the history of the Potawatomi Nation, a tribe that migrated into Wisconsin during the seventeenth century.

Lac du Flambeau Band of Lake Superior Chippewa Heritage Tour

PO Box 67, Lac du Flambeau, WI 54538
(715) 588-3303
Historical sites on the Lac du Flambeau reservation include Waswagoning, a recreated Ojibwe village of the seventeenth century, and the George W. Brown, Jr. Museum and Cultural Center, which displays a vast array of Ojibwe artifacts.

Menominee Heritage Tour

Phone: (715) 799-5217
The 46-mile auto tour includes Spirit Rock (a symbol of tribal survival), tribal war memorials, the Menominee Logging Museum (see Chapter 5), and the reservation's natural beauty. Call the number above for tour map.

Oneida Nation Museum

866 EE Road, PO Box 365, Oneida, WI 54155
(920) 869-2768
A group of the Oneida Nation, a member of the once-powerful Iroquois Confederacy of New York State, settled in Wisconsin during the 1830s. Tours of the reservation are also available. Call (920) 490-2452 for tour information.

For information about pow-wows and other cultural events, contact:

Native American Tourism of Wisconsin

PO Box 9 , Lac du Flambeau, WI 54538
(715) 588-3324 x109
natow.org/natow-bin/directory.cgi

were responsible for hunting, fishing, and diplomacy with other tribes. Women were responsible for child rearing, agriculture, and gathering. Though the chiefs were men, women's voices were respected in tribal councils.

Warfare greatly shaped the lives of Wisconsin's native peoples. Conflicts arose frequently between nations, typically concerning hunting territories. Native American warfare was much different than it was in Europe. It was typically small in scope, and involved small bands of warriors raiding an enemy village. The warrior leading the party had to first obtain permission from the war chief. War parties were typically smaller than 50 men, who fought as individuals rather than in mass formations. Once a war had been started, warriors sought revenge for losses inflicted on the families and their tribes. Because these were essentially blood feuds, women and children of the enemy tribe were considered fair targets. Across much of North America, in battle an Indian warrior often removed the scalp of an enemy warrior he had killed, which was then displayed in the village of the victor. Warriors who killed an enemy were awarded an eagle feather, which he then wore in his hair. To keep conflicts limited, Indian peoples also sought ways to end the cycle of killing. Under the practice of "covering the dead," the warrior who killed a member of an enemy tribe could offer gifts to the deceased person's family, such as food, clothing, or weapons. If the family accepted the gifts, the killing was forgiven. If not, the cycle of violence would continue. All of the tribe's adult men were expected to participate in warfare; indeed, a man's social status usually involved his skills in battle. Even today, military service is highly respected among Wisconsin's Native American peoples.

The economies of Wisconsin's Native Americans varied depending on geography. In southern Wisconsin, agriculture was an important part of the economy. Wisconsin's first farmers grew a variety of crops, including beans, squash, tobacco, and most important, corn, which was planted in widely separated mounds. Native Americans cleared farm lands using controlled fires, which also added nutrients to the soil. Once the soil began to give out, they would move their fields to another location. Northern Wisconsin's colder climate and poor soil

Wooded path in Wisconsin © *Vicki France*

precluded any substantial agriculture. In all parts of the
state, hunting and gathering remained the most important
economic activity. Deer was the most commonly hunted
animal, but moose, elk, and a variety of other animals were
also sought. Hunters often used fire to drive game or to
create open spaces to attract it. Bear were killed only
occasionally and with great ceremony, since native peoples
believed them to be of spiritual significance. Wisconsin's
lakes also teemed with fish, including perch, walleye, and
sturgeon. The Ojibwe preferred to fish in the spring and at
night, using torches to attract and illuminate their quarry.
Indian women gathered a wide variety of plants from the
wild, including cranberries, blueberries, raspberries,
grapes, wild potatoes, and a wide variety of nuts. Nature
also provided many herbs, roots, and barks used as
medicines. In the spring, native peoples tapped the maple

trees for maple sugar. The harvesting of wild rice was also important, especially in the northern part of the state.

Native peoples in Wisconsin lived in small villages, but also moved according to the rhythms of the seasons. The typical dwelling was a wigwam, a circular or oval structure made of tree saplings and bark, in which lived the nuclear family and possibly some older relatives. Transportation and communication between villages was done most easily by water. Lightweight birch-bark canoes worked well on inland rivers, while heavier dugout canoes performed better on larger lakes. Villages were also connected by a series of overland trails. Native peoples marked the trails by tying down young hardwood trees, causing them to warp into distinctive shapes recognizable to travelers. In fact, the pre-contact Native American overland transportation network is still in use today. Many present-day highways in Wisconsin began as Indian trails. The so-called Winnebago Trail crossed central Wisconsin from Lake Michigan to the Mississippi. Portions of US 151 (Manitowoc to Fond du Lac), US 45 (Fond du Lac to Oshkosh), State Highway 21 (Oshkosh to Sparta), and State Highway 16 (Sparta to La Crosse), are built upon the foundations of that trail. Motorists in Wisconsin today sometimes drive upon transportation routes that have been in use for many centuries.

In the popular mind today, Native Americans lived harmoniously with nature in a pristine wilderness. In reality, Wisconsin's pre-contact landscape was greatly shaped by human hands. Native peoples built earthworks—in some cases, large ones. The landscape was dotted with villages, fields filled with crops, and manmade clearings, all tied together by a complex transportation network. Native Americans utilized and manipulated the natural world, but did so in a way that was very different than the peoples of Europe. The arrival of Europeans during the seventeenth century would drastically alter the lives of the Native Americans and the land itself.

2

EUROPEAN EXPLORATION AND COLONIZATION

In 1492, Christopher Columbus sailed west from Spain hoping to reach the shores of Asia. On the way, he inadvertently stumbled across two continents previously unknown to Europeans—North America and South America. Columbus was not the first European to reach the Americas, but it was his voyage that permanently opened the door between the Old World and the New World. Spain—the nation that employed Columbus—conquered the great Native American empires of the Aztecs and the Incas, and established a colonial empire that stretched from Mexico to Tierra del Fuego. Spain quickly became Europe's wealthiest and most powerful nation. Other European nations hoped to duplicate Spain's tremendous feat, and European explorers fanned out across America. England founded a series of colonies along the east coast of North America. The Netherlands took the Hudson River Valley, only to lose it to England. France established a colony in the St. Lawrence River Valley in present-day Canada. Following the St. Lawrence into the interior of North America, the French were the first Europeans to reach Wisconsin.

WORLDS COLLIDE

French exploration of North America began only decades after the first Columbus voyage. Giovanni da Verrazano, an Italian sailing for France, reached the east coast of North America in 1524, exploring the region from the Carolinas to Newfoundland. In 1534, Jacques Cartier reached the Gulf of St. Lawrence in present-day Canada. Returning the following year, he sailed up the St. Lawrence River as far as what is now Montreal. It was not until the early seventeenth century that the permanent French presence in North America began. The key figure in the creation of New France was Samuel de Champlain. Born in Brouage, France in 1575, Champlain was the son of a navy captain. After a career in the army, he spent two years in Spanish America, where he became fascinated with the potential of the New World. Champlain made his first voyage to Canada in 1603, and five years later he officially founded the colony of New France at Quebec. Champlain traveled widely across New France, meeting its native peoples, learning its geography, and assessing its economic potential. His vision for New France, along with his excellent administrative skills, guided the colony during its critical early years. Although Champlain never set foot in Wisconsin, it was the force of his vision and personality that led the first Europeans to the region.

France had several goals for its North American holdings. First, they hoped to find an inland water route through North America to the Pacific, which Europeans referred to as the "Northwest Passage." The nation that discovered such a waterway would have direct access to China and India, and thus an advantage over its European competitors. France was also in the process of creating a worldwide empire. European nations believed that they needed to create large, self-sufficient empires in order to compete and survive. If an empire was large and economically diverse, so the thinking went, it was less likely to have to import goods from other nations. At the same time, the ability to sell goods to other countries brought more money into the empire, creating a favorable balance of trade. The French sought not just riches in the New World, but also converts to Christianity. The first Christian missionaries in New France were Roman Catholic priests. In 1615, Champlain brought four priests of the Recollet order to New France to minister to the Native Americans. Ten years later, missionaries from the Society of Jesus— better known as the Jesuits—arrived in Canada.

France found little in the way of gold or silver in their new colony, but it did find a rather lucrative product that justified a continued presence in North America—fur. Indeed, New France was particularly suited for the fur trade. The region contained numerous species of fur-bearing animals, and its cold winter climate made the animal pelts particularly thick, rich, and valuable. The animal most sought by Europeans was the beaver, which was abundant in the woods of North America. A large, aquatic rodent, the beaver is noted for building dams along slow-moving rivers and streams. Europeans prized the beaver's soft, dense, and waterproof pelt, which was especially suited to felting. Beaver hats were high fashion in Paris, and the prices for beaver pelts were high. The beaver had been hunted to extinction in Europe, and Russian supplies from Asia were diminishing. North America represented an untapped, seemingly inexhaustible source of beaver pelts. In addition to beaver, the French also sought the coats of bear, deer, fox, marten, muskrat, and bison.

For the French, getting the pelts of the beaver and other animals was the problem. They could send out hunting parties in a strange new land to hunt animals whose habits were unfamiliar to them, or they could enlist the help of skilled Native Americans hunters. Champlain understood that the French fur trade would not prosper without the help of the Indians. Unlike the situation in English and Spanish colonies where Europeans typically seized lands and enslaved the native peoples, the French sought amicable relations with the Native Americans in the lands they claimed. In particular, the French developed a strong trade relationship with the Huron, an Iroquoian-speaking people resident to the eastern shores of Lake Huron in present-day Ontario. An agricultural nation, the Huron had also developed strong trade links with many tribes in the Great Lakes region. The French recognized the business skills and central location of the Huron, and a commercial partnership developed. The Huron essentially became middlemen in the French fur trade. Huron traders traveled deep into the interior of North America—to places like Wisconsin—and traded with local tribes for beaver pelts. The Huron then traded these pelts to the French.

To cultivate good relations with the Native Americans, Champlain sent young Frenchmen into the wilderness to live with the Native Americans in order to learn their languages and cultures, as well as to gain information about the interior of the continent. The first of these Frenchmen was Étienne Brûlé, who may have been the first European to set foot in present-day Wisconsin. Born in 1592, Brûlé arrived in New France in 1608, and Champlain soon dispatched the adventurous teenager to live among the Huron. Spirited and independent, Brûlé quickly adopted Huron dress and assimilated into their culture, so much so that his appearance and behavior shocked a good number of his fellow Frenchmen. Brûlé left no written accounts of his journeys, so the details of his travels are sketchy. His explorations seem to have taken him to all of the Great Lakes except Lake Michigan, and as far south as the Chesapeake Bay. He apparently traveled along the south shore of Lake Superior between 1621 and 1623. No one knows if Brûlé actually reached Wisconsin. Flowing into Lake Superior in Douglas County is the Brule River. The river may have obtained its name from the French explorer or from the French term *bois brûlé* (burned wood).

Another of Champlain's young men in the wilderness was Jean Nicolet. Born in Normandy in 1598, Nicolet arrived at Quebec in 1618. Nicolet quickly gained a reputation as a skilled translator and a diplomat between the French and native peoples. Back in Quebec, Champlain had learned about a tribe in the western Great Lakes that spoke an unfamiliar language and were known as the "people of the stinking waters." Hoping that the stinking waters might be seawater, he assigned Nicolet the task of making contact with this nation and possibly finding the Northwest Passage. In 1634, Nicolet and seven Huron guides headed west from Huron lands and into Lake Michigan. Nicolet was likely the first European to see this lake, which the French called *Lac des Illinois*. Traveling along the lake's western shore and into Green Bay, Nicolet is believed to have landed at Red Banks, just north of what is now the city of Green Bay. There he met the Ho-Chunk, a Souian-speaking people among the predominantly Algonkian tribes on the western shore of Lake Michigan. Hoping to find the Northwest Passage to Asia, Nicolet carried with him a Chinese robe so that he would be suitably dressed upon his arrival in the Far East. According to legend, when Nicolet landed at Red Banks he believed he was in China, and went ashore dressed in his silk robe firing his pistols. In reality, Nicolet knew he was not in China, but he still hoped to find the passage to Asia. He

French Forts in Wisconsin

With a huge interior empire to protect, the French constructed numerous forts and military posts in the Great Lakes and Mississippi Valley regions, including several modest fortifications in Wisconsin:

Ft. LaBaye—The first French military post in Wisconsin was Ft. LaBaye, established in 1684 by Nicolas Perrot on the west bank of the Fox River in Green Bay. Today, the site is at the foot of the Ray Nitschke Bridge in downtown Green Bay, just north of the Neville Public Museum. In 1717, the facility was refurbished and renamed Ft. St. François. The British assumed control during the Seven Years' War. In 1816, the US Army built Ft. Howard on the site (see Chapter 3).

Ft. St. Antoine—Overlooking Lake Pepin on the Mississippi River, Ft. St. Antoine was erected in 1686 under Perrot's direction. A state historical marker located about three miles northwest of Pepin on State Highway 35 marks the fort's location.

Ft. St. Nicolas—Built by Perrot about 1685, Ft. St. Nicolas was near the confluence of the Wisconsin and Mississippi rivers at Prairie du Chien. The US Army established Ft. Crawford in the area in 1816 (see Chapter 3).

Ft. LaPointe—This fort was located at the southern tip of Madeline Island, the southernmost of the Apostle Islands, in Lake Superior. In 1693, officials in Quebec commissioned the construction of a fort on the island to house traders and about 30 soldiers. The fort was abandoned in 1698, but the French reestablished a military presence on the island with the construction of a new fortification in 1718.

Ft. Trempealeau—Rising 400 feet above the Mississippi River, Mt. Trempealeau had long been an important navigational landmark for Native Americans, and later for French explorers as well. The site derives its present name from the French, *la montagne qui trempe a l'eau* (the mountain that soaks in water). In 1731, Godefroy de Linctot established Ft. Trempealeau at the foot of the mountain. The French occupied the post only five years. Today, the fort site is located in Perrot State Park, named after the French trader who briefly operated a fur-trade post in the area.

ventured up the Fox River, probably as far as Lake Winnebago, before returning to Green Bay and then back to Quebec. Indeed, Nicolet's landing is an event shrouded in mystery. Some historians speculate that he never reached Lake Michigan at all, and landed at the western tip of Lake Superior near Superior, Wisconsin.

Contact with Europeans changed the lives of Wisconsin's Native Americans in numerous ways. The goods Europeans traded for beaver furs revolutionized the economies and cultures of Indian peoples. Ordinary steel implements, such as knives, kettles, and fishhooks, far surpassed in quality the goods Indians could produce themselves. Steel axes chopped down trees faster and more efficiently, for example, while steel kettles proved much more durable than those made of clay. Perhaps the most prized of all European trade goods were firearms. Those tribes with guns could not only be much more efficient hunters, but would also have an overwhelming military superiority over their rivals. Because Native Americans did not produce steel goods and firearms themselves, they quickly grew dependent on the Europeans for them. As a result, Indian life grew increasingly focused on beaver hunting. Agricultural villages began to disperse as native peoples broke up into smaller bands that were more efficient at hunting. Territorial conflicts emerged between tribes, as the competition for beaver led to incursions into the traditional hunting grounds of others. The beaver soon grew overhunted—almost extinct in some areas—as Native American peoples competed desperately for furs to exchange for European trade goods. In addition, European diseases ravaged Wisconsin's Indian population. Having been isolated from the Old World for thousands of years, Native Americans had never been exposed to many illnesses common in Europe, and thus had built up no natural immunities to them. As a result, smallpox and other maladies took thousands of lives among the native peoples. In Wisconsin, the Ho-Chunk were particularly devastated. Historian Patti Loew has suggested that thirty years after the arrival of Nicolet, disease and warfare with neighboring tribes had reduced the Ho-Chunk population to perhaps 500 people.

The fur trade also involved complex diplomacy that could sometimes lead to war. The Indians became entangled in Old World conflicts, as were Europeans in

New World conflicts, all revolving around the fur trade. European powers befriended Indian tribes, but this meant that the Europeans also became the enemies of their friend's enemies. The Huron, for example, had long had an enemy in the Iroquois—a confederation of Indian tribes resident to present-day New York State. As the French relationship with the Huron grew, so did the animosity between the French and the Iroquois. At the same time, European nations were competing for power and influence in the New World, and the Native Americans thus became tied up in Old World power struggles. The Iroquois had befriended the Dutch in the New Netherland colony of the Hudson River Valley. Just as the Huron had grown dependent on the French for firearms and other trade goods, the Iroquois depended on the Dutch. By the 1640s, the Iroquois had exhausted the supply of beaver in their own lands. To continue to trade for Dutch goods, the Iroquois turned their eyes northward to the lucrative fur-hunting areas of the northern Great Lakes that were controlled by the Huron. From the Iroquois perspective, their survival hinged upon displacing the Huron and gaining access to furs of the Great Lakes.

Beginning in 1643, the Iroquois began raiding the French–Huron trade, as well as attacking tribes allied to them. The Huron Iroquois war was far more destructive than traditional Native American wars had been. The economic necessity of obtaining furs transformed the traditionally small-scale warfare into wars of annihilation. European firearms made the fighting all the more deadly. Eventually the Iroquois gained the upper hand, burning Huron villages and slaughtering their inhabitants. By 1667, the Iroquois had essentially destroyed the Huron. The surviving Huron were forced to disperse across the Great Lakes region. Many Huron sought the protection of the French at Quebec. Others fled west to Wisconsin. Huron refugees initially established themselves along Lake Pepin on the Mississippi River, hoping to act as middlemen in the trade with the Dakota. Eventually the Huron settled on Madeline Island in the Apostle Islands along Wisconsin's Lake Superior shoreline, before the Dakota displaced them once again.

The Iroquois War had a profound effect on Wisconsin. Many Indian tribes fled to the western shore of Lake

Michigan in hopes of evading the Iroquois menace. The Potawatomi, for example, an Algonkian-speaking people originally resident to present-day Michigan, rounded the southern end of the lake and entered Wisconsin after 1640. The Potawatomi took refuge along Lake Michigan's western shore as far north as the Door Peninsula. Thanks to the decline of the Ho-Chunk, the Meskwaki, also known as the Fox Indians, established themselves along the Fox River. Other nations taking refuge in Wisconsin included the Kickapoo, Illinois, Mascouten, Miami, Odawa (Ottawa), Petun, and Sauk, as well as the Huron. The Iroquois carried their war into Wisconsin, but with little success. A band of refugee peoples representing no fewer than five Indian nations established a stockaded village on Rock Island off the tip of the Door Peninsula. In 1653, Iroquois warriors ventured westward to attack the Rock Island village, but arrived exhausted and starving. The Iroquois begged the refugees for food, but were instead killed by those they had come to attack.

Northern Wisconsin was the scene of fur trade-related warfare between the Ojibwe and the Dakota that lasted more than a century. One battle took place at St. Croix Falls on the Wisconsin–Minnesota border about 1770. The rocky shores of the river were said to be filled with the dead and wounded, and many were swept away by the river's swift currents before the Dakota were forced to retreat. The fighting in Wisconsin lasted until the nineteenth century. In 1806, a Dakota war party descended on Ojibwe rice boats on Mole Lake in Forest County. Five hundred lives were reportedly lost before the Dakota withdrew.

The Iroquois War severely hindered the fur trade, and the French sought new avenues to gain access to the northern fur areas. The Odawa, resident to the northern shore of Lake Huron, replaced the vanquished Huron as middlemen in the French fur trade. At the same time, French explorers undertook efforts to establish direct contact with western tribes. In 1654, Medard Chouart, Sieur de Groseilliers, traveled along the western shore of Lake Michigan—the first firmly documented instance of a European explorer in Wisconsin. Groseilliers and his brother-in-law, Pierre-Espirit Radisson, undertook a remarkable voyage to Lake Superior in 1659. Radisson and

Groseilliers camped for a time along the south shore of Chequamegon Bay, and traveled inland to trade with the local Indians. Desperate for European trade goods, the local inhabitants lavished their affections on the French explorers. "We were Cesars," wrote Radisson, "[there] being nobody to contradict us." From Chequamegon Bay, Radisson and Groseilliers paddled northward and established contact with the Cree Indians in northwestern Ontario. The two explorers became convinced that the rich fur-trapping regions of the north could be accessed through Hudson Bay in northern Canada. They returned to Quebec in 1661 with 60 boatloads of furs, demonstrating the potential of the area and probably saving the colony from economic disaster. But because they had made an unauthorized voyage, the governor of New France seized the furs and had the two explorers arrested. Angry and disappointed, Radisson and Groseillers took their knowledge to the English, who established the Hudson's Bay Company in 1670.

THE EXPANSION OF NEW FRANCE

In the wake of the Iroquois War, New France underwent a period of reorganization and expansion. The latter half of the seventeenth century was the age of Louis XIV, the fabled "Sun King" whose unlimited ambition led France to become Europe's preeminent power. To further the glories of France, he also pushed for the expansion of France's colonial empire, including further exploration in North America. In addition, increasing competition from the English made reinvigorating the colony a necessity. With the establishment of the Hudson's Bay Company, France lost access to some of the best fur-producing regions in the world. At the same time, England had conquered the New Netherland colony in 1664 and renamed it New York, giving England control of the east coast of North America from Maine to the Carolinas. New France now lay sandwiched between English colonies. Louis made New France a royal colony in 1663, increasing supervision of the colony from Paris. He began meager efforts at colonizing Frenchmen in the New World, mainly in the St. Lawrence River Valley between Quebec and Montreal. Louis also brought in new leadership that helped reinvigorate the colony, most notably Jean Talon and the Comte de Frontenac. The Sun King's policies pushed the French presence deeper into North America, and led to the establishment of semi-permanent settlements in Wisconsin.

Although the French continued to use Native American middlemen in the fur trade, individual French traders made their way into the *pays d'en haut* (upper country) with increasing frequency. An officially licensed trader was known as a *voyageur*. The term *coureur du bois* (runner of the woods) referred to an illegal trader, although the term was also used for legally licensed Frenchmen in the interior. Individual traders could amass large sums of money quickly, and French officials found it impossible to stop illegal trading. In addition, the Indians of the interior preferred to obtain trade goods directly from the French rather than going through Odawa middlemen. One of the first French traders to operate in Wisconsin was Nicolas Perrot, who was trading in the Chequamegon Bay and Green Bay areas as early as the 1660s, bringing numerous tribes into alliances with France. The French established numerous trading posts in the area, and fur traders often lived among the Native Americans for years at a time. Marriages to Indian women were common. Not only were native women the only marriage partners available to French men, but marriage also helped to solidify economic ties. Even today, French surnames are common among Wisconsin's Native Americans, a remnant of the colonial fur trade era. A mixed-race class known as the *Métis* emerged in Wisconsin and other parts of New France that combined elements of both cultures and provided a bridge between the French and the Native Americans.

Searching for souls instead of furs, Jesuit priests were also an important European presence in Wisconsin. The first Christian missionary in Wisconsin was Father René Ménard. In 1660, Ménard accompanied a group of French and Odawa traders to the south shore of Lake Superior, and then southward in search of a village of Christian Huron refugees then located on the Black River. Somewhere in the Wisconsin Northwoods, Father Ménard mysteriously disappeared. More successful was Father Claude Allouez. In 1663, Allouez had been named church vicar for the interior, and the priest went out to see his flock. He arrived at Chequamegon Bay, where the Christian Huron had established a new village. There Allouez built a small church made of birch bark. It was the first Christian house of worship in Wisconsin. Allouez then moved on to the Green Bay area, preaching the gospel along the shores of the bay and along the Fox River. In 1671, Allouez and another Jesuit priest, Father Louis André, built a second modest birch-bark mission near the present-day city of De Pere, which he called St. Francis Xavier. From the missions, the priests sought converts among the Native Americans and administered the sacraments to French traders, as well as the Native American and Métis faithful. Located at fur-trading centers, the Catholic missions became important gathering points for the French, Métis, and Native Americans alike. The French also established military forts at key locations in Wisconsin. The forts, missions, and trading posts formed the basis of the first semi-permanent European communities in Wisconsin.

As the French penetrated ever deeper into the interior, they gathered more geographic knowledge of the region. Native Americans told of a large river to the west. Still seeking the elusive Northwest Passage, the French hoped this river might be the Colorado River that flowed into the Gulf of California and the Pacific. In 1673, fur trader and mapmaker Louis Jolliet joined with Father Jacques Marquette, a Jesuit priest, and undertook an expedition to find this great river. Marquette and Jolliet left Mackinac in May 1673. The two explorers traveled to Green Bay and ascended the Fox River to an Indian village composed of Kickapoo, Mascouten, and Miami. This village, near the present-day city of Berlin in Green Lake County, was the limit of territory known to the French. From the village, Native American guides led Marquette and Jolliet to the source of the Fox River and over a short, swampy portage to another, much larger river. Marquette recorded the name of the river as the "Meskousing"; Jolliet as the "Miskonsing." The French would come to know the river as the "Ouisconsin," which was later Anglicized to become the Wisconsin River, from which the state derives its name. From the Fox–Wisconsin portage, the Frenchmen descended the Wisconsin River until they met the

Mississippi near Prairie du Chien. They voyaged down the Mississippi as far as Arkansas, where they encountered evidence of Spanish influence. Fearing capture by the Spanish, they returned northward, this time ascending the Illinois River, portaging at present-day Chicago, then up the western shore of Lake Michigan. Marquette spent the winter of 1673–1674 at De Pere, and died in 1675 on an expedition to convert the Illinois Indians; Jolliet eventually returned to Quebec.

Another French explorer, René-Robert Cavelier de La Salle, reached the mouth of the Mississippi and in 1682 claimed the entire Mississippi River Valley for France. A new French colony, Louisiana, was created on the Gulf of Mexico and lower Mississippi valley. The Fox–Wisconsin portage was an important link between Quebec and Louisiana. Another portage existed between the Brule and St. Croix Rivers in Douglas County, linking Lake Superior with the Mississippi River. The first European to use the Brule–St. Croix portage was Daniel Greysolon du Lhut. Du Lhut is most noted for establishing links with the Dakota in Minnesota, and even negotiated a temporary truce between the Dakota and the Ojibwe. The city of Duluth, Minnesota, was named in his honor. French explorers soon stepped out onto the Great Plains, and even reached the Rocky Mountains far to the west. By 1700, France had claimed a vast territory in the interior of North America, as well as the continent's two most important river valleys.

The reinvigoration of New France did not last very long, however. New France soon went into another period of decline. First, Louis XIV called for a halt to the French fur trade in the interior regions, including Wisconsin. The Jesuits reported how the *coureurs du bois* were corrupting the Indians with alcohol and debauching their women. The market for furs had also become glutted. The governor of New France, the Comte de Frontenac, opposed the king's policy and kept fur traders operating in the interior until he could talk the king into a compromise. The English were also applying increasing pressure on New France. English traders began moving into French-claimed territories, selling the Indians trade goods that were cheaper and of better quality than those sold by the French. After 1680, there were

The Jesuit Relations

The French missionaries who explored North America kept exacting records of their journeys, which have been collected in a series of books known as the Jesuit Relations and Allied Documents. *Below is the report of Father Jacques Marquette of his journey through Wisconsin with Louis Jolliet (spelled "Jollyet" in the text). The passage begins at the Mascouten village near present-day Berlin—the farthest western point known to Europeans at the time. From there, Marquette and Jolliet headed off into unknown territory. They were the first Europeans to cross over the Fox–Wisconsin portage and descend the Wisconsin River to the Mississippi.*

Monsieur Jollyet and I, assembled the elders together; and he told them that he was sent by Monsieur Our Governor to discover New countries, while I was sent by God to Illumine them with the light of the holy Gospel. He told them that, moreover, The sovereign Master of our lives wished to be known by all the Nations; and that in obeying his will I feared not the death to which I exposed myself in voyages so perilous. He informed them that we needed two guides to show us the way; and We gave them a present, by it asking them to grant us the guides. To this they very Civilly consented; and they also spoke to us by means of a present, consisting of a Mat to serve us as a bed during the whole of our voyage.

On the following day, the tenth of June, two Miamis who were given us as guides embarked with us, in the sight of a great crowd, who could not sufficiently express their astonishment at the sight of seven frenchmen, alone and in two Canoes, daring to undertake so extraordinary and so hazardous an Expedition.

We knew that, at three leagues from Maskoutens, was a River which discharged into Missisipi. We knew also that the direction we were to follow in order to reach it was west-southwesterly. But the road is broken by so many swamps and small lakes that it is easy to lose one's way, especially as the River leading thither is so full of wild oats that it is difficult to find the Channel. For this reason we greatly needed our two guides, who safely Conducted us to a portage of 2,700 paces, and helped us to transport our Canoes to enter That river; after which they returned home, leaving us alone in this Unknown country, in the hands of providence.

Thus we left the Waters flowing to Quebeq, 4 or 500 Leagues from here, to float on Those that would thenceforward Take us through strange lands. Before embarking thereon, we Began all together a new devotion to the blessed Virgin Immaculate, which we practiced daily, addressing to her special prayers to place under her protection both our persons and the success of our voyage; and, after mutually encouraging one another, we entered our Canoes.

The River on which we embarked is called Meskousing. It is very wide; it has a sandy bottom, which forms various shoals that render its navigation very difficult. It is full of Islands Covered with Vines. On the banks one sees fertile land, diversified with woods, prairies, and Hills. There are oak, Walnut, and basswood trees; and another kind, whose branches are armed with long thorns. We saw there neither feathered game nor fish, but many deer, and a large number of cattle. Our Route lay to the southwest, and, after navigating about 30 leagues, we saw a spot presenting all the appearances of an iron mine; and, in fact, one of our party who had formerly seen such mines, assures us that The One which We found is very good and very rich. It is Covered with three feet of good soil, and is quite near a chain of rocks, the base of which is covered by very fine trees. After proceeding 40 leagues on This same route, we arrived at the mouth of our River; and, at 42 and a half degrees Of latitude, We safely entered Missisipi on The 17th of June, with a Joy that I cannot Express.

renewed tensions between the French and the Iroquois, who were now supported by England. The numerous wars that ravaged Europe during the seventeenth and eighteenth centuries drained the French treasury and diverted the attention of officials in Paris from American affairs. The European wars also had corresponding conflicts in the American colonies. Fighting between the English and the French—as well as their Native American allies—occurred with considerable frequency in northern New England and the Gulf of St. Lawrence. The English gradually began to chip away at French holdings in Newfoundland and Nova Scotia, threatening French access to the vitally important St. Lawrence River.

Wisconsin was the scene of a war during the early eighteenth century between the French and the Mesquakie. After their arrival in Wisconsin during the Iroquois War, the Mesquakie had established a number of villages in the area of the Fox River and northern Lake Winnebago, the largest and most important of which overlooked Big Lake Butte des Morts on the Fox River, near what is now Oshkosh. The Mesquakie had never been friendly with the French, and had grown sympathetic toward the Iroquois. When French-allied tribes massacred a band of Mesquakie near Detroit in 1712, the Mesquakie began to use their strategic position astride the Fox–Wisconsin waterway to block French access to the Dakota, as well as to harass French travel and communications between Quebec and Louisiana. The French sent military expeditions into Wisconsin and Illinois to break Mesquakie power, and several battles occurred in northeastern Wisconsin. In 1716, French forces, along with Indian allies, laid siege to the large Mesquakie village at Big Lake Butte des Morts. The term *butte des morts* ("hill of the dead") suggests that a rather fierce battle took place before the Mesquakie capitulated. Archaeological excavations have yielded numerous bullets and shell fragments from the site. Unfortunately, the battlefield has since been destroyed, and is now a housing subdivision known as Bell Haven Estates.

Tensions with the French diminished for a time, but several years after the battle at Big Lake Butte des Morts the Mesquakie leader Kiala revived attempts to create an anti-French Indian confederacy. In 1728, the French sent another expedition to the Fox River Valley, but the Indians abandoned their villages before the French arrived. Two years later, French-allied Indians raided Mesquakie camps on the lower Wisconsin River. The French clashed with the Mesquakie and their Sauk allies at Little Lake Butte des Morts, near present-day Menasha, in 1733—although there is debate as to whether the battle ever took place. Fritse Park in Menasha is believed to be the site of the battle. Pressure from the French and their Native American allies had effectively subdued the Mesquakie by the mid-1730s. The Mesquakie and their Sauk allies moved in a southwesterly direction along the Mississippi River to Illinois and Iowa. Nevertheless, the Mesquakie wars had a negative impact on the development of the French regime in Wisconsin. The fighting inhibited the development of permanent French settlements in the region. The wars also forced the French to seek avenues farther to the south and east in order to link Quebec and Louisiana, in particular, the Maumee–Wabash route between Lake Erie and the Ohio River. The movement of traffic eastward was a dangerous proposition for the French. Not only was it closer to the Iroquois threat, but it also brought France into conflict with Great Britain (formed by the merger of the English and Scottish crowns in 1707). Both nations claimed the Ohio River Valley, and the struggle for control of that region had a tremendous impact on Wisconsin.

The British Era

The Seven Years' War, long known to Americans as the French and Indian War, was a significant European power conflict, but one that began over the struggle for North America. To protect access to the Ohio River, the French built a chain of forts in what is now northwestern Pennsylvania. Where the Allegheny and Monongahela rivers meet to form the Ohio River was Fort Duquesne. In 1754, the British colony of Virginia—which also claimed the region—sent a young militia colonel named George Washington to halt the French. Instead, the French sent Washington packing back to the Old Dominion. The following year, a British general, Edward Braddock, led another unsuccessful effort to take the fort. Among those fighting against Braddock in 1755 were Indians from

"Braddock's Defeat" by Edwin Willard Deming, 1755. Charles de Langlade, the Green Bay fur trader is on the left directing the attack with Indians from Wisconsin and Michigan. General Edward Braddock is just falling from his horse, the bridle of which is being caught by George Washington.

present-day Wisconsin, who were aligned with the French, led by Charles de Langlade. Born at Mackinac in 1729, Langlade was the son of French fur trader Augustin Mouet, Sieur de Langlade, and Domitille Villanueve, the daughter of the Odawa chief Kewanoquat. As a Métis, Langlade was able to move between the French culture of his father and the Native American culture of his mother, and gained a great deal of respect in both. Langlade and the Wisconsin Indians have been credited with turning the tide of battle at Fort Dusquene, and forcing the British to retreat from the Ohio Valley.

In 1756, the Franco–British skirmishing in America became a full-scale, worldwide war, and Britain eventually gained the upper hand. Fort Duquesne eventually fell to the British, which they renamed Fort Pitt in honor of the British prime minister who led the war effort. British forces from the Atlantic colonies eventually moved north, capturing Quebec in 1759 and Montreal in 1760. The French suffered a similar fate in Europe, and in 1763 they surrendered to the British. In the peace settlement, France lost almost all of its North American empire. All French territories in North America east of the Mississippi—including the area now known as Wisconsin—went to the British. French territory west of the Mississippi went to Spain. The French retained their Caribbean possessions and a few islands off Newfoundland, but its vast holdings on the continent were gone. Charles de Langlade, who had fought the British at Quebec and in numerous other battles, surrendered at Mackinac to Great Britain and then settled at Green Bay. He not only accepted British rule, but also the job of Britain's Indian agent in the Green Bay area. British troops moved into the Wisconsin region as well, establishing Fort Edward Augustus at the site of the French post at Green Bay.

Now that the British had possession of interior North America, they had complete access to the fur trade of the Great Lakes. However, the new territories posed numerous problems. In particular, the British takeover was unpopular with the Native Americans of the region. British had long been known as a land-hungry people who established large colonies of settlers, and the Indians feared—not unreasonably—that British rule would mean further encroachments on their lands. In addition, British officials, no longer in competition with French traders, conducted the fur trade in a heavy-handed and condescending manner, ending the French custom of gift giving and

Jonathan Carver,
Travels through the Interior Parts of North America

Jonathan Carver's Travels through the Interior Parts of North America, *published in London in 1778, was the first English-language description of Wisconsin. In 1766, Carver began one of many expeditions to find the elusive (and ultimately non-existent) Northwest Passage. He entered present-day Wisconsin at Green Bay, traversed the Fox–Wisconsin waterway to Prairie du Chien, and then ascended the Mississippi River. Here he describes his arrival at Lake Pepin on the Mississippi River:*

On the first of November I arrived at Lake Pepin, which is rather an extended part of the River Mississippi, that the French have thus dominated, about two hundred miles from the Ouisconsin. The Mississippi below this lake flows with a gentle current, but the breadth of it is very uncertain, in some places it being upwards of a mile, in others not more than a quarter. This river has a range of mountains throughout the whole of the way; which in particular parts approach near to it, in others lie at a greater distance. The land betwixt the mountains, and on their sides, is generally covered with grass with a few groves of trees interspersed, near which large droves of deer and elk are frequently seen feeding. In many places pyramids of rocks appeared, resembling old ruinous towers; at others amazing precipices; and what is very remarkable, whilst this scene presented itself on one side, the opposite side of the same mountain is covered with the finest herbage, which gradually ascended to its summit. From thence the most beautiful and extensive prospect that imagination can form opens to your view. Verdant plains, fruitful meadows, numerous islands, all of these abounding with a variety of trees that yield amazing quantities of fruit, without care of cultivation, such as the nut-tree, the maple which produces sugar, vines loaded with rich grapes, and plum-trees bending under their blooming burden, but above all the fine river flowing gently beneath, and reaching as far as the eye can extend, by turns attract your imagination and excite your wonder.

curtailing the flow of guns and ammunition to the Indians. Native disaffection with the British led to an event known as Pontiac's Rebellion, which broke out in 1763. Pontiac, an Odawa chief, laid siege to the British garrison at Detroit. Unrest soon spread throughout the Great Lakes region. At Mackinac, the Ojibwe seized the British fort, using a lacrosse game outside the gates of the post as a diversion for an attack. The small British garrison at Fort Edward Augustus, commanded by Lt. James Gorrell, abandoned Green Bay and headed north to relieve the siege of Mackinac. Across the Great Lakes region, Pontiac's Rebellion quickly fizzled. Many tribes sided with the British, including the Menominee. It had also become clear to the Native Americans that the French were gone forever, and that the British could not be dislodged.

But in a sense, Pontiac's Rebellion was a victory for the Indians of the Great Lakes region. Native unrest showed the British that they had to formulate new policies in order to appease the Indians and reap the benefits of the lucrative fur trade. The first step was the Proclamation Line of 1763. British officials essentially drew a line along the spine of the Appalachian Mountains. To the west of that line, further European settlement was forbidden. Trade with Indians in the west was to be strictly regulated, and British military posts were built to ensure the enforcement of the laws. Another key law was the Quebec Act of 1774. This act extended the administrative borders of Quebec from the St. Lawrence River Valley into the Great Lakes and Mississippi River Valley. Given the geography and history of the region, the law was sensible; the region was most easily accessed through the St. Lawrence River and the European inhabitants were primarily French Canadian. The Quebec Act also granted religious toleration to the Roman Catholics of Quebec, who were now under Protestant British rule, helping to diminish anti-British feeling among French-speaking residents.

Although dubious about the loyalty of the French Canadians in the Great Lakes, the British found they depended on their knowledge and connections with local Indians to continue the fur trade. But with British rule came fur traders and explorers from other parts of the British Empire. Scottish traders, in particular, came to dominate much of the Great Lakes fur trade after 1763. Several Americans from the eastern colonies also entered Wisconsin. New Englander Jonathan Carver, for example, traveled extensively through Wisconsin during the mid-1760s in an unsuccessful attempt to find the Northwest Passage to the Pacific. Indeed, Carver claimed that two Dakota chiefs had granted him 12 million acres of land in present-day Wisconsin and Minnesota. (For decades to follow, maps of Wisconsin would show "Carver's Claim" in the northwestern part of the state). Numerous trading posts sprang up in Wisconsin during the British era.

In some cases permanent settlements developed, the first of which was Green Bay. The economy continued to revolve around the fur trade, but small-scale European-style agriculture and animal husbandry also emerged. Despite being part of the British Empire, Green Bay had a remarkably French Canadian flavor. In keeping with the land holding patterns common in Quebec, Green Bay's earliest settlers settled on long, thin strips of land that emanated outward from the river's edge. Its most prominent citizen was Charles de Langlade, who died in 1802. Other prominent Green Bay families included the Grignons, the LaRoses, the Carons, and the Jourdains. The first permanent English-speaking residents did not arrive until the 1790s. Marriages between French Canadian men and Native American women were still common, and Green Bay had a substantial Métis population closely connected to nearby Native American tribes. As a remote outpost, Green Bay had no priest to perform marriages. As a result, many were married *à la façon du pays* (in the custom of the country), in which the couple simply made a verbal commitment to each other. A similar community had emerged at Prairie du Chien near the mouth of the Wisconsin River by 1780. This settlement became Britain's point of contact with the Dakota Indians and the Mississippi River, Prairie du Chien, and emerged as a bustling village and site of an important fur trade rendezvous each year.

British policy toward the Great Lakes may have stabilized the region and helped them to maximize fur trade profitability, but it stirred considerable anger in the East Coast colonies. The Proclamation Line and Quebec Act conflicted with the desire of the colonies to expand

Studio portrait of Augustin Grignon, a fur trader and settler in Green Bay, holding a tomahawk. The tomahawk was made from a gun barrel by Jourdain, the government blacksmith in Green Bay, and could be used as a pipe as well.

westward. Most eastern colonies claimed vast tracts of land in the interior of North America, from the Atlantic coast all the way to the Pacific. Oftentimes these claims overlapped. Wisconsin was claimed in its entirety by Virginia, and Massachusetts claimed the southern third of the present-day state. To pay for the maintenance of their expanded empire, the British Parliament attempted to impose direct taxes on the colonists, most notably the Stamp Act of 1765. Because Americans had no delegates in the British Parliament, the colonies believed such taxes violated their cherished rights as Englishmen, crying "no taxation without representation." Heavy-handed British attempts to make the colonists pay the taxes only inflamed American sentiments further, and in 1775 war broke out between the colonies and the mother country, ushering in the American

Fur Trade Heritage

Forts Folle Avoine
County Highway U
Danbury, WI 54830
(715) 866-8890
www.theforts.org
Forts Folle Avoine is a re-creation of an early-nineteenth-century fur-trading post located on the site of actual British trading posts operated by the North West and XY Fur Trade Companies. Costumed historical interpreters explain the workings of the post, as well as of an Indian village located nearby. Folle Avoine is the French term for wild rice, a staple of the Native Americans who inhabited the region during the fur trade period.

Madeline Island Historical Museum
La Pointe, WI 54850
(715) 747-2415
madeline.wisconsinhistory.org
Administered by the Wisconsin Historical Society, the Madeline Island Museum is located at one of the most historic—not to mention scenic—spots in Wisconsin. The museum focuses on the island's role in the fur trade under the French, British, and Americans, but delves into other aspects of the island's history, including logging, missionary activities, and the origins of summer tourism.

Prairie du Chien Rendezvous
c/o Prairie du Chien Chamber of Commerce
PO Box 326
Prairie du Chien, WI 53821
(800) 732-1673
www.prairieduchien.org
Held each June, the rendezvous features historical interpreters who recreate life during the fur-trade era.

Revolution. For the second time in less than twenty years, North America was plunged into war. The following year, on July 4, the American colonies declared independence, creating the United States of America.

The American Revolution had little direct impact on Wisconsin. At the beginning, sentiment in the region was overwhelmingly pro-British, for Europeans and Indians alike. Native Americans, in particular, feared the land hunger of the American colonists. Charles de Langlade recruited Indians to fight for the British, and the Wisconsin contingent fought in the St. Lawrence River Valley in the east and at St. Louis to the south. But after the American victory at Saratoga, New York, in 1777, support for the British began to wane. France had entered the war on the American side after Saratoga, pulling many Indians away from their allegiance to Britain. In 1779, Spain—with its colony of Louisiana on the west bank of the Mississippi— also joined the war against Britain, further eroding Indian support. The 1778–1779 Virginian George Rogers Clark invaded the Ohio River Valley, firming up Native American support for the United States in that area. After the American victory at Yorktown, Virginia, in 1781, the British gave up their attempts to win back their wayward colonies. In the 1783 peace settlement, the Treaty of Paris, the British ceded nearly all of its North American lands east of the Mississippi and south of the Great Lakes to the Americans. The area of Wisconsin was now part of the United States. To the Americans, the lands between the Great Lakes and the Ohio River became known as the Northwest Territory.

Although the British had given up their claims to the Northwest Territory, they were slow to leave it. British fur traders continued to operate in the region, in defiance of American wishes. In addition, Britain openly supported the Native Americans of the region, including the Shawnee chief Tecumseh, who formed an Indian confederacy to drive the Americans from the Northwest Territory. The British even kept military forces at Mackinac and other posts in the Great Lakes region. Still a relatively weak nation, the United States was powerless to force the British out. Under the terms of Jay's Treaty of 1794, the British began pulling its troops out of the American territories, but retained the right to keep fur traders in the region. Only slowly did American traders and American officials enter the region. The purchase of the vast Louisiana Territory in 1803 gave the United States possession of the west bank of the Mississippi, bolstering the American presence in Wisconsin. Continuing disputes over the Northwest, combined with the impressment (forced recruitment) of American sailors into the British Royal Navy, led to the outbreak of a second Anglo-American war in 1812. Once again, sentiment in Wisconsin was strongly pro-British.

Wisconsin was the scene of one minor battle during the War of 1812. In June 1814, Governor William Clark of Missouri led an expedition north from St. Louis and established Fort Shelby at Prairie du Chien—the first US military post in Wisconsin. Clark returned to St. Louis, leaving Captain Joseph Perkins in command of 60 men. The following month, a British force of 150 troops, accompanied by 400 Native American allies, traversed the Fox–Wisconsin waterway from Mackinac to attack Fort Shelby. The siege began on July 17. The outnumbered Americans put up a good fight, but by the third day of hostilities, they began to run out of ammunition and medical supplies, and were forced to surrender. Though several combatants were wounded in the Battle of Prairie du Chien, nobody was killed. The British commander, Lt. Col. William McKay, paroled most of the American soldiers, who made their way back to the safety of St. Louis.

By the end of 1814, both the British and the Americans had grown tired of the war, and in December signed the Treaty of Ghent, ending the conflict. Under the terms of the treaty, both sides returned to their pre-war borders. The ultimate effect of the War of 1812 for Wisconsin was to end British domination of the region. British traders withdrew to Canada. Most of the small French-Canadian population remained, and took oaths of loyalty to the United States. After having fomented rebellion among the Native Americans, the British left them to the mercy of the Americans, who began arriving in increasing numbers after 1815. After more than 30 years of legally being US territory, Wisconsin was about to become American in reality.

3

THE TERRITORIAL PERIOD

A fter the American Revolution, the pace of westward expansion increased dramatically. Free from imperial barriers, American settlers trekked west across the Appalachian Mountains in ever increasing numbers. The size of the American population swelled dramatically—from 3.9 million in 1790 to 17 million just 50 years later—making the nation's physical expansion all the more inevitable. During the first half of the nineteenth century, Wisconsin was on the frontier of American movement westward. The territorial period in Wisconsin saw the transition from Native American sovereignty to the emergence of American communities. It was a time of opportunity, economic growth, transformation, and great tragedy.

AMERICANS TAKE CONTROL

Although the United States had held legal title to Wisconsin since 1783, American influence in the region had been remarkably light. After 1800, the Northwest Territory was divided numerous times to create new states and territories. Ohio was the first state to be carved out of the territory, admitted to the Union in 1803. Wisconsin was, at various times, part of the Indiana and Illinois Territories. After the admission of Illinois in 1818, Wisconsin became part of the Michigan Territory. With its capital in Detroit, the Michigan Territory covered a vast region from the shores of Lake Huron to the Missouri River. Territorial status was a prelude to full statehood. The residents of the territory elected a legislature, but the president appointed the governor. Territories elected delegates to the US Congress, but they had no voting representatives. The territory had no electoral votes and thus no say in presidential elections. Once a territory's population reached 60,000, its residents could apply for statehood.

As was the case in many frontier areas, the first substantial American presence in Wisconsin was the military. With the removal of British troops after the War of 1812, Americans quickly moved in. In 1816, the US Army established two forts in Wisconsin—both at the locations of previous French and British posts. One was Fort Howard, located on the west bank of the Fox River at Green Bay. At Prairie du Chien the army established Fort Crawford. Although garrisoned only by a few hundred troops each, Forts Howard and Crawford guarded the vital Fox–Wisconsin waterway, established points of contact and supply for fur traders and Indian agents, and deterred possible Indian uprisings. But many of the soldiers stationed at the forts found their frontier assignments less than pleasing. One Massachusetts man described Fort Crawford as "the most lonesome place that Man was ever doomed to live in."

The return of peace in 1815 allowed the resumption of the Great Lakes fur trade. After the war, the Americans finally gained control of Wisconsin's trade in peltry. In particular, a German immigrant named John Jacob Astor and his American Fur Company established a virtual monopoly on the fur trade in the northern United States. Based in New York City, Astor envisioned trading operations that stretched across the continent. Astor's men established fur-trading posts all across present-day Wisconsin, from Beloit to Madeline Island. Though controlled by an American company, French Canadians—whose experience with the trade and the Native Americans was essential—continued to play a vital role in the Wisconsin fur trade. Some of the first wealthy families to emerge in Wisconsin were of French origins. In 1837, Charles A. Grignon—descended from a Métis family long active in the Wisconsin fur trade—built a graceful mansion on the Fox River at the site of a fur trading post. Known as the "mansion in the woods," the city of Kaukauna grew up around it. Green Bay fur trader Hercules Dousman moved his operations to Prairie du Chien, where he amassed a small fortune. Later in the century, his descendants built a stately mansion named Villa Louis on the banks of the Mississippi.

But the 1820s proved to be the final phase of the fur trade in Wisconsin. The resumption of the trade quickly led to a severe depletion of marketable fur-bearing animals. The American Fur Company began to look farther west for pelts and profits. The economic activity that had dominated the region's economy since the seventeenth century was dying out. But Americans found another product that made Wisconsin profitable, and stimulated the first major wave of settlers to the Wisconsin frontier. It was the rush for "grey gold."

THE LEAD MINING FRONTIER

The limestone bedrock of the Driftless Area in southwestern Wisconsin and adjacent areas of Illinois and Iowa contained extensive deposits of lead. Native Americans had mined the surface lead deposits for thousands of years before the arrival of Europeans, transforming the material into jewelry and paints. French explorers began trading with the area's Indians for lead, and dreamed of exploiting the region themselves. After France lost control of the region in 1763, other European powers hoped to exploit its ample lead supplies. During the 1780s, Julien Dubuque, a Frenchman working for Spain, obtained permission from the local Indians to begin mining on the west side of the river near the present-day city of Dubuque, Iowa. Lead from Dubuque's "Mines of Spain" was shipped down the Mississippi River to St. Louis and New Orleans. Americans were well aware of the area's rich deposits when Great Britain ceded the east bank of the Mississippi to the United States after the American Revolution. President Thomas Jefferson designated the area a national mineral reserve in 1807.

During the early nineteenth century Americans found it increasingly less difficult to get to the lead district and other areas of the frontier. New modes of transportation shortened travel times significantly, connecting remote regions to American markets. One of the first improvements was the construction of overland roads, but these early highways were usually little more than dirt paths that were impassible much of the year. Water transportation was by far the most efficient way to reach the frontier. The Mississippi River connected Wisconsin to New Orleans, and the invention of the steamboat made the voyage up the river considerably faster and more efficient.

Miners in the bowels of a lead mine circa 1900, Cassville, Wisconsin

Where rivers did not exist, Americans created them. Numerous canal building projects helped link inland waterways and spread American civilization west. No canal project was more important than the Erie Canal, completed in upstate New York during the 1820s. The Erie Canal ran 363 miles from Albany on the Hudson River to Buffalo on Lake Erie, and provided an efficient water route that connected the Great Lakes region to the major cities on the Atlantic seaboard.

Americans began arriving in the lead district in significant numbers during the 1820s. Traveling up the Mississippi, they reached the mouth of the Fever River (later renamed the Galena River) in northwestern Illinois. The city of Galena, at the confluence of the Fever and Mississippi, became the main entry point into the lead

Mining Heritage

Badger Mine and Museum
279 West Estey Street, Shullsburg, WI 53586
(608) 965-4860
www.shullsburgwisconsin.org/
shullsburgbadgerminemuseum.htm
The Badger Mine dates to 1827 and descends 47 feet below ground.
From the museum visitors can also take a driving tour of local mining
history. Call (608) 965-4401 for tour information.

Mining Museum
405 East Main Street, PO Box 780, Platteville, WI 53818
(608) 348-3301
www.platteville.com/mining_museum.htm
At the Mining Museum, visitors can descend 50 feet below ground into the
1845 Bevans Lead Mine, which once produced two million pounds of lead
in a single year.

Pendarvis
114 Shake Rag Street, Mineral Point, WI 53565
(608) 987-2122
www.wisconsinhistory.org/pendarvis/
Pendarvis is a little piece of Cornwall in Wisconsin. Cornish miners
constructed modest cottages of stone and wood, much like those they left in
the Old Country. In Mineral Point, their settlement became known as "Shake
Rag Under the Hill." As the story goes, the miners' wives signaled to their
husbands that lunch was ready by standing outside their doors and waving
a white rag in the air. Pendarvis, preserved by the Wisconsin Historical
Society, is one of the few miner cottages that still survive. The grounds
include beautiful gardens and a gift shop where one can sample saffron
cake—a favorite of the Cornish settlers. On a hill across Shake Rag Street is
the Merry Christmas Mine, and a prairie restored to the conditions before
settlement. On the prairie one can still see "badger holes"—crude pits that
served as shelter in the 1820s for the earliest settlers.

St. John Mine
129 South Main Street, Potosi, WI 53820
(608) 763-2121
This museum features a cave that produced lead from the seventeenth
through the nineteenth century.

Tower Hill State Park
5808 County Highway C, Spring Green, WI 53588
(608) 588-2116
Daniel Whitney's shot tower is preserved in this park. It also affords scenic
views of the Wisconsin River.

region. From Galena, prospectors ventured northward up the river into present-day Wisconsin, searching the hills and hollows of the Driftless Area for lead. Lead prices fluctuated, but were usually high enough to ensure a hearty profit. Because the region was a federal mineral reserve, miners had to obtain a permit, and were also obligated to turn over 10 percent of their lead to the government. Miners rushed to the area, staked their claims, and began to dig. The early miners concentrated on the abundant surface deposits of lead, digging huge pits into the earth. Life on the lead frontier was often harsh and crude. Log huts sprang up wherever lead had been discovered. Some miners simply dug shallow holes in the ground and covered them with a makeshift roof of branches, leaves, or sod. Such habitations became known as "badger holes," their inhabitants called "badgers." It is from these earliest miners that Wisconsin obtained its nickname the "Badger State."

Permanent American settlements soon emerged. New Diggings, in what is now Lafayette County, was first settled in 1824 by miners who left the "old diggings" of Galena. Colorful place names still dot the map of southwestern Wisconsin, such as Swindler's Ridge, Snake Hollow, and Nip and Tuck. The mining village of Hardscrabble later adopted the more idyllic-sounding name of Hazel Green. The center of the Wisconsin lead region became Mineral Point, which had grown to 1,000 people by 1829. Smelting facilities sprang up to refine the lead, at which point the government took its cut. Processed lead bars known as "pigs" were transported south to Galena, and then shipped down the Mississippi. At Helena on the Wisconsin River, Green Bay businessman Daniel Whitney established an enterprise to turn lead into shot. Molten lead was dropped 120 feet down a shot tower (in reality, a vertical tunnel bored through a limestone cliff) into a cooling pool of water, creating lead balls suitable for firearms. The village of Helena has since disappeared, but the shot tower still remains on what is now known as Tower Hill.

Lead miners came from many different parts of the United States. William Hamilton, the youngest son of New York Founding Father Alexander Hamilton, established mining operations near present-day Wiota in Lafayette County, long known as "Hamilton's Diggings." Many ventured up the Mississippi from the lead regions of southeastern Missouri. Others came from southern states like Kentucky and Tennessee, giving Wisconsin's lead district a distinctly southern flavor. Some of those who came from the south, such as Henry Dodge of Missouri, brought their slaves with them to the lead mining frontier. Despite the fact that federal law banned slavery in all the lands of the Northwest Territory, an estimated 150 African-American slaves worked the lead mines of Wisconsin during the 1820s. Dodge also settled on Indian lands near present-day Dodgeville, refused to pay the government its 10 percent, and dared US troops to make him, claiming that he and other lead miners could "whip any number of US soldiers sent over from Fort Crawford to collect." Dodge was not alone. Many miners thumbed their noses at the rules and regulations of the mining district, and little could be done to make them comply. Indeed, the lead frontier was as lawless and colorful as any in American history. One traveler in the region described a good many of its inhabitants as being "fugitives from justice, thieves, pirates, and deserters" who seemed to enjoy "drinking, gambling, quarreling, dueling, and pistoling one another." "Every tavern was full to overflowing," remembered another. "Mineral Point was anything but a quiet and desirable place to live in."

The questionable morals of many miners inspired Christian missionaries to invade the region. Itinerant Methodist ministers known as "circuit riders" moved from place to place in search of converts. A Roman Catholic priest, Italian-born Father Samuel Mazzuchelli, founded a number of Catholic churches in the region. St. Augustine's Church in New Diggings, for example, is the last surviving wooden structure Mazzuchelli constructed in Wisconsin. The pioneer priest also constructed a church on Sinsinawa Mound in Grant County, and founded the Sinsinawa Dominican Sisters Congregation in 1847, which still calls the mound home. In all, Mazzuchelli (whom the English-speaking denizens of the area often referred to as "Matthew Kelly") founded more than 20 churches in the Old Northwest, and influenced the landscape of southwestern Wisconsin in other ways. For example, he platted the streets of the village of Shullsburg, giving the streets such religious-sounding names as "Charity," "Hope," and "Judgment."

Mazzuchelli died in 1864. His grave is located in the cemetery behind St. Patrick's Catholic Church in Benton. Mazzuchelli is currently a candidate for sainthood in the Roman Catholic Church.

Lead mining also attracted immigrants, especially from the British Isles. Miners from Wales and Yorkshire came to the Wisconsin lead district. Beginning in the 1830s, miners from the Cornwall region of southwestern England began to arrive. Cornwall had long been known for tin mining, but by the early nineteenth century the mining economy there was in decline. The Cornish brought with them valuable mining expertise often lacking among the Americans, such as techniques for water drainage and powder blasting. While the Americans extracted lead from surface pits, the Cornish began to dig deep shafts into the earth to tap into rich underground veins, often resuming work on claims abandoned by Americans. Their skills reinvigorated lead mining in southwestern Wisconsin. When the lead began to give out, the Cornish turned to mining zinc, an industry that lasted well into the twentieth century. Some moved on to the copper mines of Michigan, and many participated in the California Gold Rush of 1949. In all, 7,000 Cornish immigrants came to the lead district, leaving a cultural imprint on the region still evident today. The architecture of Mineral Point still resembles a quiet Cornish village. The Cornish also introduced the pasty (pronounced *PASS-tee*)—a dish consisting of meat, vegetables, and seasonings baked inside a bread crust— which miners would carry with them into the mines. One can still order a pasty in Mineral Point, Shullsburg, and other locations in southwestern Wisconsin.

Thousands came to the Wisconsin lead region in search of riches—one of the first great mineral rushes in American history. Mining often took a terrible toll on the environment. Approaching Mineral Point, one traveler noted that "the hills were stripped of their trees, and windlasses, mineral holes, piles of dirt, rocks, and mineral greeted our view on all sides." As the minerals became exhausted, agriculture assumed the dominant role in the area economy. Even today one can travel though the genteel countryside of southwestern Wisconsin and still find the remnants of mine shafts, tailings, and the chimneys of old smelters. Farmers complain that cows occasionally disappear when old mine shafts collapse. To this day, the Wisconsin state seal includes the image of a miner, a testament to the importance of the mining frontier to the state's history.

THE FATE OF THE INDIANS

The arrival of large numbers of Americans after 1815 had a tremendous effect on Wisconsin's Native Americans. With the decline of the fur trade, the Indians no longer had a commodity that Euro-Americans desired, save one— their land. Indeed, most Americans no longer viewed the Indians as economic partners, but as obstacles to "progress" and "civilization." Still economically dependent on whites, Wisconsin Indians could do little but give in to American demands for land. The marginalization of the Native Americans, and in some cases their physical removal from the region, is clearly one of the most tragic episodes in Wisconsin history.

On the eve of American settlement, the federal government controlled only small portions of present-day Wisconsin around Green Bay and Prairie du Chien. A disputed 1804 treaty with the Sauk and Mesquakie gave the United States a claim to lands in the far southwestern corner of the state. The first important cessions occurred after an 1827 episode known as the Winnebago War. As lead miners moved northward in search of new mineral deposits, they began to encroach on the lands of the Ho-Chunk. In retaliation for white depredations against his people, a Ho-Chunk warrior named Red Bird led an attack on settlers near Prairie du Chien, killing two and wounding a child. Angry Ho-Chunk warriors also began to harass American keelboats on the Mississippi. The attacks sent shock waves across the frontier, and rumors spread of an all-out Indian war. In response, General Henry Atkinson headed north from St. Louis with several hundred soldiers. In addition, troops from Fort Howard moved southward, and Henry Dodge raised a militia force among the miners. Settlers erected stockades for their protection. American forces gathered at the Fox–Wisconsin portage, but war was averted when Red Bird surrendered in September, and later died in prison awaiting trial. In response to the crisis, the army began the construction of a

Juliette Kenzie,
Wau Bun, the "Early Day" in the Northwest

Juliette Kenzie was the wife of an Indian agent named John Kenzie. In 1830, the Kenzies made their way from the east to Fort Winnebago in Portage, Wisconsin, where Mr. Kenzie served as agent to the Ho-Chunk. Their home is now the Indian Agency House, a museum of frontier life. The Kenzies eventually settled in Chicago where she wrote Wau Bun—*a classic travelogue of the Old Northwest, published in 1857. In the passage below, the Kenzies arrive at the homestead of William S. Hamilton.*

Following the course of the inclosure down the opposite slope, we came upon a group of log-cabins, low, shabby, and unpromising in their appearance, but a most welcome shelter from the pelting storm. ...

We were shown into the most comfortable-looking of the buildings. A large fire was burning in the clay chimney, and the room was of a genial warmth, notwithstanding the apertures, many inches in width, beside the doors and windows. A woman in a tidy calico dress, and shabby black silk cap, trimmed with still shabbier lace, rose from her seat beside a sort of bread-trough, which fulfilled the office of cradle to a fine, fat baby. She made room for us at the fire, but was either too timid or too ignorant to relieve me of my wrappings and defences, now heavy with the snow.

I soon contrived, with my husband's aid, to disembarrass myself of them; and having seen me comfortably disposed of; and in a fair way to be thawed after my freezing ride, he left me to see after his men and horses. He was a long time absent, and I expected he would return, accompanied by our host; but when he reappeared, it was to tell me, laughing, that Mr. Hamilton hesitated to present himself before me, being unwilling that one who had been acquainted with some of his family at the east, should see him in his present mode of life. However, this feeling apparently wore off, for before dinner he came in and was introduced to me, and was as agreeable and polite as the son of Alexander Hamilton would naturally be. ...

The blowing of a horn was the signal for the entrance of ten or twelve miners, who took their places below us at the table. They were the roughest-looking set of men I ever beheld, and their language was as uncouth as their persons. They wore hunting-shirts, trowsers, and moccasins of deerskin, the former being ornamented at the seams with a fringe of the same, while a colored belt around the waist, in which was stuck a large hunting-knife, gave each the appearance of a brigand.

Mr. Hamilton, although so much their superior, was addressed by them uniformly as "Uncle Billy;" and I could not but fancy there was something desperate about them, that it was necessary to propitiate by this familiarity. This feeling was further confirmed by the remarks of one of the company who lingered behind, after the rest of the *gang* had taken their departure. He had learned that we came from Fort Winnebago, and having informed us that "he was a discharged soldier, and would like to make some inquiries about his old station and comrades," he unceremoniously seated himself and commenced questioning us.

The bitterness with which he spoke of his former officers made me quite sure he was a deserter, and I rather thought he had made his escape from the service in consequence of some punishment. His countenance was fairly distorted as he spoke of Captain H., to whose company he had belonged. "There is a man in the mines," said he, "who has been in his hands, and if he ever gets a chance to come within shot of him, I guess the Captain will remember it. He knows well enough he darsn't set his foot in the diggings...."

Having delivered himself of these sentiments, he marched out, to my great relief.

new frontier post, Fort Winnebago, at the Fox–Wisconsin portage. All that remains of the post today is the surgeon's quarters –now a museum—and the cemetery, located nearby on County Highway F.

Ho-Chunk land cessions quickly followed the Winnebago War. The first came in 1829, when they were forced to give up their claim to the lead district lands south of the Wisconsin River. In 1832, they ceded their eastern lands in the Rock River Valley. During the 1830s, dispossessing Native Americans of their lands was not confined to Ho-Chunk in Wisconsin, but had become national policy. To make room for white settlement, President Andrew Jackson signed the Indian Removal Act in 1830, mandating that nearly every Indian tribe east of the Mississippi be transported west of the river, where the government would provide them with new lands. In 1837, the government successfully pressured the Ho-Chunk to abandon their remaining lands in Wisconsin and move west. The government moved the Ho-Chunk into Iowa and then Minnesota. Forced from their Minnesota reservation after the Dakota Uprising of 1862, the Ho-Chunk trekked even further westward into present-day South Dakota, 500 perishing along the way. Several "Disaffected Bands" of Ho-

Chunk led by Chief Yellow Thunder refused to leave
Wisconsin. On several occasions, soldiers rounded up the
Ho-Chunk renegades and shipped them westward, but
Yellow Thunder and his followers always came back. It was
not until 1874 that the government abandoned its attempts to
remove the Ho-Chunk, and allowed them to maintain
homesteads in western Wisconsin.

Government pressure forced other Wisconsin nations
to give up their lands. In northeastern Wisconsin,
significant Menominee land cessions began in 1831. Led by
the capable and respected Chief Oshkosh, the Menominee
managed to avoid removal westward, and instead obtained
a reservation on ancestral lands in 1854, enabling
Wisconsin's oldest continuous residents to remain in the
state. The Potawatomie surrendered their claims in
southeastern Wisconsin in 1833. Some Potawatomie
headed west to Kansas, while others fled to the Wisconsin
Northwoods, eventually settling in present-day Forest
County. As late as the Civil War, 4,000 Potawatomie still
lived in the Milwaukee area. In northern Wisconsin, the
Ojibwe ceded a large tract of land in 1837, under the
condition that they be allowed to hunt and fish off the
reservation. Another Ojibwe cession occurred in 1842. In
an attempt to lure the Ojibwe westward, the government
forced the tribe to collect its treaty payments at Sandy Lake,
Minnesota. Four hundred Ojibwe died en route, leading
the government to end the practice. Indeed, Indian removal
from Wisconsin was largely a failure. Of all the Native
American peoples living in Wisconsin in 1830, only one—
the Dakota—was successfully dislodged from the state. In
fact, Native Americans removed from farther east were
relocated in Wisconsin. Bands of Oneida Indians, part of
the Iroquois Confederacy, settled to the west of Green Bay,
and the Stockbridge-Munsee—remnants of the Mohican
and Lenni-Lenape (Delaware)—settled adjacent to the
Menominee Reservation in Shawano County.

In 1832, Indian troubles to the south spilled over into
Wisconsin during an event known as the Black Hawk
War. The previous year, a band of Sauk and Mesquakie—
tribes once resident in Wisconsin—had been forced from
their rich farmlands in western Illinois to new lands across
the Mississippi in Iowa. But the poor quality of

government rations during the winter of 1831–1832 created a great deal of anger. In April 1832, the aging warrior Black Hawk led about 1,000 disgruntled Sauk and Mesquakie, including many women and children, back into Illinois, where they hoped to resume farming. Fearing an Indian uprising, General Henry Atkinson led several companies of infantry from St. Louis to the Rock River. His force included two young officers named Zachary Taylor (future US president) and Jefferson Davis (future president of the rebel Confederacy). The Illinois governor called up the state's militia. Among those mobilized was a militia captain named Abraham Lincoln of New Salem, Illinois, who ventured as far north as present-day Jefferson County, Wisconsin. Lincoln never saw combat in the Black Hawk War, but claimed he had fought many bloody battles with mosquitoes, as have countless other travelers to Wisconsin. Black Hawk ascended the Rock River to the north and east, hoping for aid from the Ho-Chunk and Potawatomie. On May 14 near the Kishwaukee River in northern Illinois, drunken militiamen under the command of Captain Isaiah Stillman fired on a band of Indians flying a white truce flag. Black Hawk's men then counterattacked and drove the panic-stricken militia from the field, causing the engagement to be forever known as "Stillman's Run."

After Stillman's Run, Black Hawk's bands dispersed and fled north into Wisconsin, raiding white settlements for provisions. Once again, settlers erected stockades across the lead region to protect themselves from Indian raids. Pursuing Black Hawk into Wisconsin was General Atkinson and the local militia, led by Henry Dodge. On June 16, one of Black Hawk's raiding parties ambushed three settlers near Wiota, killing two. Colonel Henry Dodge and 20 of his men happened to arrive at the scene. The raiders took flight with Dodge in pursuit. The Indians took refuge behind an embankment near an oxbow lake once connected to the Pecatonica River. A brief skirmish ensued, known locally as the Battle of the Pecatonica. Dodge's men charged with such overwhelming force that all of the Indians were killed in just a few minutes. Only three of Dodge's men were killed, and one seriously wounded. It was the first US military victory of the war.

Re-forming near Lake Koshkonong, Black Hawk's band headed northeast along the Rock River as far as Hustisford in Dodge County. When assistance from the Ho-Chunk and Potawatomie was not forthcoming, Black Hawk then turned west, hoping to re-cross the Mississippi before being captured. Food and supplies began to run out, however, and the US soldiers were able to follow Black Hawk across the Wisconsin prairies by the trail of discarded equipment, dead horses, and dying stragglers. Undisciplined militiamen sometimes scalped the Indian stragglers they encountered. Black Hawk's band was preparing to cross the Wisconsin River in the late afternoon on July 21 when US Army and militia forces under General James D. Henry

Brookes and Stevenson, Bad Axe Battleground, 1856

caught up with them. Black Hawk and several of his warriors returned to the heights above the river to delay the American soldiers so that the remainder of the band could cross. He strategically placed his men on both sides of a small ravine in hopes that the military would follow the creek bottom in between. Colonel Henry Dodge, leading the militia, led the first charge, which was repulsed. The Battle of Wisconsin Heights raged for about an hour. As sunset approached, General Henry ordered a bayonet charge, but Black Hawk's men had slipped away through the woods and

Battlefields of the Black Hawk War

The most significant military conflict on Wisconsin soil was the Black Hawk War of 1832, of which there are three important battlefields in Wisconsin:

Battle of the Pecatonica

The battlefield is located 1.5 miles northwest of Woodford on County Highway M, in Lafayette County. The battle site is part the 60-acre Black Hawk Memorial Park. The old oxbow lake, known since the skirmish as "Bloody Lake," is still there and a historical marker tells the story of the battle.

Battle of Wisconsin Heights

The battlefield is located two miles southeast of Sauk City off State Highway 78, 3/4 mile south of the County Highway Y intersection. A state historical marker indicates the entrance to the battlefield. The mound located in the ravine is where Black Hawk directed the battle. The area was restored to its original oak savannah vegetation by the Department of Natural Resources in the 1990s. There are only a few interpretive markers.

Battle of Bad Axe

The Battle of Bad Axe took place in some of Wisconsin's most beautiful countryside. Black Hawk's band approached the river along what is now State Highway 82. The fighting occurred in and around what is now the Black Hawk Park. The Vernon County Historical Society has developed a driving tour of the Bad Axe battlefield based on historical markers placed in the 1930s. Much of the battlefield is on private land.

In addition to the battlefields, Black Hawk's trail in Wisconsin is dotted by numerous historical markers and memorials, indicating the sites of skirmishes, encampments, or stockades constructed by settlers. A notable example is Fort Koshkonong, a replica of a Black Hawk War fort near Fort Atkinson in Jefferson County.

marshes. In the morning, Henry and Dodge learned that Black Hawk's band had escaped across the Wisconsin River.

On August 1, Black Hawk's starving band reached the Mississippi at Bad Axe Creek. As they approached the riverbank, Black Hawk's band was met by the steamboat *Warrior*, which was armed with a cannon. Despite the fact that Black Hawk had waved a white flag, the *Warrior* opened fire, killing 23 and delaying the crossing. The following day army and militia troops, coming overland from the east, reached the river. Particularly desperate fighting took place in what is now known as "Battle Hollow" leading down to the river. Just as American troops had driven the Indians to the river's edge, the *Warrior* returned with reinforcements. Black Hawk's band was overwhelmed. Indians—men, women, and children— were shot trying to cross the river. John H. Fonda, whose account of the battle has been preserved in *Wisconsin Historical Collections*, recalled a particularly brutal scene involving an aged warrior and his sons:

> The old man loaded his guns as fast as his sons discharged them, and at each shot a man fell. They knew they could not expect quarter, and they sold their lives as dear as possible; making the best show of fight, and held their ground the firmest of any of the Indians. But, they could never withstand the men under Dodge, for as the volunteers poured over the bluff, they each shot a man, and in return, each of the braves was shot down and scalped by the wild volunteers, who out with their knives and cutting two parallel gashes down their backs, would strip the skin from their quivering flesh, to make razor straps of.

Black Hawk himself escaped Bad Axe, but surrendered at Prairie du Chien a few weeks later. In all, 72 whites were killed (soldiers and civilians), and anywhere from 450 to 600 Indians died in the conflict. The Black Hawk War marked the end of armed hostilities between Indians and whites in Wisconsin, and was one of the last Indian wars fought east of the Mississippi. The path was now open to extensive white settlement in the region.

Henry R. Schoolcraft and the
Treaty of Prairie du Chien

Henry Rowe Schoolcraft was one of the most important American explorers of the present-day Midwest. His accounts of his expeditions in the region are notable for his keen observations of the region's Native American peoples. In 1825, Schoolcraft was present at the negotiations for the Treaty of Prairie du Chien. The stated purpose of the treaty was "to promote peace among these tribes, and to establish boundaries among them." With boundaries established, the treaty also provided a basis for Indian land cessions. Schoolcraft described the remarkable diversity of Native American peoples gathered there:

We found a very large number of the various tribes assembled. Not only the village, but the entire banks of the river for miles above and below the town, and the island in the river, was covered with the tents. The Dakotahs, with their high pointed buffalo skin tents, above the town, and their decorations and implements of flags, feathers, skins and personal "braveries," presented the scene of a Bedouin encampment. Some of the chiefs had the skins of skunks tied to their heels, to symbolize that they never ran, as that animal is noted for its slow and self-possessed movements. ...

The Chippewas presented the more usually known traits, manners and customs of the great Algonquin family—of whom they are, indeed, the best representative. The tall and warlike bands from the sources of the Mississippi—from La Point, in Lake Superior—from the valleys of the Chippewa and St. Croix rivers, and the Rice Lake region of Lac du Flambeau, and of Sault Ste. Marie, were well represented.

The cognate tribe of the Menomonies, and the Potawattomies and Ottowas from Lake Michigan, assimilated and mingled with the Chippewas. Some of the Iroquois of Green Bay were present.

But no tribes attracted as intense a degree of interest as the Iowas, and the Sacs and Foxes—tribes of radically diverse languages, yet united in a league against the Sioux. These tribes were encamped on the island, or opposite coast. They came to the treaty ground, armed and dressed as a war party. They were all armed with spears, clubs, guns and knives. Many of the warriors had a long tuft of red-horse hair tied at their elbows, and bore a neck lace of grizzly bears' claws. Their head-dress consisted of red dyed horse-hair, tied in such manner to the scalp lock as to present the shape of the decoration of a Roman helmet. The rest of the head was completely shaved and painted. A long iron shod lance was carried in the hand. A species of baldric supported part of their arms. The azian, moccason and leggins constituted a part of their dress. They were, indeed, nearly nude, and painted. Often the print of a hand, in white clay, marked the back of shoulders. They bore flags of feathers. They beat drums. They uttered yells, at definite points. They landed in compact ranks. They looked the very spirit of defiance. Their leader stood as a prince, majestic and frowning. The wild, native pride of man, in the savage state, flushed by success in war, and confident in the strength of his arm, was never so fully depicted to my eyes. And the forest tribes of the continent may be challenged to have ever presented a spectacle of bold daring, and martial prowess, equal to their landing.

Their martial bearing, their high tone, and whole behavior during their stay, in and out of council, was impressive, and demonstrated, in an eminent degree, to what a high pitch of physical and moral courage, bravery and success in war may lead a savage people. Keokuk, who led them, stood with his war lance, high crest of feathers, and daring eye, like another Coriolanus, and when he spoke in council, and at the same time shook his lance at his enemies, the Sioux, it was evident that he wanted but an opportunity to make their blood flow like water. Wapelo, and other chiefs backed him, and the whole array, with their shaved heads and high crests of red horse-hair, told the spectator plainly, that each of these men held his life in his hand, and was ready to spring to the work of slaughter at the cry of their chief.

CREATION OF THE WISCONSIN TERRITORY

Before the land could be sold and settled, it had to be surveyed. Wisconsin, like all the lands of the Old Northwest, was mapped using a grid. The Northwest Ordinance of 1785 mandated that the lands of the Northwest Territory be divided into townships of six square miles each. Each township was then divided into 36 sections of one square mile each. Sections were then further subdivided, the typical purchase of land being a section of 40 acres. Land surveying in Wisconsin began in 1831 when surveyor Lucius Lyon built a mound at the Illinois border and the intersection of the Fourth Principle Meridian, near Hazel Green on the present-day Grant–Lafayette County line. This was the "point of beginning" for mapping Wisconsin. Using the Illinois border as a baseline, surveyors plotted township lines northward from the border every six miles. Running east or west from the Fourth Principle Meridian every six miles were range lines. Any location in Wisconsin today can be located using the township and range system begun in 1831. The checkerboard pattern is clearly evident to anyone who has flown over Wisconsin or any of the other states of the Old Northwest, and many of today's roadways follow the section lines drawn in the nineteenth century.

Once the land was surveyed, land purchases could begin. The federal government opened land offices in Green Bay and Mineral Point in 1834. Between 1834 and 1837, the government sold more than one million acres of land in Wisconsin. Fully two-thirds of the land sold went to land speculators, who possessed the capital necessary to purchase large tracts. Many speculators had worked as surveyors, providing them with an abundance of information about the economic potential of certain locations. The speculators were not just interested in obtaining prime farming and timber lands, but also potential sites for cities and villages. One area on the Lake Michigan shoreline received particular attention. Three rivers met the lake at this spot, creating a fine harbor necessary to bring in settlers and ship out produce. The surrounding prairies and woodlands provided excellent agricultural opportunities. The area had long been a fur trading entrepôt, which the Potawatomie referred to as

Mahn-ah-wauk (meaning "council grounds"), and known today as Milwaukee.

In 1818, Solomon Juneau, a French Canadian employed by the American Fur Company, established a trading post at the mouth of the Milwaukee River. As the fur trade waned and the pressures of settlement grew, Juneau found that he had peremptory rights to some of the most prized land on the western shore of Lake Michigan. In 1833, Green Bay speculator Morgan Martin proposed to Juneau a partnership to transform the land between the Milwaukee River and Lake Michigan into a settlement that became known as Juneautown. At the same time, Connecticut-born speculator Byron Kilbourn established another village on the west bank of the river, which became known as Kilbourntown. Evidence of the rivalry between the two settlements can still be found on the landscape of downtown Milwaukee. Each settlement platted its streets independently of the other, forcing the bridges across the Milwaukee River that link the two former towns to be at odd angles. A third settlement emerged on the south bank of the Menomonee River known as Walker's Point, named after Virginia speculator George H. Walker. Southeastern Wisconsin became the focus of a land boom in the 1830s, and Milwaukee—created by the merger of the three competing settlements—quickly emerged as Wisconsin's leading city.

Settlers would require roads to enter the new lands, and the federal government began an effort to construct them. The first important thoroughfare, known as the Military Road, linked Forts Howard, Winnebago, and Crawford. Work began in 1832 under the direction of Lt. Alexander Center. The soldiers stationed at the forts did much of the labor. The Military Road was hardly a great engineering project. It was little more than a dirt and log thoroughfare, typically made impassable by snowmelt and storms. Center charted the path of least resistance, bypassing hills and swamps and often following ancient Indian trails. Nevertheless, when completed in 1837, the Military Road provided a useable overland route from Green Bay to Prairie du Chien and the lead district. Some of Wisconsin's present-day highways are built on the foundations of the Military Road, such as a stretches of US Highway 18 from Prairie du Chien to Mount Horeb. The highlands along the south bank of the Wisconsin River on which this portion of the road was built is still known as the Military Ridge. Other segments of the old Military Road over which the automobile tourist can still travel today include portions of US 151 north and south of Fond du Lac, and State Highway 55 along the eastern shore of Lake Winnebago.

Between 1835 and 1836, the army constructed another road from Green Bay to Chicago, linking Forts Howard and Dearborn. Later military roads penetrated into northern Wisconsin and Upper Michigan. The federal government sponsored the building of other roads. State Highway 11, for example, generally follows the course of a federal road constructed to link the lead district with the growing lake port cities. Private companies sprang up to build wooden plank roads, which charged a toll. In all, Wisconsin chartered 135 plank-road projects between 1836 and 1871. Inns and other establishments served weary travelers on Wisconsin's early highways, like the Wade House in Sheboygan County, completed in 1850. Canal building was of little consequence in Wisconsin. Milwaukee businessman Byron Kilbourn dreamed of a canal network linking Milwaukee with the Rock River, but little came of it. The logical place for a canal was at the Fox–Wisconsin portage. Construction began on the 2.5-mile-long canal in 1849, but by then it was too late. Chicago had already emerged as the most important link between the Great Lakes and the Mississippi Valley. The slow, meandering headwaters of the Fox were unsuited for heavy barge traffic anyway. Chicago, of course, went on to become the great metropolis of the Midwest and one of the world's great cities. Visitors today can still stroll along the banks of the Portage Canal, and think about what Portage might have become.

Settlers to Wisconsin came from many different places, but those who dominated the earliest years of settlement were the "Yankees"—those descended from New England stock. After the American Revolution, New Englanders began to leave the rocky soils of that region for the fertile farmlands of New York State. The migration of Yankees continued westward with the frontier, channeled into the Great Lakes region by the Erie Canal. Yankees were prominent in the settling of Ohio, Michigan, and northern

Illinois, and by the 1830s the flood of Yankees hit the southeastern portions of Wisconsin. New York State sent the largest share of migrants to Wisconsin, more than 68,000 by 1850. Numerous Wisconsin cities, towns, and villages bear the names of localities in New York, such as Albany (Green County), Brooklyn (Dane County), Genesee (Waukesha County), Otsego (Columbia County), and Rochester (Racine County). The influence of the Empire State was so strong that Wisconsin was sometimes referred to as "New York's Daughter." The New England states sent a good number of migrants to Wisconsin as well. Dane County, for example, contains place names such as Fitchburg, Springfield, Deerfield, Roxbury, Windsor, Rutland, and Vermont—all reminiscent of the New England countryside that many migrants to Wisconsin left behind. The Yankees in the eastern part of the region soon began to outnumber the Southerners and others in the lead district. The Yankees brought with them a system of values that would greatly shape Wisconsin history. Descended from the Puritans, they had a sense of Christian piety and a divine mission to improve the world. Yankee culture stressed literacy and education, as well as a strong spirit of community responsibility. The Yankees also had a reputation for industriousness and entrepreneurial acumen. Their presence would further link Wisconsin to the northeastern states, politically and culturally as well as economically.

By 1836, the population of Wisconsin had reached 11,000, leading to the creation of the Wisconsin Territory that year. Although still a part of the Michigan Territory, residents west of Lake Michigan began to complain that the territorial government in Detroit was too distant and did not consider their interests. East of the lake, Michiganders began to press for statehood, drawing up a constitution and demanding admission to the Union. Boundary disputes and sectional politics delayed statehood until 1837, but by 1836 Michigan statehood was all but assured. On July 3, 1836, the Wisconsin Territory was officially created. The new territory extended from Lake Michigan westward to the Missouri River, encompassing the present-day states of Wisconsin, Iowa, and Minnesota, as well as portions of the Dakotas.

President Andrew Jackson appointed his friend and protégée Henry Dodge to be the first territorial governor.

Aside from being Democrats, Jackson and Dodge were remarkably similar in other ways. Both had gained reputations as Indian-fighting frontiersmen. Governor Dodge was frequently spotted wearing pistols and Bowie knives while conducting official government business. Both men were also slaveholders from the upper South, though Dodge emancipated his slaves upon his appointment as governor of a northern territory. The hero of the Black Hawk War, Dodge was popular with the territory's residents, but his administrative and political skills were sometimes lacking. A proponent of the lead district, Dodge established a temporary capital at Belmont in Lafayette County. The Yankees along the lakeshore complained that Belmont was too distant, and the absence of any substantial settlements nearby made the site seem remote and impractical to all involved with territorial government. "The accommodations at Belmont were most miserable, there being but a single boarding house," wrote one delegate. "Our beds were all full, and the floor well spread with blankets and overcoats for lodging purposes."

One of the top priorities of the territorial legislature was to designate a permanent capital. The legislators at Belmont were besieged with proposals for capital sites from across the territory, each promoter touting the advantages of his location. The winner in this competition was federal judge and land speculator James Duane Doty, who owned land on an isthmus between Lakes Mendota and Monona in south-central Wisconsin. Located roughly half way between the lead region and the lakeshore, Doty's site was an excellent regional compromise. A shrewd political operator, Doty bribed legislators with plots of land in his proposed capital city and even provided them with warm buffalo robes in the dead of winter. Doty's site, named Madison in honor of constitutional architect and former president James Madison, was approved as the new capital in December 1836. The capital was moved from Belmont to Burlington, Iowa, while development of the Madison site was underway. In Madison, the capitol building would be situated on a glacial drumlin overlooking the isthmus and surrounding prairies. The streets of the new city were named for the signers of the US Constitution (although one street on the Capitol Square was later named for Doty). In 1838, lands west of the Mississippi were split off from Wisconsin to form the Iowa Territory, and the Wisconsin territorial government took up its permanent residence in Madison.

Wisconsin's population continued to swell. By 1840, the Wisconsin Territory had a population of 30,945. Just six years later, Wisconsin contained 155,247 persons—well above the 60,000 required for statehood. Most of the new arrivals were Yankees, although others came as well, including Europeans, especially from Great Britain, Norway, and Germany (European immigration will be explored in more detail in the next chapter). Nineteenth-century America, with its emerging democracy and fluid social order, seemed like one massive social experiment. Inspired by the sense of change and feeling of human liberation of the day, several new religious movements and utopian societies emerged, both in America and in Europe. Wisconsin was home to several such groups. One of the most notable was the Church of Jesus Christ of Latter-Day Saints—better known as the Mormons. A small group of Mormons settled in Lafayette County during the 1840s. Because of their unorthodox religious ideas, as well as the controversial practice of polygamy, the Mormons faced bitter persecution and were driven from place to place until they established a colony at the Great Salt Lake in the remote deserts of the American West. Graceland Cemetery in Blanchardville is one of the last remnants of early Mormonism in Wisconsin. In 1844, a utopian society known as the Wisconsin Phalanx founded a commune in Fond du Lac County named Ceresco, based on the ideas of French philosopher Charles Fourier. Phalanx members lived communally, holding all property in common and sharing equally in labor and its profits. Ceresco was more successful than most communal experiments, but the creation of the rival village of Ripon nearby doomed its future. The commune broke up, but one of its dormitories still stands on the west side Ripon's Ceresco Park.

By the mid-1840s, Wisconsinites began to call for statehood. In 1846, 124 delegates gathered in Madison to write a state constitution. Although the overwhelming majority of Wisconsin residents were Democrats, the convention was nevertheless fraught with division. In particular, the constitution created by the 1846 convention banned the chartering of banks, which many viewed as tools of the wealthy. Yankee opposition to the banking prohibition led to the defeat of the constitution in an 1846 referendum. Lawmakers met again in 1847, watering down the failed constitution of the previous year by deferring the banking issue and other thorny problems to later referenda. In March 1848, voters approved the constitution 16,754 to 6,384. On May 29, 1848, President James K. Polk signed legislation that made Wisconsin the 30th state in the Union. Wisconsinites were now able to participate fully in the political life of the nation. Nelson Dewey, a Yankee who owned a large estate on the Mississippi River he called Stonefield, was elected Wisconsin's first governor.

Wisconsin entered the union at a particularly dramatic moment in American history. By 1848, the sectional crisis over slavery, brewing since the time of the American Revolution, could no longer be contained. Wisconsin would play a significant role—and sometimes take center stage— in the great drama that was the American Civil War.

4

THE CIVIL WAR ERA

The Civil War that broke out in 1861 was the bloodiest and most destructive conflict in American history. The primary cause of the war was slavery, an issue about which increasing numbers of Americans were unwilling to compromise. "A house divided against itself cannot stand," stated Abraham Lincoln in 1858. "I believe this government cannot endure permanently half slave and half free. I do not expect the Union to be dissolved; I do not expect the house to fall; but I do expect it will cease to be divided. It will become all one thing, or all the other." Lincoln, who would lead the Union through the war, proved to be right. As the sectional crisis brewed and then exploded, Wisconsin was a young state. Its economy and its society were in flux. Some parts of the state had just passed through the frontier stage; some parts had yet to be settled. Like it or not, Wisconsin and its people were thrust into the greatest crisis the nation had ever known. The young Badger State would have to grow up fast.

A MATURING ECONOMY

In the decades after statehood, Wisconsin's economy revolved around agriculture. Even though it is known today as the "Dairy State," Wisconsin was a wheat-growing state during the Civil War era. Wheat was a hearty crop that grew well in the changeable climate of the Upper Midwest. It required little capital outlay on the part of the farmer, and once planted it needed little maintenance until harvest time. The country was growing quickly and wheat was in high demand. Indeed, Wisconsin wheat was also exported overseas, connecting Badger State farmers to worldwide markets. In 1850, Wisconsin farmers produced 4.2 million bushels of wheat; by 1860 that figure had climbed to 14 million. Wisconsin wheat contributed mightily to the feeding of Union troops during the Civil War. By the 1870s, Wisconsin had nearly two million acres of land devoted to wheat cultivation, nearly all of it south of the Fox–Wisconsin waterway. Other economic activities sprang up to support wheat production. Grist mills emerged to grind the wheat into flour, for example. Mills were usually located along fast-moving rivers to take advantage of water power, and formed the basis of many of Wisconsin's present-day cities and towns. One of the best surviving examples of a pre–Civil War mill is a five-story grain mill dating to 1855 that still overlooks downtown Cedarburg.

The origins of industrialization in Wisconsin can also be traced to the state's agricultural economy. The Industrial Revolution—an economic shift from handicraft manufacturing to mass production in factories—began in Great Britain in the eighteenth century and spread to America by the 1820s. New industrial inventions made farming the American frontier more efficient and profitable, such as John Deere's steel plow, which tilled prairie soils more effectively, and Cyrus McCormick's mechanical reaper. In 1842, a New York migrant named Jerome I. Case founded a company to manufacture threshing machines in Rochester, Wisconsin. The J.I. Case Company eventually moved its operations to nearby Racine and became one of the nation's most innovative manufacturers of farm equipment, and Case amassed one of Wisconsin's first great industrial fortunes. Frontier Wisconsin had a good supply of livestock, which in turn supported several industries. Milwaukee became a regional meatpacking center, for example. The availability of animal skins, as well as ample supplies of hemlock, oak, and tamarack bark made Milwaukee the leading center of the leather tanning industry in the United States. Indeed, by 1900 Wisconsin produced 15 percent of the nation's raw leather. Tanning, in turn, led to the rise of boot and shoe manufacturing in Wisconsin. Many of the boots worn by Civil War soldiers were made in the Badger State.

Wisconsin was increasingly connected to national and even international markets. Port cities sprang up along the Lake Michigan shoreline to export the state's agricultural produce and manufactured goods. Places like Kenosha (originally known as Southport), Racine, Port Washington,

Sheboygan, and Manitowoc all owe much of their early development to maritime activities. Wisconsin's main port was Milwaukee, with its harbor protected from vicious lake storms. The bounty of Wisconsin was shipped east to Buffalo, then across the Erie Canal to New York City. The wheat boom of the 1850s made Milwaukee one of the busiest ports on the Great Lakes, and grain elevators dotted the Milwaukee skyline. Indeed, for a brief time Milwaukee was a busier port than Chicago.

But no transportation development was more important than the railroad. Rail lines slowly snaked their way westward, connecting Chicago to the East Coast by 1852. Railroads could carry a larger bulk of goods faster than traditional road and water transportation methods. They were also less affected by weather conditions and could run all year long. The railroads carried passengers as well, and travel times across the country lessened considerably. By the time of the Civil War, it took just days to reach Wisconsin from New York, rather than weeks. Railroads were incredibly expensive to build, however. Huge amounts of capital had to be raised long before profits could ever be realized. Because most state governments (like Wisconsin) forbid the use of state tax money for internal improvements, America's railroads were built by private corporations, which were typically engaged in cutthroat competition characterized by periods of boom and bust.

Wisconsin's first railroad—a mere ten-mile stretch between Milwaukee and Waukesha—was completed in 1851. Just six years later Wisconsin had 688 miles of track, with lines connecting Chicago and Milwaukee, and traversing the state from Lake Michigan to the Mississippi River. Towns and villages competed fiercely for rail connections, issuing subsidies to attract rail connections. Farmers, recognizing the advantages of railroads to ship their crops to market, often mortgaged their farms to buy stock in railroad companies, and even provided the labor needed to build the lines in their localities. But the railroads soon gained an unsavory reputation in the eyes of many Wisconsinites. Company owners openly bribed lawmakers for favors, especially when government land grants to rail companies began in 1856. During the Panic of 1857 every

*The first Milwaukee railroad depot, which was used by the Milwaukee &
Waukesha and the Milwaukee & Mississippi railroads. After the Milwaukee
Road acquired the Milwaukee & Mississippi Railroad in 1868 and diverted
the passenger trains to the Union Depot on Reed Street. The presence of
passenger cars to the north of the depot suggest that this picture was taken
shortly prior to that move.*

rail company in Wisconsin went bankrupt, leaving
thousands with worthless stocks and bonds. After the
panic, Milwaukee banker Alexander Mitchell, an
immigrant from Scotland, bought up numerous Wisconsin
railroads, eventually consolidating them as the Chicago,
Milwaukee, & St. Paul Railroad, commonly known as the
Milwaukee Road. Mitchell also had interests in the Chicago
& Northwestern Railroad, which also owned tracks in
Wisconsin. Mitchell soon dominated all rail traffic in the

Badger State, and his companies began to penetrate into the northern woodlands and onto the Great Plains. Farmers complained that Mitchell used his monopoly power over Wisconsin railroads to overcharge his customers and to influence politicians to prevent regulation. In the coming decades, the power of the railroads and other corporations would become a dominant issue in Wisconsin politics.

The opening of new farmlands, combined with the development of manufacturing, made Wisconsin's economy boom, attracting an ever-increasing stream of migrants from the east. Wisconsin also attracted thousands of immigrants, who would shape the course of Wisconsin history in countless ways.

Land of Immigrants

Wisconsin opened for settlement at the dawn of a massive worldwide movement of people. Between 1820 and 1920, roughly 36 million people came to the United States, mainly from Europe. Europe's population increased dramatically after 1800, nearly doubling in just 50 years. At the same time, the nature of the European economy was changing. The subsistence farming practiced by European peasants for centuries was giving way to commercial agriculture. Small plots of land were being consolidated into larger, more efficient farms. In short, it took fewer peasants to produce more food. Those peasants who owned their own land were usually able to sell it at a profit; others were

Ethnic Heritage

America's Black Holocaust Museum
2233 N. 4th Street
Milwaukee, WI 53212
(414) 264-2500
www.blackholocaustmuseum.org
The museum chronicles the experience of African peoples not just in Wisconsin, but in all of America. It contains exhibits on the forced immigration of slaves from Africa, slave life, and the struggle for freedom. It also contains exhibits about its founder, Dr. James Cameron, the only person known to have survived a lynching. Cameron passed away in 2006.

Little Norway
Blue Mounds, WI 53517
(608) 473-8211
www.littlenorway.com
Originally a Norwegian pioneer homestead, Little Norway contains numerous buildings related to Norwegian-American heritage—including a reconstruction of a Norwegian church displayed at the 1893 World's Fair in Chicago—as well as a vast collection of Norwegian folk artifacts.

Swiss Historical Village
612 Seventh Avenue
New Glarus, WI 53574
(608) 527-2317
www.swisshistoricalvillage.org
Founded in 1942, the Swiss Historical Village recreates the world of the Swiss immigrants who founded New Glarus. The whole village gets into the act as well, its architecture attempting to imitate a rural Swiss atmosphere—without the Alps, of course.

Norskedalen
N455 O. Ophus Rd
P. O. Box 235
Coon Valley, WI 54623
(608) 452-3424
www.norskedalen.org
Meaning "Norwegian Valley" in English, Norskedalen re-creates Norwegian frontier life with authentic Norwegian- constructed

buildings from the surrounding area that have been relocated to the site.

Old World Wisconsin
S103 W37890 Highway 67
Eagle, WI 53119
(262) 594-6300
www.wisconsinhistory.org/oww/
Old World Wisconsin, a program of the Wisconsin Historical Society, is a living history museum that depicts the lives of rural immigrants in the nineteenth century. On the grounds of this 576-acre facility are historic buildings gathered from across the state and painstakingly rebuilt. Costumed interpreters carry out the day-to-day tasks of the immigrant farmers—farming, cooking, cleaning, and caring for livestock. In addition to European immigrant groups, the facility also portrays the experiences of Yankee and African-American migrants. In the center of Old World Wisconsin is "Ethnic Crossroads Village," a collection of typical village buildings such as a blacksmith shop, an inn, a town hall, and church—places a frontier farmer would visit on an excursion into town.

Wisconsin's Ethnic Settlement Trail
5900 North Port Washington Road Suite 146
Milwaukee, WI 53217
(414) 961-2110
www.ethnicwisconsin.org
A heritage tourism project of the Wisconsin Department of Tourism, Wisconsin's Ethnic Settlement Trail guides travelers through the unique ethnic patchwork that is eastern Wisconsin from the earliest days of settlement to the present. Many tours focus on specific groups, including Czechs, Danes, Dutch, French Canadians, Icelanders, Irish, Italians, Norwegians, Poles, and Swedes. There are several related to the Germans. Native Americans are also included. Other tours focus on multi-ethnic neighborhoods, such as the Bay View section of Milwaukee. The tours lead visitors to churches, museums, cultural organizations, and other significant sites.

In addition, Wisconsin cities and villages host numerous ethnic festivals. Visit the Wisconsin Department of Tourism's website at www.travelwisconsin.com for listings.

simply forced from their homes. Most displaced peasants sought factory jobs in European cities, but for those who could afford the voyage, emigration to America—and the Wisconsin frontier—was another option. Wisconsin's growing cities offered jobs, often at better pay and under better conditions than those available in Europe. Especially appealing to displaced peasants was the opportunity to own land. There was virtually no available farmland left in Europe, but the American frontier had countless acres of prime land available at cheap prices. In America, a lowly peasant could become a free and prosperous farmer.

Many were drawn to the United States by so-called American letters—correspondence from immigrants to friends and relatives back in Europe describing the numerous opportunities available in the United States. "Yes, it really is good here," wrote one German immigrant back home about Wisconsin. "There are no dues, no titles here, no taxes... no [mounted] police, no beggars." "It is almost unbelievable how fortune has gone for us the whole time in the new world," wrote an immigrant from Norway. "There is no one of our ages here who have climbed upward as fast as we." Such tales of freedom and good fortune attracted thousands from Europe to Wisconsin. By the time of the Civil War, roughly one-third of Wisconsin's population had been born in another country.

During the nineteenth century, most immigrants to Wisconsin came from northern and western Europe. Great Britain in particular was a significant source of immigrants. Because of their close cultural links to their American cousins, British immigrants had many advantages over their continental European contemporaries. They spoke the same language as native-born Americans, and shared common Protestant religious traditions. The British also understood the basics of the American political and legal system, which are based largely on British models. British immigrants often came with a little money or a skill, and quickly found a stable place in the economy. The British were sometimes referred to as the "invisible immigrants" because of their tendency to blend into American society so easily. "There is ten scotch families all within a few miles of us," wrote Scottish immigrant James Douglas from his new farmstead outside Milwaukee. "We have two scotchmen for neighbors. Their land joins mine and we have two Englishmen on the other side." Douglas also confided that "I like the yankes better than either the scotch or english for neighbours." Ethnic enclaves of British immigrants were rare, but several emerged in Wisconsin. Miners from Cornwall settled in southwestern Wisconsin during the lead rush of the 1820s and 1830, for example (see Chapter 3). Clusters of Welsh settled around Wales (Waukesha County) and Cambria (Columbia County). Place names like Caledonia (Racine County) and Argyle (Lafayette County) indicate the presence of Scottish settlers.

Another group of immigrants from the British Isles, but one distinctive in many ways, was the Irish. The Irish maintained their culture, including their Roman Catholic faith, in the face of centuries of English invasion and occupation. England ruled Ireland like a conquered colony, seizing its land and trapping its peasants in poverty. Compounding the misery of Ireland was the Potato Famine of the 1840s. The potato, which was the staple crop of the Irish peasant, suffered from a severe blight that led to massive crop failures and widespread hunger. Many starved to death, while others left Ireland altogether. The Irish were the single largest immigrant group to the United States before the Civil War; nearly two million arrived between 1820 and 1860. They were also the poorest group, often arriving with nothing but the clothes on their backs. Irish immigrants flooded into the cities of the east, and ended up with the dirtiest, lowest-paying jobs. Because of their poverty it was difficult for the Irish to make their way to the Wisconsin frontier, but many did nonetheless. Some took railroad jobs that brought them west, while others simply moved from town to town seeking employment. In Wisconsin, Irish immigrants took manufacturing jobs in the growing cities, or worked as itinerant farmhands. Irish neighborhoods sprang up in several Wisconsin cities, such as in Milwaukee's Third Ward on the lower east side of the city. In some places rural Irish enclaves emerged, such as the Town of Erin in Washington County and the area around Dundee along the Sheboygan–Fond du Lac County line.

Most immigrants to Wisconsin came from continental Europe, and the largest immigrant group to Wisconsin was the Germans. By 1860, nearly a quarter of Wisconsin

Must-See Sites: Milton House

In 1838, a Yankee migrant named Joseph Goodrich settled at the crossing of two Indians trails, a place known as Prairie du Lac in Rock County. Goodrich opened a frontier inn, and the village of Milton grew up around it. By all accounts, Goodrich's inn was usually filled to capacity. In 1844 he completed work on a much larger stagecoach inn, a distinctive hexagonal building that became known as the Milton House. Touring the restored inn, visitors can get a first-hand idea of what it was like to travel across frontier Wisconsin. Visitors are guided through all surviving sections of the inn, including the lobby, guest rooms, blacksmith shop, and many other features.

But what is really special about the Milton House lies in the basement. Joseph Goodrich was a staunch abolitionist, and it is widely believed that he was a conductor on the Underground Railroad. The Milton House

is the best documented of all Underground Railroad stations in Wisconsin. After touring the inn, visitors are guided to the basement. Located there are small displays related to slavery, abolitionism, and the Milton House's role in the struggle to free the slaves. Visitors are also shown the inn's storage areas, where runaways were believed to have stayed.

How did the escaped slaves get into the Milton House without being detected? Located about 40 feet behind the inn is the Goodrich Cabin. Connecting the two structures is an underground tunnel, through which visitors can walk. This tunnel, it is believed, was used to conceal Underground Railroad activities. Under cover of darkness, runaways were spirited into the cabin. Once in the cabin, the runaways would then be guided through a trap door in the cabin's floor, through the tunnel, and into the Milton House basement. To resume their journey, the escapees were guided back through the tunnel, and away from the Milton House toward their next stop on their journey to freedom.

residents had been born in Germany, and by 1890 the figure reached 35 percent. According to the 2000 census, 42 percent of Wisconsin residents still reported German as their primary ethnic identification. German immigrants were a remarkably diverse people. Germany was not a unified empire until 1871, and many immigrant Germans identified with their home province and not "Germany" at all. To Wisconsin came Bavarians, Hessians, Pomeranians, Saxons—even Hamburgers and Frankfurters. German immigrants were often bitterly divided along religious and regional lines. Prior to 1860, Catholics from the Rhineland and southern Germany predominated; thereafter Protestants from northern and eastern Germany prevailed. In addition, German Jews arrived in Wisconsin along with their Christian countrymen, and some German immigrants were "freethinkers" who rejected organized religion altogether. A small but prominent group of Germans were liberal political refugees from the failed revolutions of 1848. Most notable among these "Forty-Eighters" to come to Wisconsin was Carl Schurz, who lived in Watertown from 1855 to 1861. Schurz served as a Civil War general, ambassador, and US senator from Missouri. His wife, Margarethe Meyer Schurz, is said to have founded America's first kindergarten in Watertown in 1856. Not until they arrived in America did most of these immigrants even think of themselves as "German."

Wisconsin's first German settlement, Freistadt, was founded by Lutherans from Pomerania in 1839. The settlement is in the present-day city of Mequon in Ozaukee County. In nearby Germantown in Washington County, a number of German hamlets emerged, such as Dhiensville and Kirchhayn, both of which still exist today. Germans promptly spread throughout Wisconsin, but tended to congregate in specific areas. German farmers settled mainly in the counties of eastern Wisconsin, especially along the Lake Michigan shoreline, where they constituted the majority in many areas. Here the settlers found a temperate climate and fertile landscape shaped by glaciers, much like they had known back home. Even today, one can drive through the countryside of eastern Wisconsin and be reminded of a pastoral German setting with green fields, Holstein cows, wooded lots, and hilltop churches. In particular, a region known as the "Holy Land" in northeastern Fond du Lac County and nearby areas was settled by German Catholics who retained the old custom of naming their villages after their churches, such as St. Joseph and Mt. Calvary. German place names are common across eastern Wisconsin, such as Kiel (Manitowoc County), New Holstein (Calumet County), and Rhine (Sheboygan County). Germans were also numerous in Sauk and Grant Counties in the southwest, Marathon County in the north-central region, and many other areas of the state. Nearly every city had a German neighborhood. In Milwaukee, the Germans were concentrated on the north side of town.

The Germans influenced life in Wisconsin in countless ways. Having gained a reputation for efficiency and industriousness, Germans contributed significantly to the state's economic development. German entrepreneurs established some of Wisconsin's most profitable companies. In 1848, German immigrant Frederick Vogel founded a tannery—one of many Germans to enter that occupation. He sold his products in the store of another German, Guido Pfister. The Pfister and Vogel Leather Company that emerged from the partnership became Milwaukee's largest tanning operation and one of the largest in the world. The Pfister family would later build the Pfister Hotel in Milwaukee, which remains one of the state's most elegant and luxurious. Indeed, German immigrants brought to Wisconsin its most famous industry of all—beer brewing—which before the Civil War served only the local market. German farms were said to be clean, efficient, and very productive. Germans seemed to have an eye for good land, selecting farm plots near market centers and transportation routes, and with sufficient supplies of wood for building and for fuel. Germans were less likely than Yankees to go into debt to finance their farm operations. Wisconsin's Germans enjoyed a vigorous social life, consisting of literary societies, musical clubs, and numerous other organizations. Milwaukee was known as the "German Athens" because of the vast number of German cultural organizations active in the city. One of the most popular clubs among Germans was the *Turnverein*, a gymnastic society. Wisconsin's oldest surviving Turner Hall, dating to 1867, is in the Hamilton section of Cedarburg. Many

German culinary traditions persist in Wisconsin, perhaps most notably a type of sausage known as the *bratwurst*. Wisconsinites prefer the "Sheboygan-style" bratwurst, which is unique to the American Midwest, and remains the focus of any summer cookout in the Badger State.

Numerous other groups from northwestern Europe made their way to the Wisconsin frontier during the middle of the nineteenth century. Second in numbers to the Germans were Norwegians, who settled mainly in south-central and western Wisconsin. The Norwegians were overwhelmingly a farming people who lived in tight-knit, isolated communities. Danish immigrants settled in Brown County, as well as in Racine, where one can still enjoy a Danish pastry known as a *kringle*. In fact, the Danish neighborhood of Racine was long known as "Kringleville." German-speaking immigrants from Switzerland settled New Glarus in Green County in 1845. Czechs, known to Americans in the nineteenth century as Bohemians, were concentrated in Manitowoc and Kewaunee Counties. Immigrants from the Netherlands came as well. The Dutch, like the Germans, settled in separate communities divided along religious lines. In 1848, Father Johannes VandenBroek established a colony of Dutch Catholics along the Fox River in Outagamie County. Kaukauna, Little Chute, and nearby cities remain heavily Dutch today. Dutch Protestants settled southwest of Fond du Lac, as well as in southern Sheboygan County in the area of Oostburg and Cedar Grove. Belgians—both French and Dutch speaking—settled along the shores of Green Bay in Brown and Door Counties. French-Canadian fishermen came to Two Rivers seeking better opportunities. Even people from the tiny country of Luxembourg settled in the Badger State, especially in southern Sheboygan and northern Ozaukee Counties. Many ethnic traditions, like Swiss yodeling and the crafting of Dutch wooden shoes, were reported in Wisconsin as late as World War II. Perhaps no place outside of New York City can boast of the diversity of pre–Civil War immigrant groups than Wisconsin.

The State of Wisconsin actively promoted immigration. It flooded Germany and other parts of Europe with guidebooks to the state, and opened an immigration office in New York. Not everyone welcomed the newcomers, however. Immigrant cultures often clashed with American ways. Many Americans insisted that immigrants speak English, for example. Alcohol was another point of contention. Germans of nearly all backgrounds enjoyed drinking beer. (The countless number of taverns in Wisconsin today stands as a testament to the continuing influence of German culture on Wisconsin life.) However, native-born Americans were often aghast at German drinking habits, especially the practice of the "continental Sunday," where German families gathered in the local beer hall after church. To many Yankees, the consumption of alcohol on Sunday was little short of blasphemy—especially in the presence of children. In fact, a temperance movement grew in strength among Yankees during the nineteenth century. Religion was perhaps the greatest source of contention, in particular the Roman Catholic faith of the Irish and a good many others. Believing that all Catholics were unquestionably loyal to a "foreign potentate" (the Pope), some saw Catholic immigration as part of a papal conspiracy to snuff out American democracy and turn the United States into a papal dominion. Yankees hoped that public schools would Americanize the newcomers, especially the Catholics. In response, immigrants tended to favor church-run parochial schools that stressed their own religious values, and which were often conducted in native languages. In politics, immigrants favored the dominant Democratic Party, which pledged to keep government power as limited as possible. Social reformers like temperance and public-school activists gravitated to the opposition Whigs.

Immigration was not the only factor changing the ethno-cultural makeup of Wisconsin. Migrants from other parts of the United States continued to come as well, especially Yankees from the Northeast. African Americans also began to filter into the Badger State. People of African descent had lived in Wisconsin long before 1848. Among the French fur trappers, for example, were "Black Métis" of mixed African and Indian ancestry. A few army officers stationed at Fort Crawford brought their slaves with them to Wisconsin, as did some southern lead miners such as Henry Dodge (see Chapter 3). Dodge and other Wisconsin slaveholders had freed their slaves before statehood in 1848,

Wisconsin's Civil War Training Camps

During the Civil War, numerous training camps emerged to turn Wisconsin's young men into soldiers. None are well preserved, but Civil War enthusiasts can still visit many of their locations:

Camp Barstow (Janesville)—The site of Camp Barstow is located south of downtown Janesville on the banks of the Rock River, just northwest of the intersection of Delavan Drive and Beloit Avenue. Located on part of the grounds is the present-day Rotary International Botanical Gardens.

Camp Bragg (Oshkosh)—Located on the west side of Oshkosh, the site of the camp is today Camp Bragg Memorial Park, which is at the northeast corner of Hazel and Cleveland streets in Oshkosh.

Camp Harvey (Kenosha)—The First Wisconsin Cavalry organized at Ripon, but, finding no suitable place there to train, the regiment relocated to Kenosha. The new camp was named after the popular Wisconsin Civil War Governor Louis P. Harvey, who died in an accident while visiting Wisconsin troops in Tennessee in 1862. It was located on the south side of Kenosha, on a site now within the borders of Kenosha's Green Ridge Cemetery. A stone monument marks the location.

Camp Randall (Madison)—The Camp Randall site is bounded by Monroe Street on the south, University Avenue to the north, Breese Terrace to the west, and Randall Ave to the east. Today Camp Randall is part of the University of Wisconsin, occupied mainly by the University's Athletic Department, including Camp Randall Stadium—home of the Wisconsin Badgers football team. Remnants of the area's Civil War heritage are confined to a small park in the southeastern corner of the facility, consisting of a memorial arch at the foot of Dayton Street, several cannon, a smattering of monuments, and reproductions of the cabins in which Confederate prisoners were held. After World War II, parts of the site were used to house returning veterans attending the University of Wisconsin on the G.I. Bill.

Camp Scott (Milwaukee)—The site of Camp Scott is located near downtown Milwaukee. The camp was located just northwest of the intersection of Wisconsin Avenue and 12th Street. Today, West Wells and West Kilbourn Streets run through the former camp, and the area is part of the Marquette University campus.

Camp Sigel (Milwaukee)—The site of Camp Sigel is located on the northeast side of Milwaukee, in an area today bounded by Prospect and Bartlett avenues (east and west borders) and Lafayette and Royal Places (north and south). Initially named **Camp Holton**, the grounds were renamed in honor of General Franz Sigel, a prominent German-American politician, and were the training grounds for most of the state's German regiments. Late in the war, the facility was renamed again, this time **Camp Reno**. The area is today a residential district.

Camp Tredway (Janesville)—Located on the east side of Janesville, the site of Camp Tredway is presently occupied by the Rock County Fair Grounds, at the intersection of East Milwaukee Street and Randall Avenue.

Camp Utley (Racine)—The site of Camp Utley was located between 17th and 23rd streets (north to south), with Lake Michigan to the east and railroad tracks to the west. Today the area is largely residential, though a park now exists along the lakeshore.

Camp Washburn (Milwaukee)—This camp was located at the Cold Spring Race Track on Vliet Street just west of North 27th Street.

Camp Wood (Fond du Lac)—Originally known as Camp Hamilton, this camp was located on the west side of the city between Johnson and Division Streets; and from Lincoln Avenue (then Waupun Street) to Hickory Street. A stone marker commemorates the camp, though, oddly, it is located in Playmore Park, some distance from the camp location.

and many of these ex-slaves remained in the Badger State. After 1848, free blacks migrated into the state, as did increasing numbers of runaway slaves seeking freedom from the slave states of the South. Small black communities emerged in Milwaukee and Racine. Southwestern Wisconsin contained African-American farming settlements at Pleasant Ridge and Patch Grove in Grant County, and Cheyenne Valley in eastern Vernon County. Wisconsin's African Americans frequently experienced bitter racial discrimination. The state constitution specifically barred them from voting, and subsequent efforts to provide black suffrage before the Civil War all ended in failure. It was not until after the Civil War that black Wisconsinites could vote. Although Wisconsin's African Americans were not slaves, they still faced numerous obstacles to full equality.

WISCONSIN AND THE SECTIONAL CRISIS

Ever since the American Revolution, the United States tried to exist with the South dependent on slave labor and the North free from it. As the nineteenth century progressed, Northerners increasingly saw slavery as a moral abomination and a barrier to economic development. A vocal few were abolitionists, who wanted to end slavery immediately and unconditionally. At the same time, Southerners were just as determined to hold on to their "peculiar institution." At the conclusion of the Mexican–American War in 1848, the United States gained a vast stretch of land running from Texas to California. Southerners demanded the right to bring their slaves into the new territories, but Northerners vowed to stop them.

To smooth over the crisis, Congress enacted a series of laws known as the Compromise of 1850, giving each side a little something. One victory for the South was a new fugitive slave law. Prior to 1850, slaves who escaped from the South to a free state were subject to being captured and sent back into slavery, but enforcement of fugitive slave laws in the North was often lax. The Fugitive Slave Act of 1850 had more teeth. The cases of runaways were taken out of state courts and tried by special federal commissioners, who were paid more if they ruled against the accused runaway. Ordinary citizens in the North could now be deputized and compelled to help capture a runaway, despite moral objections they might have against slavery. Many Northerners saw the Fugitive Slave Act of 1850 as a perversion of American political principles and a violation of their own civil liberties. Some suspected that a "slave power conspiracy" secretly controlled the country.

Wisconsin's abolitionists defied the fugitive slave laws. In the Badger State, abolitionists tended to be Yankees, though immigrants—most notably the German Forty-Eighters—were active in the movement as well. Throughout the North, an "Underground Railroad" existed to help runaway slaves escape to Canada. Harboring a fugitive slave was a federal crime. To avoid detection, escapees had to be spirited from safe house to safe house, usually under the cover of night. Several "stations" on the Underground Railroad existed in Wisconsin, especially in Milwaukee and in the Yankee strongholds in Kenosha, Racine, Rock, and Walworth Counties. Runaway slaves arrived mainly from the Mississippi Valley, and entered Wisconsin via Chicago or the Rock River Valley. At the lake ports, runaways were then smuggled onto ships bound for Canada. Documenting the existence of Underground Railroad stations is a difficult task. Since harboring fugitive slaves was illegal, few abolitionists kept records of their activities. To confirm the existence of an Underground Railroad site, historians often must depend on "soft" evidence like reminiscences written or dictated years after the events transpired, evidence which can often be subject to exaggeration, faulty memory, or outright fabrication. Legends of Underground Railroad activities are often attached to older homes in the Yankee districts of southern Wisconsin, but such claims often turn out to be unverifiable.

Many fugitive slaves never made it to Canada, but remained in northern cities. Life for an escaped slave in the North could be precarious. Slave catchers roamed the North seeking runaways, and many Northern citizens turned in fugitives for the reward money. The case of one slave who sought freedom in Wisconsin put the Badger State in the national spotlight. Joshua Glover escaped his master in Missouri and made his way to Racine, where he landed a job at a mill. His master, B.S. Garland, soon discovered his location, however. In March 1854, Garland

and two deputy US marshals burst into Glover's cabin and beat him into submission. They then brought Glover to the Milwaukee jail, and arranged his transportation back to Missouri. An antislavery mob of more than 100 people led by Sherman Booth, the editor of a Wisconsin abolitionist newspaper, descended on the jail and freed Glover, who was soon placed on a boat headed for Canada and freedom. Indicted for his actions under the Fugitive Slave Law of 1850, Booth argued that the law was unconstitutional. A sympathetic Wisconsin Supreme Court agreed, but the US Supreme Court, in the case *Ableman v. Booth* (1859), overruled the Wisconsin court decision, stating that states had no jurisdiction over federal laws. The Booth case was an important legal challenge to the powers of the federal government, although interestingly, in this case it was a Northern state claiming "states' rights" and the Southerners calling for federal supremacy.

The year 1854 also saw a realignment of the political order, and once again Wisconsin played a key role in national affairs. The spark for the 1854 crisis was the Kansas–Nebraska Act, engineered by Illinois Senator Stephen Douglas. The law potentially opened the Kansas and Nebraska Territories to slavery—lands where slavery had previously been banned. Northerners were outraged. Dissatisfied with both major parties, antislavery Northerners broke away. On March 20, 1854, disgruntled Whigs and Democrats, as well as members of the small antislavery Free Soil Party, gathered at Ripon. The meeting was organized by a New Yorker named Alvan Bovay and took place in a local school, a diminutive building known today as the "Little White School House." They adopted the name "Republican" for their new party. A larger meeting took place in Madison that July, and similar gatherings had taken place across the North. Ripon's claim to be the birthplace of the Republican Party has not gone unchallenged. In fact, communities in Michigan and New Hampshire also make this claim. Whatever the case, by the end of 1854 a national Republican Party had been organized, and quickly grew into the nation's second-largest party. The Whigs never recovered from the defections to the Republicans and disbanded, and the Democrats fell increasingly under the influence of the

Southern slaveholders. The Republicans soon became dominant in the North, capturing majorities in state legislatures and Northern congressional delegations. In 1856, the Republican presidential candidate nearly won the White House.

The Republicans quickly gained supremacy in Wisconsin politics, capturing a majority in the state legislature, the governorship and a US Senate seat in 1855, and the entire US congressional delegation by 1860. Many in Wisconsin remained loyal to the Democrats, however, especially German Catholic and Irish voters. For these immigrants, their concerns were not so much about slavery as they were about preserving their cultures. Many of those who became Republicans were Whig social reformers who had long been active in the temperance movement and hostile toward the Roman Catholic Church. Some immigrants, poor Irish laborers in particular, also feared economic competition from free blacks should slavery be ended. Republicans tried to shake their image as a nativist party by reaching out to immigrants. The German Forty-Eighters were solidly in the Republican camp. Some German Protestants, spurred on by their anti-Catholicism, signed on as well. Indeed, German Protestants became a key swing vote in Wisconsin, actively courted by both parties.

By the late 1850s, the whispers of civil war had turned into open discussion. Wisconsin's Republican governor, Alexander Randall, was an impassioned abolitionist who threatened to pull Wisconsin out of the United States if the federal government continued to support slavery. Randall understood that war was on the horizon, and by 1860 began to wonder about the readiness of the state's volunteer militia should a conflict break out. On the eve of the Civil War, militia units—which existed for local defense in case of invasion or rebellion—had become little more than social organizations, often with strong political and ethnic affiliations. Many units had colorful names, such as the Fox River Zouaves, the Eau Claire Badgers, and the Ripon Roughs and Readies. When Governor Randall began his efforts to shore up the state's militia, he met resistance from the Union Guards, a unit of Irish Democrats from Milwaukee. Randall asked the organization's commander, Garret Barry, whether he would defend Wisconsin if a conflict broke out between the state and the federal government. Barry responded that while he disliked slavery, he would not do so if he thought it violated the US Constitution. This was not the answer Randall wanted, and he promptly disbanded and disarmed the Union Guards. In the early morning hours of September 7, 1860, the Union Guards set sail for Chicago on the sidewheeler *Lady Elgin* to attend a Democratic rally and to raise money for new weapons. Leaving Chicago just before midnight, the *Lady Elgin* steamed north toward Wisconsin. The weather grew stormy, and at 2:30AM on September 8 the *Lady Elgin* was rammed by another ship off Winnetka, Illinois. Approximately 300 people died in the disaster, including Barry.

The presidential election of 1860 was the most divisive in American history, given that it led to civil war. After bitter debate the Democrats, divided between North and South, could not agree on a candidate and ended up nominating two—one for each section. The Republicans nominated Abraham Lincoln of Illinois, who had seen militia service in Wisconsin during the Black Hawk War. In his quest for the White House, Lincoln toured southeastern Wisconsin in September 1859. Speaking in Milwaukee, he expressed his distaste for a system of labor in which workers were driven "without their consent," and his preference for "free labor," which would "secure an individual, social, and political prosperity and happiness, whose course shall be onward and upward." The elegant Lincoln-Tallman home in Janesville is the last surviving private residence in which Lincoln slept during his campaign swing through Wisconsin. Lincoln was a moderate on the slavery issue—at least by Northern standards—pledging only to stop the spread of slavery, not abolish it. Southerners believed, however, that if the Republicans won the election, slavery would no longer be safe in the United States, and threatened to leave the Union if Lincoln was victorious. Even though Lincoln's name did not appear on the ballot in many Southern states, he won a victory in the Electoral College due to the North's population advantage. As promised, most of the slave states pulled out of the Union and formed the Confederate States of America. President Lincoln, fearing the breakup of the

United States would endanger the cause of representative government worldwide, vowed to hold the country together. The stage was set for civil war.

WISCONSIN GOES TO WAR

On April 12, 1861, Confederate forces attacked the federal post of Fort Sumter in Charleston, South Carolina. The Civil War had begun. News of Fort Sumter sent shocked Wisconsin, as it did all of America. The overwhelming sentiment in the Badger State, among people of both parties and across ethnic lines, was to support President Lincoln and his pledge to preserve the Union. The North seemed to have all the advantages—in manpower, in industry, and in agricultural production. But the Confederacy was a vast area stretching from Virginia to Texas, and Confederate soldiers would be fighting on their home soil. The South was also the home of many of the nation's best military minds, who opted to fight for the Confederacy.

President Lincoln's call for volunteers to crush the Confederate rebellion was enthusiastically received in Wisconsin—at first. During the Civil War, the regular army was very small. Local militia units were forged into regiments that were raised and trained by the states, and then turned over to the federal government for war service. Wisconsin's main training ground was located on the fair grounds of the Wisconsin Agricultural Society on the southwest side of Madison. The facility was named Camp Randall in honor of the state's abolitionist governor. Camp Randall became a collecting point for militia units and volunteers from across the Badger State—farm boys, lumberjacks, the rich and the poor. In all, 70,000 men trained there. The camp was erected hastily and conditions for the soldiers could often be quite spartan. There were not enough barracks for all, forcing some to live in tents. Soldiers complained (and sometimes rioted) about the poor food. Sanitation left much to be desired, resulting in the spread of diseases. Then there were the countless hours of marching and drilling, in all kinds of weather, which were necessary to turn civilians into soldiers, but monotonous and exhausting for the men. Soldiers sometimes escaped the confines of the camp and sneaked into Madison for some unofficial recreation—much to the alarm of the city's young women and their parents. In addition to training Union soldiers, Camp Randall also held Confederate prisoners for a time. One hundred and thirty-five died in captivity and were buried at "Confederate Rest" in Madison's Forest Hill Cemetery—the northernmost Confederate cemetery. In all, Wisconsin raised 53 infantry regiments, four cavalry regiments, and fifteen batteries of artillery. Many other Wisconsinites served in regular army and navy forces. About 82,000 Wisconsin men saw service, comprising nine percent of the state's overall population.

Although Wisconsin was a relatively small state remote from the rest of the country, its soldiers certainly contributed their fair share to the Union war effort. One of the most famous and respected of all Union fighting units was the Iron Brigade. Composed of the 2nd, 6th, and 7th Wisconsin Infantry Regiments, as well as one regiment each from Michigan and Indiana, the Iron Brigade fought in the campaigns of the east, and played a pivotal role at the battles of Antietam (1862) and Gettysburg (1863), both considered key turning points in the war. At Gettysburg, the 2nd Wisconsin suffered 77 percent casualties. Although some Wisconsin regiments fought in the campaigns in the east, most served in the Mississippi River Valley. In the west, Wisconsin troops took part in such notable battles as Shiloh (1862) and Vicksburg (1863), the latter battle giving the Union control of the Mississippi River. With the Mississippi secure, many Wisconsin regiments made their way eastward. At the Battle of Missionary Ridge in Tennessee in 1863, an eighteen-year-old lieutenant named Arthur MacArthur of

The men in this tintype image were among 500 soldiers taken prisoner at Brentwood on March 25, 1863 and sent to Richmond. They were exchanged for Confederate prisoners and released, and were back in Nashville by June 15, 1863. Private Porter Wait, Company C, of the 22nd Wisconsin Infantry, is the second from the right (with beard).

the 24th Wisconsin Infantry grabbed the regimental flag from the wounded color bearer and shouted to his comrades, "On Wisconsin!" MacArthur's heroics rallied his troops, and inspired the state's official song. Several Wisconsin regiments took part in General George T. Sherman's infamous 1864 "March to the Sea" from Atlanta to Savannah in 1864, wreaking havoc and destruction across the Georgia countryside. By the end of the war, Wisconsin troops had fought in every Confederate state except Florida. Twenty-one Wisconsin men received the

Medal of Honor—the nation's highest military decoration—including Lieutenant MacArthur.

During the Civil War, military units were often organized from specific cities and villages, allowing men to serve alongside friends, neighbors, and even brothers. Many of Wisconsin's regiments were raised along ethnic lines. The 15th Wisconsin, for example, was composed primarily of Norwegians. Its commander, Colonel Hans Heg, was killed at Chickamauga. A statue of Heg today overlooks the east corner of the Capitol Square in Madison. Irish immigrants organized the 17th Wisconsin, which had a green battle flag decorated with Gaelic emblems. The Germans organized numerous regiments. One of the most battle-tested of the German regiments was the 26th Wisconsin, which covered the withdrawal of the Iron Brigade at Gettysburg and then later served in Sherman's March to the Sea. In addition to serving in ethnic units, immigrants served alongside their native-born neighbors in nearly every Wisconsin regiment. Native Americans volunteered, too. Company K of the 37th was composed mainly of Menominee Indians, for example. African Americans were barred from military service until President Lincoln issued the Emancipation Proclamation in 1862, effectively ending slavery and transforming the war into a crusade to end that evil institution. Once allowed to do so, black Americans rushed to the colors. Wisconsin's African-American community was not large enough to create an entire regiment, but 250 black Wisconsinites fought with the 29th US Colored Troops, which was devastated at the Battle of the Crater in Virginia in 1864.

The war was not universally popular in Wisconsin. A few Northerners, known as Copperheads, were openly sympathetic to the South. Resistance to the war grew when the government began drafting young men into military service. At the beginning of the war volunteers were plentiful, but as the war dragged on and casualty counts rose, recruits became increasingly scarce. Some objected to the draft as a violation of civil liberties. Further enraging many were loopholes that favored the wealthy. One could hire a substitute to serve in one's place, for example, or pay a commutation fee to avoid military obligation altogether. The draft was especially unpopular in the immigrant communities, where support for the war was weakest. The lakeshore counties north of Milwaukee, heavily populated by immigrants, were not fertile recruiting grounds. Resistance to the draft broke out quickly, most notably in Port Washington, where in November 1862 mobs of German and Luxembourger immigrants attacked the local draft commissioner, destroyed records, and burned down the homes of several prominent Republicans. Order was restored with the arrival of troops from Madison. More than 100 were arrested and marched through the streets of Milwaukee as an example to potential rioters in that city.

After four long years of bloody warfare, the Confederates finally surrendered in April 1865. The Union had been preserved, as had America's experiment with democracy. Slavery was ended, and four million African American slaves were now free. The cost of victory was tremendous, however. Nationally, more than 600,000 Americans had died, constituting approximately two percent of the nation's entire population. Nearly as many Americans died in the Civil War as in all of America's other wars combined. Of Wisconsin's 82,000 troops, 12,216 perished during the war, fully two-thirds from disease. Another 15,000 returned to the state with amputated limbs and other physical disabilities. The war had temporarily arrested the fast-paced development of the young and vigorous Badger State, but with the conclusion of hostilities Wisconsin got back to work. As the nineteenth century drew to a close, Wisconsin would continue to be a land of great development and change, but it would also experience severe growing pains along the way.

Old Abe the War Eagle

One of Wisconsin's most famous Civil War veterans was not a soldier or even a human being, but a bald eagle named Old Abe. In 1861, the tiny eaglet was captured by an Ojibwe Indian named Ahgamahwegezhig and given to settlers Dan and Margaret McCann of Jim Falls in exchange for some corn. The McCanns treated the young eagle as a family pet, but the eagle grew quickly and it became too difficult to care for him. When the Civil War broke out, McCann gave the eagle to an Eau Claire militia company, which became Company C of the 8th Wisconsin Infantry. The soldiers named their new mascot bird "Old Abe" in honor of President Lincoln. He was assigned to the color guard and a special perch was constructed for him.

Old Abe served for three years and participated in 37 battles and skirmishes. At Corinth, Tennessee in 1862, Confederate bullets severed Old Abe's tether and the bird lost some feathers, but was otherwise fine. His most notable battle was at Vicksburg in 1863. After the war, Governor James T. Lewis authorized the construction of a special apartment for Old Abe in the basement of the State Capitol. The eagle attracted thousands of visitors. In 1876 he traveled to Philadelphia to represent Wisconsin at the nation's Centennial celebrations, where he signed "autographs" by pecking on photographs of himself. Old Abe died in 1881. His remains were stuffed and placed on view at the Capitol. When fire gutted the building in 1904, Old Abe was gone.

Old Abe–related historic sites may be found in many parts of Wisconsin. He was most likely born and captured in Eisenstein Township in Price County, lands that are today part of the Chequamegon National Forest where bald eagles—perhaps Old Abe's distant relatives—still soar. The Old Abe State Trail runs 19.5 miles from Chippewa Falls to Cornell. Along the banks of the Chippewa River at Jim Falls, the local Lions Club has erected an Old Abe monument. A highway wayside just north of Jim Falls on State Highway 78 is the location of the McCann homestead. In Madison, replicas of Old Abe may be found in the assembly chambers of the State Capitol and at the Wisconsin Veterans Museum across the street, and his likeness also keeps watch above the Camp Randall Memorial Arch at the corner of Dayton and Randall Streets. Old Abe also appears on the Wisconsin Memorial at Vicksburg. The J.I. Case Company of Racine adopted Old Abe as the logo for their company, and the US Army's 101st Airborne Division's insignia is based on the Civil War "veteran" from Wisconsin.

For more on Old Abe, see Richard H. Zeitlin, *Old Abe the War Eagle* (1986).

Old Abe, Wisconsin War Eagle, perched on cannon near the Wisconsin Capitol with a flag in background.

5

Gilded Age Wisconsin

In American history, the last decades of the nineteenth century are often referred to as the "Gilded Age." The phrase was coined by Mark Twain and Charles Dudley Warner, whose book of that title was sharply critical of the attractive yet deceptive nature of American society at the time. On the surface America seemed a wonderful place. The economy grew at a tremendous rate. New technologies like the telephone and the phonograph made life easier and more pleasurable. Entrepreneurs amassed some of the greatest fortunes the world has ever seen. But beneath the veneer of progress lay an unfortunate side. This was an age of ruthless, unregulated economic competition in which men sought profits and power at any cost. The political system grew ever more corrupt, and became little more than a tool of financial interests. Life in Wisconsin followed national trends. The state experienced important changes that diversified its economy. But while some Wisconsinites saw tremendous benefits, those benefits often came at the expense of their neighbors.

America's Dairyland

Agriculture remained an integral part of the Wisconsin economy after the Civil War. But the types of crops the Badger State's farmers grew underwent an important transition. Wheat, the mainstay of Wisconsin agriculture since statehood, began to decline in importance after 1870. Though relatively easy to grow, wheat also exhausts the soil of nitrogen and other nutrients rather quickly, diminishing yields. Rusts, smuts, and other diseases also took their toll, as did insects such as the cinch bug. After the Civil War, Wisconsin wheat production began to shift from southern Wisconsin to new lands in the northwestern parts of the state. By the 1870s, vast new wheat lands opened up farther west in Minnesota and Iowa, and eventually on the Great Plains. The wheat frontier had passed Wisconsin by. The nearly two million acres of wheat-producing land in the mid-1870s had declined to just 750,000 acres by 1900, and by the 1920s to below 250,000.

The decline of wheat forced Wisconsin farmers to seek out new crops, leading to the diversification of agriculture during the Gilded Age. Some farmers experimented with cereals such as barley, corn, and oats. Vegetables such as beans, cabbage, and peas became common along the Lake Michigan shoreline. Orchards of cherries and apples grew up; scenic Door County is today known for its beautiful cherry orchards. Some switched to tobacco farming, particularly Norwegian immigrants. Tobacco took root in Dane and Rock Counties in southern Wisconsin, and in Vernon County in the west, both regions inhabited by Norwegians. Edgerton once boasted of being the "tobacco capital of the world," though Virginia and North Carolina certainly had good reason to chuckle at such a claim. In addition to crop diversification in settled areas, new lands were opening up to the north and west, further expanding Wisconsin's agricultural offerings. Potatoes were well suited to the sandy soils of central Wisconsin, for example. Marshlands in the west-central part of the state developed into cranberry bogs. In later years, cranberry bogs would also emerge in the Northwoods. Wisconsin is today the nation's second-greatest producer of cranberries.

But it was dairy—milk, butter, and cheese—that came to dominate Wisconsin agriculture, leading to the state's well-known moniker, "America's Dairyland." The advent of dairy marked an important change in the lives of Wisconsin farmers. Unlike wheat, which is relatively easy to grow, dairy is a labor-intensive, year-round occupation that revolves around the needs of the milk cows. Dairying also entails significant outlays of capital for cows, barns, and various kinds of equipment. The production of butter and cheese requires a great deal of skill; the quality of Wisconsin's earliest dairy offerings varied considerably. Wisconsin butter, for example, earned the unenviable nickname "western grease" and was more commonly used as a lubricant than as food. But Wisconsin's cool climate was well suited for the preservation of dairy products, and the growing cities of the

Midwest provided a regional market. With the development of refrigerated railroad cars in the 1870s, Wisconsin dairy products could reach national and even world markets. Today, Wisconsin is internationally recognized as a leader in dairy production and innovation.

In the transition to dairy, Wisconsin once again followed in the footsteps of New York State. Upstate New York had undergone the transition from wheat to dairy several decades before, and migrants from that region brought valuable knowledge and skills. The father of Wisconsin dairy farming was a transplanted New Yorker named William Dempster Hoard. Born in Stockbridge, New York, in 1836, Hoard was raised on a farm and moved to the Wisconsin frontier at the tender age of eighteen. After service in the Civil War he returned to the Badger State, where he founded a newspaper, the *Jefferson County Union*, and began to preach the benefits of dairying. He argued, for example, that dairy would not only revitalize the state's sagging farm economy, but also its exhausted soils. In 1872, Hoard took the leading role in founding the Wisconsin Dairyman's Association, and in 1885 began publishing *Hoard's Dairyman*, a magazine devoted to the concerns of the dairy farmer. Hoard was politically savvy as well, and was elected governor in 1888. Wisconsin's farmers were at first suspicious of Hoard's message, but as wheat yields continued to decline, more and more farmers heeded his call. Wisconsin's population of milk cows increased as wheat yields fell, and more and more acres were devoted to hay and other feed crops. Cheese factories sprang up across the countryside. The modern Wisconsin countryside—its sights as well as the smells (natives often joke about the state's "dairy air")—slowly began to emerge in the late nineteenth century, thanks to Hoard's vision.

The University of Wisconsin also helped make Wisconsin a leader in dairy production. Research conducted at the university helped increase the quality and quantity of the state's dairy products. One problem that had traditionally vexed dairy producers was determining the butterfat content of milk; the higher the content, the better the quality of the product. In 1890, Stephen M. Babcock developed a test to determine milk's butterfat. The Babcock Test was quick, simple, and most importantly, reliable. The price of milk could now be determined by butterfat content, not by weight, eliminating the practice of adding water to the milk, as some unscrupulous farmers had done. As one historian phrased it, the Babcock Test did "more for the honesty of the dairyman than the Bible." The university also pioneered research on the use of the silo—tall, round storage bins for animal feed. Many farmers did not believe that cows would eat stored grain until UW researchers showed that they would. Silos began to spring forth from the Wisconsin landscape. The ruins of early cement silos are still a common sight in Wisconsin today. In short, the rise of dairy went hand in hand with the growth of the university's agriculture school. The University of Wisconsin remains one of the leading agricultural research institutions in the world. The western end of the campus contains many agriculture-related buildings that date to the turn of the century, including the Stock Pavilion—known to generations of students simply as the "Cow Palace."

By 1900, dairying had become the dominant form of agricultural enterprise in Wisconsin, and the Badger State grew to become the nation's largest dairy producer. The signature country landscape of Wisconsin—the rich, rolling green pastures dotted with black-and-white Holstein cows, red barns with silos reaching skyward—had taken shape by 1900. Today Wisconsin is one of the leading states in milk and butter production, and until recently was America's top producer of cheese. On a casual drive through nearly any part of Wisconsin, visitors can sample a bewildering variety of cheeses—brick, brie, cheddar, Havarti, Limburger, Monterrey Jack, Muenster, Swiss, even (believe it or not) chocolate cheese. One type of cheese, Colby, was developed in Colby, Wisconsin in 1874. The natives also enjoy cheese curds (fresh, pre-aged cheese), which are eaten raw or deep fried. A trip to Wisconsin can frustrate even the most disciplined dieter.

"Timber!"

Although dairy was on the rise, agriculture was losing its dominant place in the Wisconsin economy. At the turn of the century, lumbering and related industries constituted the most important part of the state's economy. The Badger State had an immense number of trees, especially in the

Thirty-nine lumberers posed in front of a large stack of cut logs

northern half of the state. Pine was the most sought-after wood. Pine is soft and easily worked, and because wood floats, it was relatively easy to transport by river. Being resinous, pine is also resistant to weathering, which made it especially attractive as a building material. In particular, lumber men sought out the white pine (*pinus strobes*), which can grow to heights of more than 100 feet, providing ample amounts of wood. Because it also grows relatively straight, white pine had long been in demand for ship masts. By the mid-nineteenth century, stands of white pine in New England and New York were dwindling, but they were still plentiful in the Great Lakes region. Numerous other kinds of trees native to Wisconsin—both evergreen and deciduous—had commercial value as well.

The lumbering potential of the Wisconsin Northwoods had been understood since colonial and territorial times. Fur traders had been traversing the region for centuries, and with the decline of the fur trade many began to turn to lumber. Green Bay business-man Daniel Whitney had built a saw mill on the Wisconsin River at Nekoosa in 1831. Treaty negotiations with the Ojibwe and Menominee in the north were often aimed at getting access to their timber. As Euro-American settlement began in the 1830s and 1840s, areas of dense forest had to be cleared away for farmlands, especially along the Lake Michigan shore. Lumber mills sprang up at lake port cities such as Green Bay, Manitowoc, and Sheboygan. It was the eventual penetration into the Northwoods after the Civil War, however, that led to the heyday of Wisconsin lumbering. Several lumbering districts emerged along major rivers, with each region containing several lumber milling centers. Marinette and

its sister city of Menominee, Michigan, took in timber from the Menominee River basin. Lumber harvested in the Wolf River watershed made its way to Oshkosh, which was nicknamed "Sawdust City" because of its numerous lumber mills. On the Wisconsin River, cities such as Wausau and Stevens Point grew up around lumber mills. The Chippewa River district—considered to be Wisconsin's most lucrative—was centered on Eau Claire.

The task of chopping down the trees and transporting them to the saw mill fell to the lumberjack. Trees were typically cut in the dead of winter. Downed trees were shorn of their branches and divided into sections of twelve to sixteen feet. Animal power then dragged the logs to a nearby river, a chore that was more easily done on top of a slippery snow pack. With the spring thaw, the logs were then floated down the swollen rivers to the saw mills. Great

Field of tree stumps with row of trees in background showing land use

logjams occurred often. In 1869, one logjam on the Chippewa River was reportedly thirty feet high and fifteen miles long. Logjams often had to be broken up using dynamite. Indeed, the life of a lumberjack was a dangerous one; scores of men were drowned, crushed, cut, or were injured and killed in numerous other ways. The men who worked in the lumber camps were a varied group. Many came from eastern states where logging had fallen on hard times. Many were immigrants; French-Canadian lumberjacks, in particular, were attracted to the Wisconsin Northwoods. Often farm boys who wanted extra money might join a logging camp in the winter and return to the plow in the spring. When camp broke in the spring, many lumberjacks made their way into town with their winter savings; sometimes these lumberjacks gained an unsavory reputation for wild life in the lumber towns after months of isolation in the winter woods.

The fast-paced growth of the nation meant an unquenchable demand for lumber. After being processed at places such as Eau Claire, Marinette, and Oshkosh, much of the state's lumber was shipped to national market centers. The primary destination was Chicago, the railroad hub of the Midwest. From Chicago, Wisconsin lumber could be shipped to the burgeoning cities of the east or to the increasing number of settlers on the treeless Great Plains. Lumber was often shipped by rail, but on Lake Michigan "lumber schooners" also carried the timber to Chicago or ports eastward. In western Wisconsin, St. Louis was another important market destination. By the 1870s, railroads began to penetrate into the Wisconsin Northwoods. No longer dependent on river transportation and the rhythms of the seasons, lumbering after 1870 became a year-round activity. The forests of northern Wisconsin were felled at an incredible rate. Wisconsin led the nation in lumber production throughout most of the 1890s. In 1892, the Badger State produced more than four billion board feet of lumber.

A large amount of capital was needed to finance logging ventures. A small group of men known as the "lumber barons" were among the wealthiest and most influential men in nineteenth-century Wisconsin. Many of Wisconsin's lumber barons came from the east. Canadian-born Isaac Stephenson controlled vast amounts of timber in Wisconsin and Michigan out of his base in Marinette. Wisconsin's most notable lumber baron was Philetus Sawyer—a man aptly named for a career in lumber. As a young man, Sawyer took a job in a saw mill in Crown Point, New York, and through shrewd business skills he managed to purchase the mill before the age of 21. As the New York lumber trade declined, Sawyer sold his mill and migrated to Wisconsin. Settling in Oshkosh, he operated a saw mill in partnership with his son Edgar. Sawyer purchased prime timberlands in northern Wisconsin and other areas of the Great Lakes, and he quickly became one of Wisconsin's wealthiest men. Visitors to Eau Claire,

Marinette, and Oshkosh can still see beautiful Victorian mansions, a testament to the riches generated by logging. The lumber barons were also politically influential. Sawyer represented Wisconsin in the US Senate, and by the 1890s, Sawyer had emerged as the "boss" of Wisconsin's Republican Party. In an age noted for its rampant political corruption, the lumber barons were not shy about using their political influence to help their business interests.

Lumbering took a tremendous toll on the natural environment. By 1920, the great northern forests, which had seemed inexhaustible just decades before, had largely been reduced to vast stretches of stumps and brush. Northern Wisconsin became known simply as the "Cutover" district. Very few stands of "old-growth" forest remain. One remnant is the so-called Cathedral of the Pines in the Nicolet National Forest near Lakewood in Oconto County. Even more impressive is the Menominee Indian Reservation. In sharp contrast to the white loggers' clear-cutting, the Menominee developed a concept of "sustained yield." The practice was the vision of Chief Oshkosh, who feared that clear-cutting would lead to forest depletion and ultimately economic ruin for the tribe. Instead, the Menominee carefully selected the trees to be harvested and limited the number of trees to be cut each year, thus ensuring a continual supply. The thoughtful lumbering practices of the Menominee made them one of the most prosperous Indian tribes in the United States, and their logging techniques have been studied by foresters around the world. The character of the primeval forest on Menominee lands has also been largely preserved. Travelers through the reservation cannot help but notice the stark contrast between the dense forests on the reservation with the surrounding cleared land. In fact, the Menominee reservation is clearly visible from space.

To add to the environmental tragedy of clear-cut logging, much of Wisconsin's natural bounty in timber was wasted—by one estimate as much as 40 percent of it. Untold numbers of logs reached the milling centers waterlogged or too damaged for use. Considerable amounts of timber were also lost to fires, which were often caused or exacerbated by logging practices. Once the trees had been removed, loggers left behind branches and other debris to

Logging Heritage

Camp Five Museum
5480 Connor Farm Road, Laona, WI 54541
(800) 774-3414
www.camp5museum.org
Camp Five is a logging museum located on the site of an actual Northwoods logging camp dating to 1872. Visitors travel to the camp on an authentic steam train.

From the Pineries to the Present Heritage Area
PO Box 38, Shawano, WI 54166
(800) 235-8528
A heritage tourism project of the Wisconsin Department of Tourism, the Pineries to the Present Heritage Area highlights the logging heritage of Shawano and Menominee Counties. Included on the tour are local railroad depots, lumber mills, and the Menominee Logging Museum.

Historic Point Basse
364 Wakely Road
PO Box 295, Nekoosa, WI 54457
(715) 886-4202
www.historicpointbasse.com
The focal point of this living history museum is the Wakely House, a tavern that dates to the 1840s. Point Basse was the site of Daniel Whitney's 1831 saw mill, and became an important meeting place for the peoples of central Wisconsin, including Native Americans, French Canadians, and Yankee pioneers.

Oshkosh Public Museum
1331 Algoma Blvd., Oshkosh, WI 54901-2799
(920) 236-5761
www.oshkoshmuseum.org
Although not specifically focused on logging, this facility—dedicated to the history of "Sawdust City"—certainly has a lot to say about the topic. The museum also contains exhibits about the Sawyer family.

Peshtigo Fire Museum
400 Oconto Avenue, Peshtigo, WI
(715) 582-3244
www.peshtigofire.info/museum.htm
Housed in the first church to be rebuilt after the disaster, this museum chronicles the story of that hellish evening in this small frontier community in 1871.

Timber Trails in the Chippewa Valley
3625 Gateway Drive, Suite F, Eau Claire, WI 54701
(800) 344-FUNN x300
A heritage tourism project of the Wisconsin Department of Tourism, Timber Trails in the Chippewa Valley guides visitors to the numerous historic sites in northwestern Wisconsin related to its lumber industry, such as historic homes and mills. Several logging museums are also included on the tour, such as the Chippewa Valley Museum (Eau Claire), Empire in Pine Logging Museum (Downsville), and the Paul Bunyan Logging Camp (Eau Claire).

dry in the hot summer sun. Brush fires were common across the Cutover. The drought of 1871 made a bad situation worse, and disaster ensued. On October 8, Wisconsin experienced what may have been the world's deadliest forest fire—the Great Peshtigo Fire. Flames raged on both sides of Green Bay, in Door, Kewaunee, Brown, Oconto, and Marinette Counties, as well as portions of Upper Michigan. The fire claimed anywhere from 1,200 to 1,500 lives, 600 in the village of Peshtigo alone. The Peshtigo Fire was just one of many that broke out across the Great Lakes region that year. The Great Chicago Fire, which claimed 250 lives, raged at very same time as the Peshtigo conflagration, and stole the national headlines from the deadlier calamity in Wisconsin.

Industrial Expansion

Lumber was just one of many industries that grew in Wisconsin after 1870. Industrialization was nothing new to Wisconsin in the Gilded Age, but what had changed was the scale of manufacturing enterprises. Most of Wisconsin's early industries—such as beer brewing, flour milling, and meatpacking—emerged to meet local needs. However, as the nineteenth century wore on, business corporations in Wisconsin and across the United States grew larger and began to serve national rather than local markets. Larger companies began to devour smaller ones, resulting in economic power being concentrated in fewer and fewer hands. In many industries, small groups or even individuals controlled entire industries, stifling competition and keeping prices unnecessarily high.

Wisconsin was geographically well suited to become an industrial powerhouse. The Great Lakes, Mississippi River, and numerous other waterways provided inexpensive bulk transportation, both for shipping raw materials into Wisconsin factories and finished products to market. The continuing growth of the railroads, and Wisconsin's proximity to the railroad hub of Chicago, further integrated the state into the national economy. Yankee migrants brought with them entrepreneurial skill and capital, as did a good number of German immigrants. Wisconsin's factories churned out more and more manufactured goods and a greater variety of products than ever before.

Wisconsin's farm economy continued to influence its industrial development. The proliferation of rail lines and the development of refrigerated rail cars meant that Wisconsin farm products could reach national markets. After the Civil War, Milwaukee became an important national meatpacking center, especially for hogs. By 1880, Milwaukee's Plankinton and Armour had become one of America's largest pork-processing companies. Philip Armour abandoned Milwaukee for Chicago—the heart of the nation's meatpacking industry—and Plankinton retired and transferred his interests to his junior partner, Patrick Cudahy. In 1892, Cudahy constructed a spacious plant on a railroad line just south of Milwaukee, around which the company village of Cudahy grew.

Beer brewing saw a similar transformation. After the Civil War, Milwaukee brewing companies such as Miller, Pabst, and Schlitz became household names across the country. In the aftermath of the Chicago fire of 1871, Joseph Schlitz sent wagonloads of his beer to Chicago for the residents left without water. The gesture was well received, and Schlitz became known as "the beer that made Milwaukee famous." Men like Schlitz became wealthy, powerful, and politically influential, earning themselves the nickname the "beer barons." Captain Frederick Pabst, founder of one of Milwaukee's largest breweries, built a stunning mansion on Milwaukee's Grand (now Wisconsin) Avenue that boasted 37 rooms. Milwaukee's Pabst Theater, a remarkable example of Victorian elegance, became the center of high culture for the city's German-American community.

The decline of wheat forced flour millers to seek alternative occupations. In the Fox River Valley in northeastern Wisconsin, paper mills replaced flour to become the dominant industry of the region. Paper production in Wisconsin dated to the 1840s. In the mid-nineteenth century, paper was made from rags, but by 1870 a technique using wood pulp had become practical and cost effective. The Fox Valley was ideally suited for wood pulp paper production. The Fox River watershed included vast stretches of northern Wisconsin timber. The fast-moving waters of the lower Fox—which drop 170 feet between Neenah and Green Bay—provided both a plentiful source of power and the large amounts of water necessary for paper production. The proliferation of newspapers and magazines, as well as technological advances like the typewriter (invented in Milwaukee in 1869), created an unquenchable demand for paper during the late nineteenth century. Wood pulp paper mills sprang up along the length of the lower Fox. The largest of these companies, Kimberly-Clark, was founded in Neenah in 1872. Paper mills also emerged in the Wisconsin River Valley. Paper remains a vital part of Wisconsin's economy; the Badger State produces a vast array of paper products, such as newsprint, notebooks, facial tissues, toilet paper, and diapers. For generations, Wisconsin's paper products have touched the lives of Americans in the most intimate of ways.

Agriculture and lumber also led to the production of heavy machinery. In 1860, Edward P. Allis, a migrant entrepreneur from New York State, purchased a failed Milwaukee iron foundry. Allis understood that Wisconsin flour and saw mills needed increasing amounts of power from a source more reliable than water, so Allis began to manufacture steam engines. The Edward P. Allis Company (known as the Allis-Chalmers Company after a 1901 merger) produced a wide variety of engines used in industrial power plants, mines, and public utilities across the nation. The company also produced other kinds of industrial machinery, including band saws for lumber mills and grain-rolling machinery for flour mills. In 1900, the company moved its operations to lands just west of Milwaukee; the city that grew up around the plant became known as West Allis—today one of Wisconsin's largest cities. The Allis-Chalmers Company no longer exists, but its West Allis facility, located at the corner of 70th and Greenfield, has been renovated into an office park that retains the site's industrial heritage. Allis-Chalmers was only the largest of many heavy machinery companies to originate or operate in Wisconsin. In 1884, a German immigrant named Henry Harnischfeger teamed up with Alonzo Pawling and founded a small machine shop that grew into one of the world's largest manufacturers of cranes and mining equipment. Milwaukee became one of the nation's largest producers of machine tools and industrial equipment. America was quickly becoming the world's leading industrial power, and Milwaukee made the machines that made America work.

Agricultural Heritage

Babcock Hall Dairy Plant
1605 Linden Drive, University of Wisconsin-Madison
Madison, WI 53706-1565
(608) 262-3045
www.wisc.edu/foodsci/store
Visitors to Babcock Hall can watch ice cream being made. Locals
rave about Babcock ice cream, for sale in the dairy store. The
facility is named after Steven Babcock, a UW professor and the
inventor of a test to determine the butterfat content of milk.

Cheese Country Heritage Trail
c/o Green County Tourism
N3510B Highway 81, Monroe, WI 53566
(888) 222-9111
www.cheesecountryheritage.com
A heritage tourism project of the Wisconsin Department of
Tourism, the Cheese Country Heritage Trail guides visitors
through the history of Green County, one of the state's most
important cheese-producing areas.

Edgerton Tobacco Heritage Days
PO Box 252, Edgerton, WI 53534
(608) 347-4321
www.tobaccoheritagedays.com
When it comes to tobacco many see nothing to celebrate, but
Edgerton does. Each August the small city holds a festival to
celebrate the region's signature agricultural product.

Hoard Historical Museum and Dairy Shrine
407 Merchants Avenue, Fort Atkinson, WI 53538
(920) 563-7769
www.hoardmuseum.org
The Hoard Museum focuses on the history of Jefferson County,
but features the life and career of William Dempster Hoard,
Wisconsin dairy promoter and one-time Wisconsin governor.
The attached Dairy Shrine Visitor Center contains several
exhibits about the development of Wisconsin's dairy industry.

Mount Horeb Mustard Museum
100 West Main Street, Mount Horeb, WI 53572
(800) 438-6878
www.mustardmuseum.com
Although mustard has never been a major part of Wisconsin's agricultural history, this quirky little museum is nevertheless worth a visit. The museum claims the largest collection of prepared mustards in the world, boasting more than 4,000 different brands on display (including more than 200 made in the Badger State), as well as mustard pots, tins, and other kinds of mustard paraphernalia.

Stonefield Village
PO Box 125, Cassville, WI 53806
(608) 725-5210
www.wisconsinhistory.org/stonefield/
Stonefield was the home of Nelson Dewey, Wisconsin's first governor. Dewey's home was destroyed but has been reconstructed on its original foundations. Stonefield is also home to the State Agricultural Museum and a re-created farming village from the turn of the twentieth century.

Wisconsin Cranberry Discovery Center
204 Main Street, Warrens, WI 54666
(608) 378-4878
www.discovercranberries.com
The museum details the harvesting of cranberries in Wisconsin, from Native Americans to the present, and features a "Taste Test Kitchen." Held each September, the Warrens Cranberry Festival attracts more than 100,000 people annually. For more on the festival, visit www.cranfest.com, or call (608) 378-4200.

World Dairy Expo
3310 Latham Drive, Madison, WI 53713
(608) 224-6455
www.world-dairy-expo.com
Wisconsin is internationally recognized as a leader in dairy production and innovation. Each September dairy men and women from across the globe congregate in Madison to exchange ideas and learn the latest in dairy technology. The World Dairy Expo is open to the public.

The key ingredients to the emerging industrial economy were iron and steel, and Wisconsin played an important part in their production. Small iron foundries dotted the state before the Civil War, but such small operations could not keep pace with the ever-increasing demand. In particular, railroad expansion required iron in quantities only large factories could produce. In 1866, Michigan businessman Eber Brock Ward teamed up with Milwaukee railroad baron Alexander Mitchell to form the Milwaukee Iron Company in order to meet Mitchell's need for iron rails. Their massive Bay View Iron Works, located south of the city on Lake Michigan at Bay View, opened in 1870. Although Milwaukee became an important iron-making center, it never rivaled Pittsburgh, where Andrew Carnegie used the new Bessemer process to produce steel (a purified, more durable form of iron), making that city the center of the steel industry. Wisconsin, however, played a part in making Pittsburgh what it was. Iron ore mined from the Lake Superior region was shipped through the Great Lakes to Pittsburgh. The Gogebic Range, which runs along the south shore of the lake in Wisconsin and Upper Michigan, became an important source of iron ore. At the turn of the twentieth century, Wisconsin was fourth among the states in iron-ore mining. Hurley in Iron County was the heart of the Wisconsin mining district. Following the long-established pattern of mining booms, Hurley gained a reputation as a town notorious for drinking, gambling, and prostitution. By 1893, Hurley had one saloon for every 38 residents, mostly along a five block stretch of Silver Street. Transient iron miners and lumberjacks with "a winter's pay in their pockets and pent-up hungers in their blood," as one observer phrased it, gave Hurley's the reputation of being Wisconsin's "sin city" in the Northwoods.

The Great Lakes played a crucial role in Wisconsin's industrial story. Although the Badger State is located nearly a thousand miles from any ocean, it has a rich maritime history. Wisconsin's port cities were not just entry and exit points for people and products; maritime industries also flourished in the Badger State. Shipbuilding in Wisconsin dates back to territorial days. Skilled shipwrights in Manitowoc, Two Rivers, and Sturgeon Bay, in particular, were noted for constructing wooden sailing schooners. By 1900, Wisconsin's shipbuilders had converted to steel-hulled steamships and Superior had become one of the largest shipbuilding centers on the Great Lakes. Thousands of vessels plied the lakes, shipping iron ore from the Lake Superior region to the steel mills of Chicago and Pittsburgh, and grain from the Great Plains and Midwest to markets in the East. Beginning in the 1890s, railroad companies began running car ferries between ports in Wisconsin and Michigan, conquering a major barrier in east–west travel in the northern United States. Commercial fishing was important on the Bayfield Peninsula on Lake Superior, and from Lake Michigan ports Sturgeon Bay, Two Rivers, Manitowoc, and Port Washington, until overfishing and pollution decimated the fish population after 1900. Wisconsin's rich maritime heritage is still evident. Scenic lighthouses—some dating to the mid-nineteenth century—grace Wisconsin's lakeshore regions. The treacherous waters of the Great Lakes have produced numerous shipwrecks, especially around the Apostle Islands in Lake Superior and the *Port des Morts* ("Door of Death" in French) between Washington Island and the Door Peninsula. These wrecks are popular with sport divers today.

Numerous other kinds of business enterprises grew in Wisconsin. In 1873, an Austrian immigrant named John Michael Kohler purchased the Sheboygan Union Iron and Steel Foundry, and began producing farm implements and decorative iron works. Ten years later, Kohler coated an ordinary feed trough with enamel and produced his first bathtub. The Kohler Company went on to become one of the world's premier manufacturers of bathtubs, sinks, toilets, and other plumbing products. In Racine, Samuel Curtis Johnson bought a parquet flooring company in 1886. Two years later, Johnson's company began to produce floor wax to protect those floors. Advertising his product nationally, Johnson Wax quickly grew into one of Wisconsin's largest companies, producing a wide range of household products familiar to Americans today. Driving through the Badger State today, travelers will likely encounter some kind of manufacturing enterprise in nearly every town they travel through. Wisconsin was on the leading edge of industrial change and development in the Gilded Age.

Maritime Heritage

Discovery World at Pier Wisconsin
500 North Harbor Drive, Milwaukee, WI 53202
(414) 765-9966
www.discoveryworld.org
Discovery World features numerous educational exhibits, many of
which are related to Wisconsin's maritime history, most notably the
Denis Sullivan, a re-creation of an 1880s Great Lakes schooner.

Door County Maritime Museum
120 North Madison Avenue, Sturgeon Bay, WI 54235
(920) 743-5958
www.dcmm.org
This museum explores the nautical history of one of Wisconsin's most
important maritime locations. In addition to the Sturgeon Bay facility,
the Door County Maritime Museum also administers a smaller
museum in Gills Rock and preserves a lighthouse on Cana Island in
Lake Michigan.

Hokenson Fishery Historic Site
Apostle Islands National Lakeshore
Route 1, Box 4, Bayfield, WI 54814
(715) 779-7007
www.nps.gov/apis/hokenson.htm
Located at Little Sand Bay on the Bayfield Peninsula, the Hokenson
Fishery preserves the heritage of a Swedish immigrant family's fishing
enterprise that harvested Lake Superior waters for 30 years. Also
located in the national lakeshore is the Manitou Fishing Camp, located
on remote Manitou Island in the scenic Apostle Islands.

Lake Michigan Car Ferry
Box 708, Ludington, MI 49431
(800) 841-4243
www.ssbadger.com
The SS *Badger* is a car ferry that once carried train cars across Lake
Michigan. Today she takes passenger cars and their occupants across
the lake between Ludington, Michigan and Manitowoc. The ship is a
historical artifact itself, and the four-hour voyage (the *Badger* has a
top speed of eighteen miles per hour) is also a trip back in time to the
heyday of Great Lakes shipping. In addition to recreational facilities,
the *Badger* also holds a small museum of car ferry history.

Port Washington Fish Days
www.portfishday.com
The city of Port Washington, once a substantial fishing center, claims the "world's largest fish fry," held annually in July.

Rogers Street Fishing Village
2010 Rogers Street, Two Rivers, WI 54241
(920) 793-5905
www.rogersstreet.com
Located on the banks of the East Twin River, the Rogers Street Fishing Village displays the ships and equipment the Two Rivers fishermen used, as well as an authentic lighthouse.

SS *Meteor* Museum
Barker's Island, Superior, WI 54880
(715) 392-5764
www.ssmeteor.org
Superior was once one of the most important shipbuilding centers on the Great Lakes. The SS *Meteor* is the last surviving whaleback, a common lake freighter that was built in Superior.

Wisconsin Maritime Museum
75 Maritime Drive, Manitowoc, WI 54220
(920) 684-0218
www.wisconsinmaritime.org
Located on the banks of the Manitowoc River in one of the state's most important maritime centers, the Wisconsin Maritime Museum chronicles the history of shipbuilding in Manitowoc and across the Great Lakes from the days of wooden schooners and clippers to the age of steel-hulled freighters. It also highlights Manitowoc's unusual role as maker of submarines during World War II (see Chapter 8).

Wisconsin's Maritime Trails
c/o Wisconsin Historical Society
816 State Street, Madison, WI 53706
(608) 271-8172
www.maritimetrails.org
A partnership between the Wisconsin Historical Society and the University of Wisconsin Sea Grant, Wisconsin's Maritime Trails provides essential information for divers interested in visiting the many shipwrecks in the Great Lakes waters off Wisconsin. For non-divers, the project maintains a database of lighthouses, ships, waterfront parks, and museums related to the state's rich maritime history.

INDUSTRIALIZATION AND SOCIETY

Industrialization had important social effects in Wisconsin and across the nation. One important consequence was urbanization. Factories concentrated jobs in cities and towns. The percentage of Wisconsinites who lived in cities rose with industrial development. In 1850, just 9.4 percent of Wisconsin residents lived in urban areas. By 1870 that figure had reached 19.6 percent, and by 1900 38.2 percent. Contributing to the growth of Wisconsin's cities was continuing immigration. As the nineteenth century wore on, the nature of immigration underwent some important changes. The volume of immigration increased to unprecedented levels. The new arrivals tended to be more urban than their predecessors—there being little farm land available—taking jobs in the state's burgeoning factories. Immigrants were also increasingly more likely to be sojourners than settlers, planning to return to their homelands once they made some money in America. Steamships cut the transatlantic journey from weeks to days, and frequent sailings lowered the costs of coming to America. Many immigrants did indeed come to Wisconsin only temporarily, but a good many stayed permanently.

Northwestern Europe remained an important source of immigrants to Wisconsin. Germans still came in large numbers. The new German arrivals tended to be more Protestant than previously, and also less well off economically. Political turmoil in Germany also generated immigrants. German unification in 1871 did not bring peace to the region. The nation's chancellor, Otto von Bismarck, began his *Kulturkampf* (cultural struggle) against groups he viewed as hindering national unity, notably the socialists and religious groups such as Catholics and dissident Lutheran factions. Many found refuge in Wisconsin's rich German community. Irish immigrants continued to come as well, on average better off economically than those who came escaping the famine of the 1840s. Scandinavia also remained an important source of immigration. In particular, immigration from Sweden increased after the Civil War. The Swedes arrived just as new lands in northwestern Wisconsin were opening up. Polk and Burnett Counties along the Minnesota border had high concentrations of Swedish settlers. Finns did not arrive in substantial numbers until after 1880, settling mainly along the Lake Superior shoreline where farmlands were still available. Because of their late arrival, Swedes and Finns were more likely to take non-farm jobs in mining, lumber, fishing, or as laborers in factories or on the docks. Even immigrants from Iceland made their way to Wisconsin after 1870. The oldest Icelandic settlement in the United States was located on Washington Island on the tip of the Door Peninsula, and Icelanders also worked on the Milwaukee docks.

As the twentieth century neared, immigrants from Southern and Eastern Europe began to arrive in Wisconsin. The largest of the Eastern European groups was the Poles. In the nineteenth century, Poland was not an independent country. Ethnic Poles lived in lands controlled by the German, Russian, and Austrian empires. Poles first came to Wisconsin along with German immigrants before the Civil War, but Polish immigration increased dramatically after 1870. Agricultural settlements of Poles grew up in northeastern and central Wisconsin. Country villages like Krakow (Shawano County), Poniatowski (Marathon County), Polonia (Portage County), Pulaski (Brown County) and Sobieski (Oconto County) indicate the presence of Polish settlers. There being little available farmland available in Wisconsin, most Polish rural settlements were in the marginal lands of the Cutover region. The majority of Poles settled in the cities, however. Arriving in America a poor peasant people with few urban skills, Poles were typically forced to take the lowest-paying factory jobs. In Milwaukee, Poles quickly dominated the south side. Poles also became an important presence in industrial cities like Manitowoc, Racine, Stevens Point, and Wausau. Today, Poles are the second largest ethnic group in Wisconsin.

Milwaukee's Polish heritage is still clearly evident on the city's landscape. St. Stanislaus Church was founded by Polish immigrants in 1866. In 1901, St. Josaphat Church was completed. Both churches, which are easily recognizable by their prominent domes, still dominate the south side skyline. St. Josephat is one of Wisconsin's architectural wonders. In 1896, Father William Grutza purchased the Chicago post office and customs house, which was about to be demolished, and had it shipped piece by piece to Milwaukee, where it was reconstructed,

modified, and transformed into St. Josephat Church.
Modeled on St. Peter's in Rome, St. Josephat contains a
hand-carved marble pulpit, ornate painting and stained
glass, Polish inscriptions and depictions of Polish
Catholicism, and one of the largest domes in the United
States. In 1928, Pope Pius XI elevated St. Josephat to the
status of a basilica, an honor bestowed only upon churches
of special religious significance and architectural beauty. It
was only the third basilica in the United States.

Eastern Europe is a remarkably diverse place, and
many other peoples made their way from that region to
Wisconsin, including Croats, Hungarians, Latvians,
Lithuanians, Romanians, Russians, Serbs, Slovaks,
Slovenes, and Ukrainians. Most took low-wage factory jobs
in Milwaukee or in the nearby cities of Racine and
Kenosha, but some managed to settle in rural areas of
northern Wisconsin. Jews from Eastern Europe also began
to arrive in substantial numbers. The Jewish population of
Wisconsin was small, but its history long. The first Jews in
Wisconsin were fur traders in territorial days. As German
immigration increased, German Jews came with them.
Several farming settlements of Jews emerged in Wisconsin.
Jews were also noted for becoming itinerant peddlers or
establishing retail businesses. One Jewish newspaper in
Philadelphia lamented in 1848 that the "religious state" of
Wisconsin's Jews was "deplorable," but religious life
quickly improved. Wisconsin's first congregation, Imenu-
Al, was organized in Milwaukee in 1850. After 1890,
Eastern European Jews swelled Wisconsin's small Jewish
community. The Jews of the Russian Empire and other
regions of Eastern Europe—where the great majority of
Europe's Jews lived—faced bitter religious persecution. Of
all turn-of-the-century immigrant groups, Jews were more
likely to immigrate in family units, and had the lowest
remigration rates. By 1900, Milwaukee was the home of
several thriving congregations, and modest Jewish
communities also emerged in Appleton, Kenosha,
Madison, Manitowoc, Racine, and Sheboygan.

Immigration to Wisconsin from the Mediterranean also
increased. Greeks settled in the southeastern cities, such as
Racine, Kenosha, Sheboygan, and most notably Milwaukee.
By far the largest contingent from the Mediterranean region

came from Italy. The first Italians in Wisconsin settled in a small fishing village on the Mississippi River in Vernon County before the Civil War. Located near the site of the climactic battle of the Black Hawk War, the village was originally known as Bad Axe City, but in 1868 residents renamed it Genoa. Italians did not arrive in significant numbers in Wisconsin until after 1890. Most were peasants from Sicily and the impoverished rural areas of the south, although some northerners came as well. The majority of Italians came to the industrial cities of the southeast, especially Milwaukee and Kenosha. In Milwaukee, Italians settled mainly in the Third Ward section abandoned by the Irish. After 1900, Italians moved into the Greenbush section of Madison just south of the University of Wisconsin campus. However, Italians also settled in many other parts of the Badger State. In Hurley, they worked in the iron mines. Whenever possible, Italian immigrants preferred to continue working in agriculture. Marinette and Barron Counties in the Cutover saw sizeable colonies of Italian farmers. With their knowledge of cheese making, Italians also helped to diversify Wisconsin's dairy offerings, introducing such cheeses as parmesan, provolone, and ricotta.

Immigrants formed the backbone of a new American working class, which grew in direct relation to the expansion of industry. The lives of Wisconsin's workers were frequently very difficult. Many factory workers labored ten to twelve hours per day, six days a week. Industrial plants were apt to be dirty, smelly, and generally unpleasant places to be. Factory owners often paid little attention to workplace safety, and industrial accidents were common, with sawmills and railroads probably being the most dangerous places to make a living. Industrial work took a physical toll on the workers. "There are few boilermakers who are not more or less deaf," one worker told state inspectors, "while their eyesight is often impaired by flying particles of steel." The workers were paid very little for their labor, sometimes less than a dollar a day. Because wages were so low, all members of a working man's family were usually required to work. By 1890, there were 12,751 documented women industrial workers in the Badger State, mainly in the manufacture of clothing. Thousands of children also worked—some under the age

of thirteen, in industries ranging from iron production to
candy making. Only by pooling their meager resources
could many working class families survive.

Fighting back was difficult for the workers.
Wisconsin's working class was divided along numerous
lines. Ethnic and religious differences sometimes separated
workers, for example. Because many immigrant workers
planned to return to their homelands, they felt little
incentive to improve labor relations in the United States.
There were also differences between skilled and unskilled
workers. Those workers with a trade, such as cigar makers,
iron workers, and printers, could bargain their know-how
into better pay and working conditions. Trade unions
emerged to protect the interests of skilled workers. Union
organizing in Wisconsin began in Milwaukee as early as
1847. The Knights of St. Crispin, a union of shoemakers,
was a national trade union organized in Milwaukee in
1867. In the days before social welfare programs, trade
unions also provided aid to skilled workers and their
families in case of illness, injury, or death. Toward the end
of the nineteenth century, trade unions saw their power
diminished as mechanization made many skilled workers
obsolete. The growing body of unskilled workers had
virtually no leverage over their employers at all. They could
easily be fired and replaced, making unionizing difficult. In
addition, employers sometimes forced workers to sign
"yellow dog contracts" in which they promised not to strike
or join a union, and circulated among themselves
"blacklists" of known union organizers, preventing them
from finding employment. In addition, business leaders
had the ear of the state's political leaders—indeed, business
and political leaders were often the same people—and had
the power to call out police or the National Guard in the
event of a strike, bring in strikebreakers, and obtain court
decisions favorable to the companies.

Strikes broke out nonetheless. Milwaukee shipbuilders
were the first to walk off the job in 1848. As conditions for
workers worsened, strikes became more frequent. In 1881,
1,000 sawmill workers in Eau Claire staged a strike to win
a cut in hours from twelve to ten per day. The mill owners
brought in strikebreakers and called up the National
Guard. In the years after the Civil War, a national

View of the J.S. Morris Carriage and Sleigh Factory, a two-story frame building on Franklin Street in Waupun. Carriages and men in work aprons are in front of the building. Circa 1875.

movement emerged among workers to institute an eight-hour workday. "Eight hours for work, eight hours for sleep, eight hours for what we will" became the battle cry of workers across the nation. Labor organizers set a deadline of May 1, 1886. As the deadline approached, management refused to budge and hundreds of thousands of workers walked off the job nationwide. In several cases, the strikes turned violent. In Chicago, police killed four strikers at the McCormick Harvester plant on May 3. The following day, workers held a rally at Haymarket Square in that city. When the police arrived, an unknown person exploded a bomb that killed seven officers. The tragedy at Haymarket led to a public backlash against unions, whom many began to associate with radicalism and violence. It was a major setback for the American labor movement.

Overshadowed by Haymarket was another bloody labor incident in Milwaukee known as the "Bay View Massacre." On May 1, an estimated 10,000 workers walked off the job in Milwaukee. In the following days the number of workers on strike only grew. On May 4, a large crowd of workers gathered at St. Stanislaus Church and marched down Mitchell Street to Kinnickinnic and then to South Bay Street, leading to the Bay View Iron Works, one of the last factories still operating. The Milwaukee police soon found themselves overwhelmed, and Governor Jeremiah Rusk called in the National Guard. In particular, Rusk deployed the "Kosciuszko Guards," a unit containing many ethnic Poles, further enraging the large number of Polish workers on the picket lines. As the crowd grew angrier, the Guards fired into the air, effectively dispersing the strikers. The following day, strikers gathered again at St. Stanislaus and marched to Bay View. As the crowd approached the plant, Major George Traeumer ordered them to halt. They did not. The Kosciuszko Guards lowered their guns and fired. The volley killed seven people—including two bystanders—and injured more than ten. A state historical marker at the corner of Russell and Superior Streets marks the site of Wisconsin's greatest labor tragedy. Located nearby are seven flowering pear trees—a memorial to each of those killed—and a commemorative marker placed by the Wisconsin Labor History Society.

GILDED AGE POLITICS

In the nineteenth century, few Americans looked to the government to solve the problems the changing economy had created. The Gilded Age was the time of *laissez faire*— the idea that government should not interfere with the market economy. Neither the Democrats nor the Republicans had any desire to police economic competition. Both parties were composed of broad coalitions representing a wide range of interests and ideological perspectives. Generally speaking, the Democrats— composed of white Southerners and Catholic immigrants—favored a weak government that would not interfere with local customs. The Republicans advocated a somewhat stronger government that would promote (but not regulate) business, as well as social reforms such as public education and temperance. The result was a period of unregulated economic competition.

In the Gilded Age, the Republicans dominated Wisconsin politics. Only twice during the period did the Democrats win the governorship. In the post–Civil War years, however, the balance between the Democrats and the Republicans was more equal than it seemed on the surface. Democrats had a strong base of support in Milwaukee and in the German Catholic counties along the Lake Michigan shoreline, and any shock to the existing balance of power between the parties could tip the scales in favor of the Democrats. For example, the 1872 Graham Law—a Republican attempt to tighten the state's liquor laws—led many German Protestants to bolt from the party, contributing to the election of a Democrat as governor the following year. In 1889, the Republican-dominated legislature passed the Bennett Law, a compulsory education bill that required all certified schools to use English as the language of instruction. Once again, German Protestants crossed over to the Democrats. In the 1890 elections, the Republicans lost the governorship, control of the state legislature, and nearly all of its congressional representatives.

In order to maintain internal peace and avoid alienating key groups of swing voters, both parties tended to offer bland, watered-down platforms. The political rhetoric of the late nineteenth century was anything but bland, however. The Gilded Age was noted for its harsh

Must-See Sites: Brewery Tours

Wisconsin is famous for its beer, and no trip to the state could be complete without a brewery tour. Below is a list of the most popular:

Capital Brewery
7734 Terrace Avenue
Middleton, WI 53562
(608) 836-7100
www.capital-brewery.com

Jacob Leinenkugel Brewing Company
1 Jefferson Avenue
Chippewa Falls, WI 54729
(715) 723-5557
www.leinie.com

Miller Brewing Company
4251 West State Street
Milwaukee, WI 53208
(800) 944-5483
www.millerbrewing.com

Sprecher Brewing Company
701 West Glendale Avenue
Glendale, WI 53209
(414) 964-2739
www.sprecherbrewery.com

Stevens Point Brewery
2617 Water Street
Stevens Point, WI 54481
(800) 369-4911
www.pointbeer.com

For a complete list, visit the Wisconsin Department of Tourism website, www.travelwisconsin.com.

political demagoguery. Bitter memories of the Civil War were still fresh in the minds of many voters, and the Republicans perfected the campaign technique of "waving the bloody shirt"—rekindling wartime animosities for political gain. For example, Wisconsin Governor Lucius Fairchild told audiences that "every rebel, every Copperhead, every draft sneak, every dirty traitor" was a Democrat. His words were made all the more dramatic by the empty sleeve pinned to his chest; Fairchild lost his arm fighting the Confederates at Gettysburg. The Grand Army of the Republic (GAR), an organization of Union veterans, urged their fellow veterans to "vote the way you shot" and oppose the Democrats. Many Republicans continued to attack the drinking habits of immigrants and claim that American Catholics were part of a "papal conspiracy" to extinguish Protestantism and democracy in the United States. Such inflammatory rhetoric mobilized the party's core supporters, and kept those vulnerable to defections from straying from the fold.

The period was also known for its pervasive political corruption. Corporations bought influence or provided other favors to compliant lawmakers. Railroads, for example, often gave free passes to their political friends—a valuable plumb for lawmakers. Politicians also paid off key constituent groups. Wisconsin's GAR turned out Civil War veterans to vote for the Republicans, and in turn the veterans received an array of government benefits. Perhaps the most notable achievement of Wisconsin's GAR was the creation of the Grand Army Home (later Wisconsin Veterans Home) in Waupaca County in 1887. Many of the home's original cottages, as well as the commandant's Victorian residence, still exist on the campus. Wisconsin's GAR also received a Memorial Hall in the State Capitol building, which for many years was a military museum and is today a hearing room. The federal government also established a branch of the National Soldiers' Home on a bluff overlooking Milwaukee. Many of the home's original buildings remain, and the grounds (today administered by the US Department of Veterans Affairs) still afford a quiet respite from the hustle and bustle of the city.

In both the Republican and Democratic parties, power was concentrated in the hands of a small group of men known as the "bosses," who dispensed government jobs in exchange for political favors. The bosses were also the ones who selected the party's candidates for office, and anyone who wanted to be a candidate on election day needed to go through them. One of Wisconsin's most notorious bosses was Republican Elisha Keyes. From his seemingly harmless position as Madison postmaster, Keyes wisely used his powers of patronage (the ability to make appointments to government jobs) to head the so-called Madison Regency faction of Wisconsin Republicans. In 1880, Keyes's faction was eclipsed by Senator Philetus Sawyer's "Sawdust Contingent," dominated by lumber and railroad men. In such an atmosphere, government regulation of the economy was impossible. Many of Wisconsin's most important Gilded Age politicians lived just north of the Capitol in a section of Madison known as Mansion Hill. Today one can stroll through the area and still see the stately homes once occupied by some of Wisconsin's most powerful (and sometimes ruthless) leaders. The home of "Boss" Keyes is located at 102 East Gorham Street.

In their battles over the Civil War and liquor, political leaders—in Wisconsin and across the nation—ignored many important but potentially divisive issues, such as the growing power of business corporations and the numerous social consequences of industrialization. The political system seemed unresponsive and undemocratic, and was instead up for sale to the highest bidder. Wisconsin's citizens began to demand change, and pressure mounted on the state's corrupt politicians. Change finally came after 1900, and when it did, Wisconsin was on the leading edge of political reform in the United States.

6

The Progressive Era

America's demand for political change was finally met as the twentieth century dawned. The Progressive Era brought sweeping reform to American politics that affected the lives of all Americans. Progressivism is complex. Often described as a movement, progressives were never unified by an agreed-upon reform agenda. What linked the disparate branches of progressivism was a desire for change, a belief that change was possible, and a faith in the power of government to act in the public interest. Progressivism brought America into the modern world. Historian John M. Cooper, Jr. of the University of Wisconsin has called the first two decades of the new century the "second golden age of American politics," and Wisconsin was at the very heart of it all. The Badger State was a leader in progressive reform. Its citizens experienced the tremendous benefits of progressivism as well as its great costs. The state became one big experiment and provided a model for the rest of the nation. It was perhaps Wisconsin's finest hour.

RUMBLINGS OF DISSENT

During the late nineteenth century, several movements emerged in Wisconsin to protest the sorry state of Gilded Age politics. Protest came from many quarters, particularly farmers, workers, and the middle class. These movements were not coordinated in any way, and none succeeded in significantly changing the political system. But their criticisms raised many new ideas about the role of government in the economy, and began to erode Americans' faith in the doctrine of *laissez faire*, thus paving the way for progressivism.

The first rumblings of dissent came from the countryside. During the 1870s, an agrarian society called the Patrons of Husbandry, better known as the Grangers, pressured lawmakers for railroad regulation. Farmers depended on the railroads to ship their grain to market. But railroad companies usually had a monopoly on traffic in a particular region, and charged shipping rates that many ordinary farmers found outrageous. Granger activity in Wisconsin began in 1872, and within a few years farmers organized 500 chapters throughout the state. The Grangers formed farmer cooperatives to pool their resources, and they also became politically active. In 1872, angry farmers joined with German Protestants upset with Republican attempts to control liquor to create a Reform-Democratic ticket that ousted the Republicans from power. The reformers pushed the Potter Law through the state legislature, which created railroad rate caps and established a state railroad commission. The reform coalition was a shaky one, however, and quickly fell apart. When it did, the Republicans resumed control of the legislature and promptly revoked the Potter Law. The Granger movement also flourished in surrounding states, but had little more success than in Wisconsin. By the end of the 1870s, the Grangers had ceased to be an important political force.

Angry farmers were also an important part of the Greenback Party, one of many third-party movements that emerged in Wisconsin during the late nineteenth century. The Greenback Party grew out of the Panic of 1873 and the depression that followed. Many farmers had borrowed money to purchase farm machinery and other necessities, but as farm prices plummeted these farmers had increasing difficulty paying off those debts. Many began to advocate the liberal printing of paper money, an inflationary measure that would raise farm prices and decrease the debt burden of many farmers. The leadership of both the Democrats and Republicans—all sound money men—rejected the idea, and the Greenback Party was born. In 1877, Milwaukee industrialist Edward P. Allis ran for governor on the Greenback ticket, winning 15 percent of the vote. As the economy recovered, Wisconsin's Greenback movement faded.

In Milwaukee, socialism provided another alternative. German immigrants brought socialism to Wisconsin in the nineteenth century—working men as well as a few Forty-

Eighters and other educated intellectuals. The socialist world has long been subject to intense factionalism, and Wisconsin's small socialist community was no exception. Very few of Milwaukee's socialists were hard-line communists, but rather were gradualists in the tradition of Germany's Social Democrats, who believed that through the vote the workers could convert government into an instrument for the public good. Socialism had little impact on Wisconsin politics until after 1890, when an Austrian Jewish immigrant named Victor Berger emerged as its most important leader. Berger understood that for socialism to succeed in the United States it would have to shed its image as being ethnic and radical. Under Berger's leadership, Milwaukee's socialists began to hammer away at the issue of political corruption, which was rampant in Milwaukee city government. Socialists promised clean and efficient government, including the revitalization of the city's police and fire departments. Socialists also called for the public ownership of utilities, which in many cities were run by private companies. Clearly bucking the *laissez-faire* attitudes of the day, socialists wanted to prove that government could be run effectively and efficiently in order to set the stage for a larger, more activist government. The socialist emphasis on utilities and social services gained them the nickname "sewer socialists." It was a message many fed-up Milwaukeans wanted to hear. In 1904, several socialists were elected to the city council, and in 1910 had taken the mayor's office. Milwaukee gained a reputation for fair and functional government, and Berger became a key figure in the national socialist movement. Elected to the House of Representatives in 1910, Berger was the first socialist to serve in the US Congress.

The middle class was also growing restive. From the rise of large, national corporations emerged armies of bureaucrats, such as accountants, administrators, lawyers, and other "white collar" professionals. The middle class was educated, and often steeped in the latest social science theories. Many middle-class Americans no longer saw the world as governed by fixed and unchanging natural laws. Rather, they believed that through scientific investigation—collecting and analyzing statistics and developing theories—they could understand *how* the world operated. They also tended to believe that people had the intellectual and moral capacity to develop more efficient social systems. The economy was not a naturally functioning, self-regulating system, in the view of many, but rather a social construction that could be manipulated. Social institutions could be altered to solve social problems and provide opportunities for all. Having administered corporate bureaucracies effectively, the middle class was mystified by the waste and corruption of government and believed that through "administrative efficiency" and "rational planning," government could be made to function better and in the public interest. In addition, the middle class represented an important group of affluent consumers who resented paying artificially high prices for shoddy products and social services. They also aspired to upward social mobility. Although growing in numbers and in economic power, the middle class felt shut out of the political system, and wanted more of a voice in the political arena.

By 1890 there were numerous calls for political reform in Wisconsin, but those seeking reform often had little in common. It was the depression that struck America in 1893 that helped bring reformist elements together and give progressivism the kick start it needed. The depression of the 1890s was the worst the nation had yet seen, and second only to the Great Depression of the 1930s in severity. By the end of 1893, a quarter of Wisconsin's banks had failed. Major companies like E.P. Allis and the Milwaukee Road had laid off workers and cut wages 10 percent for those who remained. In Milwaukee, an estimated 40 percent of workers were out of a job. In Racine, La Crosse, Sheboygan, and Beloit, the figure reached 50 percent. Some communities reported hordes of "tramps" who stole farm animals to keep from starving. Strikes and riots broke out in Milwaukee and other places. The hard working as well as the indolent lost their jobs. People did not feel in control of their own destinies. This depression, like no other event, challenged the predominant *laissez-faire* attitudes of the day and laid the groundwork for progressivism. More people than ever before demanded that government take action.

But government was slow to do so. Business and political leaders (usually the same people) believed that the depression was a natural market correction that would soon right itself.

Indeed, as unemployment went up, businesses often received tax breaks, shifting the tax burden onto the hard-pressed citizens. Utility companies raised rates and cut services. When the citizens of Oshkosh complained about electricity rate hikes, the local utility company cut the power to most parts of the city. Corporate arrogance and government complicity led to grassroots activism on the part of many citizens. Joining the socialists in calls for local government reform were middle-class organizations like the Milwaukee Municipal League, a nonpartisan pressure group that lobbied lawmakers for anti-corruption legislation, municipal ownership of utilities, and electoral reforms to break the power of party bosses. Reformers were often successful. As the twentieth century dawned, public service commissions and regulatory laws kept watch on utility companies. Wisconsin's urban dwellers enjoyed a host of new social services, including public health agencies, garbage collection, improved public schools, libraries and museums, parks and pools, and many others. Some municipalities elected aldermen at large to break the power of ward bosses, or hired professional "managers" to run the city rather than an elected mayor. Nobody was yet using the term "progressive," but progressive reform was underway. Before long, the progressive impulse hit the State Capitol in Madison.

ROBERT M. LA FOLLETTE

Robert Marion La Follette is the most important individual in Wisconsin history. The name is synonymous with Wisconsin's unique brand of progressive reform. La Follette led a crusade to "restore representative government" in Wisconsin and then took that crusade to the nation. La Follette is a study in contradictions. A tireless campaigner to break the power of political machines, he built his own machine-like organization around himself and his vibrant personality. A champion of democracy, he brooked no dissent among his troops and did not like to share the limelight with others. Proclaimed politically dead several times, "Fighting Bob" always bounced back. Despite the copious amounts of ink historians have spilled on the study of his career, La Follette is still steeped in myth and legend. "Seldom has a major American political figure so successfully converted his campaign autobiography into the commonly accepted story of his political career," according to historian John M. Cooper, Jr. The myth endures because it is positive and inspirational. La Follette symbolizes Wisconsin's contribution to making America a better place, as well as the political and social values many Wisconsinites still hold dear.

La Follette was born in a log cabin on June 14, 1855 in Primrose Township, Dane County. His early life is one of hardship but also persistence. His father died soon after his birth, and his stepfather passed away when he was sixteen, leaving him a teenaged farmer and head of household. In 1873 the family moved to Madison so young Bob could attend the University of Wisconsin. La Follette was a poor student but a popular figure on campus. He considered a career in acting but discovered that his greatest talent lay in oratory. In 1879, La Follette won the Interstate Oratorical Contest, and was treated to a grand reception in the State Assembly chambers. While in college he met Belle Case, the first woman graduate of the university's law school. The couple soon wed. After completing law school himself, La Follette entered politics. He was a rather conventional Gilded Age Republican, with a deep faith in America as a land of unlimited opportunity and the belief that a person's lot in life was determined by his or her own talent, determination, and willingness to work hard. La Follette was also an ambitious young man in a big hurry. He was elected Dane County district attorney in 1880, and in 1884 was elected to the US House of Representatives. At age 29, Robert La Follette was America's youngest congressman. He served three terms in Washington, but was ousted in the Democratic triumph of 1890.

In 1891 La Follette's political career took a dramatic turn. The circumstances surrounding his awakening to reform politics will be forever shrouded in mystery. On September 17, La Follette met with Senator Philetus Sawyer—the acknowledged "boss" of Wisconsin's Republican Party—in the lobby of the Plankinton Hotel in Milwaukee. The two men gave very different accounts of what transpired. La Follette claimed that Sawyer offered him a bribe to fix a railroad case in which his brother-in-law was the presiding judge. Sawyer denied the charge and claimed he was simply trying to retain La Follette's legal

Portrait of Robert M. La Follette, Sr. at the age of 29 when elected to Congress in 1884.

services. "If you struck me in the face you could not insult me as you insult me now," La Follette reportedly told Sawyer, and stormed from the hotel. "I had been subjected to a terrible shock," he later wrote of the incident, "that opened my eyes" to the pervasiveness of corruption in American politics, shaking his faith in America as a land of opportunity. Birth and bank accounts seemed to matter more than talent and hard work. Just how shocked an experienced politician like La Follette really was about being offered a bribe during an age of rampant political corruption is open to question, but whatever the case, he seized upon the issue to wage war against the party bosses. "I determined that the power of this corrupt influence, which was undermining and destroying every semblance of representative government in Wisconsin, should be broken," he wrote. Reforming the political system, according to La Follette, was the only way to make the American dream of unlimited opportunity come true.

Throughout the 1890s, La Follette led an insurgency against the Republican machine. Much of his success can be attributed to his charismatic personality and engaging speeches. La Follette traveled throughout the state speaking with voters and shaking their hands. He also tapped into a large reservoir of discontent among groups of Republican voters. Crucial to La Follette's political career were farmers, who were angry at the railroads and suspicious of urban financial institutions. Fighting Bob always reminded audiences that he was a farm boy himself. In particular, he made an alliance with former governor and dairy promoter William Dempster Hoard, who was angry with the Republican machine's connections to the meatpacking industry and its promotion of oleomargarine as a substitute for butter. Norwegians were the most loyal of Republican voters in Wisconsin, but seldom received positions of power. The Norwegians felt that the machine was preoccupied with holding the German Protestant vote but took them for granted. La Follette, who grew up amid Norwegians and even spoke a little of their language, assured them a key role in his coalition. Younger Republicans—like himself—felt that the older bosses shut them out of power. While courting these disaffected voters, La Follette assiduously avoided temperance, women's suffrage, and other cultural issues that had traditionally split the party.

At the 1894 state Republican convention, La Follette's choice for governor, Norwegian Nils Haugen, lost to the machine candidate. La Follette ran himself in 1896 and lost, claiming that the party bosses had bribed the delegates to back their candidate. He ran again in 1898 and lost. But with each challenge to the bosses he gained more recruits, who were attracted by La Follette's spellbinding oratory and their growing dislike of the Republican leadership. Before 1897, La Follette had yet to embrace explicitly the cause of political reform, but that changed with a speech he gave in Chicago that year entitled "The Menace of the Machine." Political machines were corrupt and un-democratic, he claimed, and had to be crushed in order to restore democracy in America. La Follette kept his reform agenda simple, focusing on two main issues. One was the direct primary. Allowing party members to choose candidates was not only democratic, he argued, but would also break the power of the bosses and their corrupt caucus system. His second issue was railroad reform, popular with farmers and many others angry with corporate arrogance and influence. The year 1900 finally belonged to La Follette. Sawyer had passed away, leaving a leadership vacuum. At the same time, he had mended fences with key party leaders. Fighting Bob received the Republican nomination, and cruised to ultimate victory in November. He was the first Wisconsin governor born in the state, and the first governor of the twentieth century. There was a palpable sense of newness and change in Madison. With Fighting Bob in the governor's office, Wisconsin would never be the same again.

Once La Follette became governor, the infighting among Republicans reached a fever pitch. Party conservatives blocked his attempts at any meaningful reform, and the party devolved into squabbling factions. La Follette's people adopted the name "progressives," the first reformers anywhere in America to use that term. Party conservatives became known as the "stalwarts." Claiming to represent "the people vs. the interests," La Follette worked so hard that he collapsed from nervous exhaustion several times. In the 1902 governor's race, many stalwarts voted for the conservative Democratic candidate, but those defections were offset by what La Follette called "fair-minded" Democrats who voted for him. In his second term he managed a revision of railroad tax rates and got his direct primary placed on the 1904 ballot as a referendum, but stalwarts still blocked railroad regulation.

The legislative logjam was finally broken after the 1904 gubernatorial race. The Republican convention took place in the Old Red Gym on the University of Wisconsin campus. Progressives guarded the entrances with barbed wire, the largest university athletes they could find, and even some street thugs, to keep out stalwarts without proper credentials. The stalwarts cried foul and elected their own slate of delegates, but the state supreme court ruled that the Red Gym convention—which nominated Fighting Bob for a third term—was legitimate. La Follette won the general election handily and carried a progressive majority into the state legislature. Voters also approved the direct primary. Now La Follette could institute substantive reforms. In 1905, the legislature established a state railroad commission with the power to revise (but not set) shipping rates. Other accomplishments that year included a bill to control the influence of lobbyists in order to minimize corporate influence, and a comprehensive civil service law to promote competence rather than political connections in government jobs. Wisconsin was not the only state pursuing reform. Progressives had taken charge in several other states, and in Washington President Theodore Roosevelt had gained the nickname "trust buster" for going after corporate monopolies. Progressivism was flourishing across the nation.

One of the defining characteristics of Wisconsin progressivism was the frequent use of experts. The University of Wisconsin had a tremendous influence on Wisconsin progressivism. La Follette appointed Charles Van Hise, a former classmate from his college days, to the presidency of the university. Van Hise set about reforming the university, attracting some of greatest talent in American academics and transforming it from an ordinary state school into one of the nation's premier research institutions. Faculty members often played a vital role in designing progressive legislation. Economics professor

Robert M. La Follette, Sr., speaking to a crowd from the back of wagon. This image is one of a series of six photographs taken at the Cumberland fair that illustrate his vigorous speaking style. Circa 1897.

John R. Commons, for example, was instrumental in revising the state's civil service laws. Ideas and information traveled back and forth along Madison's State Street between the "twin domes" of Bascom Hall on the campus and the State Capitol. It was said that the University of Wisconsin was "the university that ran a state." La Follette sought expert advice off the campus as well. Founded in 1901, the Legislative Reference Library provided lawmakers with a nonpartisan source of information, rather than depending on lobbyists. Experts at the library also drafted legislation, earning the nickname the "bill factory." The cooperation of lawmakers and scholarly experts to create reform legislation became known as the "Wisconsin Idea" and influenced progressives across the United States.

Must-See Sites:
Circus World Museum

During the nineteenth and early twentieth centuries, circus shows traveled from small town to small town providing local residents with excitement and exotic sights. The first circus came to Wisconsin as early as 1840. The Ringling Brothers of Baraboo began their own circus show in the 1870s and made Baraboo their headquarters. The Ringling Brothers Circus soon became of the most popular in the United States. In 1907, the Ringling Brothers bought out the "Greatest Show on Earth," developed by P.T. Barnum and James A. Bailey. After years of running separate shows, the two circuses were formally merged and became the Ringling Brothers Barnum & Bailey Circus—probably the most famous circus in the world.

Like many Wisconsinites, the Ringling Brothers relocated to the warmer climate of Florida, but Circus World Museum has kept alive Baraboo's rich circus heritage. The atmosphere of a turn-of-the-century circus is richly re-created at Circus World Museum, including clowns, a carousel, animals, and displays of various human oddities. The highlight of the day at Circus World is a performance under an actual big-top tent. Younger visitors may also ride camels and elephants. The museum owns a unique collection of circus wagons, the kind used when circuses traveled from town to town.

Circus World Museum
550 Water Street (Highway 113)
Baraboo, WI 53913
(866) 693-1500
www.wisconsinhistory.org/circusworld/

In five years as Wisconsin governor, La Follette had broken the power of the old bosses and opened up the state's political system to more citizen participation. His hard work had gained him national attention. Journalist Lincoln Steffens credited La Follette with "restoring representative government in Wisconsin." Fighting Bob, in turn, set his sights on the national arena. He became a popular speaker on the national Chautauqua circuit, and in 1906 left for Washington to serve as one of Wisconsin's US Senators. With the retirement of President Roosevelt in 1909, La Follette was widely viewed as America's leading progressive politician.

La Follette made a run for the White House in 1912. Fighting Bob believed he had the backing of Roosevelt, and was shocked to learn that the former president had decided to come out of retirement and enter the race himself. A larger-than-life figure with a proven record of reform, Roosevelt elbowed La Follette out of the way rather handily. La Follette never forgave him. Roosevelt failed to win the Republican nomination, so he simply formed his own Progressive Party, better known as the "Bull Moose Party." On October 14, Roosevelt made a campaign appearance in Milwaukee. That evening, he left the Hotel Gilpatrick (where the Milwaukee Hyatt Regency now stands) en route to a speaking engagement at the Milwaukee Auditorium. Lurking in the crowd was a deranged man named John Schrank, who shot at Roosevelt with a .38 caliber pistol. The former president was hit in the chest, but the eyeglasses and speech in his vest pocket slowed the bullet's momentum. Wounded and bleeding, Roosevelt insisted on giving his speech. In fact, he even joked about the assassination attempt in his remarks, claiming that "it takes more than one bullet to kill a bull moose." Despite such heroics, Progressive Democrat Woodrow Wilson emerged the victor on election day. La Follette never gave up his ambition of winning the White House.

THE LABORATORY OF DEMOCRACY

Robert La Follette had earned Wisconsin the nickname "laboratory of democracy," but progressive reform in the Badger State continued after he went to Washington. La Follette tried to maintain control of Wisconsin's progressives from Washington, but with mixed results. His successor, Norwegian-born James O. Davidson, was sympathetic to progressivism but resented Fighting Bob's imperious attempt to control him, and gravitated toward the stalwarts. La Follette then joined forces with Francis E. McGovern, Milwaukee's leading progressive and a long-time La Follette rival. McGovern represented a different strain of Badger State progressivism. La Follette's base of support was in the countryside, but McGovern was more urban in orientation, concerned with issues like industrial relations and city services. In particular, McGovern's greatest fear was the rise of socialism in Milwaukee and what the "reds" might do if in power. McGovern made a name for himself fighting political corruption in Milwaukee as district attorney. In 1904 and 1905, he brought indictments against 24 people involved with municipal corruption. He was elected governor in 1910.

In his two terms in office, McGovern achieved a reform record equal to La Follette's. He continued to utilize the University of Wisconsin and keep the Wisconsin Idea alive. McGovern's record clearly indicates his urban perspective and his desire to court the working class and steal the thunder from Victor Berger and the Milwaukee socialists. The 1911 legislative session proved to be the most productive in Wisconsin history. The crown jewel of the session was America's first workers' compensation law, developed under the guidance of John R. Commons. Other 1911 laws included:

- Workplace safety regulations
- A state life insurance fund
- Laws to regulate the working hours of women & children
- Creation of the Wisconsin Industrial Commission to oversee industry practices
- State aid for highway improvement and construction
- America's first state-run vocational education program
- Wisconsin's first income tax

McGovern's reforms went beyond La Follette's concern for restoring democracy and competition, but delved into the arena of social welfare. Despite—or perhaps because of—McGovern's successes, relations between the governor and the senator deteriorated. Making matters worse was McGovern's support of Theodore Roosevelt for president in 1912. In 1914, the feud between McGovern and La Follette split Wisconsin's progressives. At the same time, stalwarts charged that the progressives had raised taxes too much and driven jobs and businesses out of the state, an assertion that began to resonate with many voters. That year, McGovern lost the governorship to stalwart Republican Emanuel Philipp. Wisconsin's progressives were not yet politically dead, but their best days were behind them.

Golda Meir

Golda Meir, one of the most important world leaders during the 1960s and 1970s, once called Milwaukee home. She was born Golda Mabovitz in Kiev, Ukraine in 1898. Her father, Moshe, came to Milwaukee in 1903. In 1906, Golda and the rest of the family arrived.

Golda's time in Milwaukee was brief in comparison to her long life, but those years were important ones. By all accounts she was a bright and vivacious girl; her mother nicknamed her *kochleffl* (stirring spoon) because of her turbulent nature. She dreamed of becoming a teacher, but her parents arranged for her to become a seamstress instead. Golda ran away from home in protest in 1913 to live with an older sister in Denver. She returned to Milwaukee the following year only after her parents acceded to her demands. She graduated from North Division High School and enrolled at the Milwaukee State Teachers' College, known today as the University of Wisconsin–Milwaukee. Her desire to teach was overtaken by another cause. Golda became involved with Zionism—a movement among Jews to establish a homeland in Israel. In 1917, she married Morris Myerson, fellow Zionist, whom she had met while in Denver. In 1921 the Myersons moved to what is now Israel—then known as Palestine, controlled by the British, and populated primarily by Arabs. She later Hebraized her last name to Meir.

In Palestine, Meir became a leader in the movement for Israeli independence, a goal achieved in 1948. That year, she sneaked across the border into Jordan dressed as an Arab woman in an unsuccessful attempt to dissuade King Abdullah from joining an Arab attack on the fledgling state. Israel survived, and Meir became a key figure in that country's Labor Party, serving as ambassador to the Soviet Union, labor minister, and foreign minister. She became prime minister at the age of 70—one of just a handful of women heads of state. She guided Israel to victory in the 1973 Arab–Israeli War. She died in Jerusalem in 1978. Today, UW–Milwaukee's campus library is named in her honor, as is an elementary school on the north side of town that Meir attended as a girl.

Progressivism was about more than just regulating the economy. Evidence of progressive thinking can still be seen on the Wisconsin landscape. Progressives believed that nearly any problem could be managed through efficient bureaucracy. In addition to cleaning up city government, many reformers wanted to make cities pleasant places to live. Madison stands as an example of what thoughtful urban planning could accomplish. By the 1890s, local businessmen, concerned about the city's appearance, formed the Madison Improvement Association, which raised money to construct fountains and boathouses throughout the city. The Madison Park and Pleasure Drive Association, founded in 1894, acquired lands and turned them into city parks. The association hired nationally renowned urban planner John Nolen to make recommendations for shaping the future growth of Madison. Nolen was highly impressed with the city. "Madison is one of the most striking examples that could be selected in the United States of a city which should have a distinct individuality, marked characteristics separating it from and in many respects elevating it above other cities," he wrote in his 1911 report to the association. "No other city of the world, so far as I know, has naturally such a unique situation on a series of lakes, with an opportunity for so much and such direct relationship to beautiful water frontages." Nolen made seventeen recommendations in all, concerning the creation of parks, playgrounds, and the protection of waterfront lands, many of which the city adopted. Madison today is a city of unusual beauty, replete with parks and other recreational facilities, owing in large part to wise progressive planning in the early twentieth century.

Madison is not the only place in Wisconsin visitors can see the legacy of the progressive mind on the landscape. Industrialization had taken a tremendous toll on the natural environment. In Wisconsin, perhaps the greatest ecological catastrophe was the destruction of the great northern forests. Economic progress often meant an ugly landscape and the depletion of vital natural resources. In Washington, President Roosevelt enacted a series of conservation laws, including the establishment of the US Forest Service in 1905. Wisconsin's progressives took action as well. Efforts to create a state park system dated to the Gilded Age, but by 1900 only one park had been created—

Interstate State Park on the Wisconsin–Minnesota border. The La Follette administration formed a commission to study the feasibility of creating state parks and forests. The first state forest, Brule River, was established in 1907. That same year Governor Davidson formed a state park board, which hired John Nolen to develop a plan of action. Nolen recommended four sites as state parks: Devil's Lake in Sauk County, Fish Creek in Door County, the Wisconsin Dells in central Wisconsin, and the confluence of the Wisconsin and Mississippi Rivers. Acting on Nolen's plan, the state began to purchase lands for parks. The Fish Creek site became Peninsula State Park in 1910. Devil's Lake joined the list the following year. Wyalusing State Park (the Wisconsin–Mississippi confluence) was established in 1917. In later years, numerous other state parks and forests would be created. (The Wisconsin Dells would elude park status, though it would eventually become a protected area). The state created the Conservation Commission in 1915, which evolved into the present-day Department of Natural Resources. Anyone who visits a Wisconsin state park or forest today can thank the progressives for their foresight.

One must always keep in mind that progressivism was not a unified movement. What one progressive saw as a necessary reform others saw as a threat to progress. One contentious issue during the progressive era was suffrage for women. For many, progressivism was about the expansion of democracy, and it did not take a great legal mind to see that denying women the right to vote was undemocratic. Many progressives saw women's suffrage as a way to expand American democracy and make the country live up to is founding principles. Women had long been involved in social reform movements, and many progressives welcomed their support at the polling place. For others, voting rights for women was not that simple. Many men viewed women as being too "weak" and "soft" to withstand the rigors of the political process. Women voting, some believed, would threaten the stability of the family and confuse the strict gender divisions upon which they believed society was founded. Because of women's involvement in the temperance movement, many immigrants—especially Germans—opposed a woman's right to vote. German men were heard to complain that

Frank Lloyd Wright

Frank Lloyd Wright is considered by many to be the greatest architect of the twentieth century, and his genius cannot be understood without reference to his Wisconsin roots. Wright was born in Richland Center on June 8, 1867. At the age of 12 the Wright family moved to Madison, but young Frank spent summers on a relative's farm near Spring Green. He attended the University of Wisconsin, but in 1887 moved to Chicago to pursue a career in architecture. A dynamic city recovering from the devastating fire of 1871, Chicago was one of the world's leading centers of architectural innovation. There he worked under the tutelage of Louis Sullivan, whose maxim "form follows function" strongly influenced Wright. He soon became one of Chicago's most popular architects, and in 1893 left Sullivan's firm and struck out on his own.

Wright is noted for the development of the "Prairie School" of architecture. Wright wanted to move away from European influences and develop a style of architecture that was particularly American. The Prairie School buildings are characterized by low, horizontal lines and made from native materials. Wright believed in an "organic" kind of architecture in which the building stands in harmony with the natural environment. One of the best examples of Prairie School architecture is Taliesin, the home Wright built near Spring Green on the farm he worked as a young man. Wright designed more than just homes. His Imperial Hotel in Tokyo (1915) was one of the few buildings to withstand that city's devastating earthquake of 1923. His Guggenheim Museum (1942) remains one of the most distinctive buildings in New York City.

Wisconsin has one of the highest concentrations of Frank Lloyd Wright–designed buildings in the world. The Frank Lloyd Wright Heritage Tour highlights some—but not all—of Wright's creations in the Badger State, including the Annunciation Greek Orthodox Congregation in Milwaukee, the S.C. Johnson Wax building in Racine, and the Unitarian Meeting House in Madison. One of the most accessible—if not spectacular—of Wright's creations is Madison's Monona Terrace, which was not constructed until long after his death. Completed in 1997 after years of debate and extensive modification of Wright's original plans, Monona Terrace extends from the Lake Monona shoreline into the lake itself, accomplishing a marriage between Madison and its beautiful lakes. It is a wonderful example of how Wright was able to blend his buildings into the natural environment.

Frank Lloyd Wright Heritage Tour
PO Box 6339
Madison, WI 53716
(608) 287-0339
www.WrightinWisconsin.org

Partial view of a boathouse designed by Frank Lloyd Wright and built for the city of Madison. The University of Wisconsin campus is seen in the distance across Lake Mendota.

women should be concerned only with *Kinder, Kirche, Küche* (children, church, kitchen). Suffrage activists pressed on nonetheless. Elizabeth Cady Stanton, Susan B. Anthony, and other women traveled throughout the United States in the nineteenth century crusading for a woman's right to vote, including visits to the Badger State. Before 1900, several western states had provided women the ballot, but Wisconsin was not one of them.

Many Wisconsin women were deeply involved in the women's movement. Carrie Chapman Catt, for example, one of America's leading feminists at the turn of the century, was born in Ripon. Groups like the Women's Christian Temperance Union (WCTU), led nationally by Janesville-born Frances Willard, were also active in Wisconsin. Momentum in Wisconsin for women's suffrage grew during the Progressive Era, especially in areas originally settled by

Yankees. Leaders of Wisconsin's suffrage movement included Racine Unitarian minister Olympia Brown (the first Wisconsin woman ordained by a major religious denomination) and Belle Case La Follette, wife of Robert M. La Follette. Among Germans, Meta Berger, wife of socialist leader Victor Berger, also fought for women's suffrage. Even Fighting Bob himself eventually came out publicly for suffrage. In 1912, the question of votes for women was put on the ballot as a referendum. The result was a resounding no. Only 37 percent of voters favored a women's right to vote; 63 percent did not. It was a stunning defeat for suffrage advocates. As one disillusioned activist said, "The last thing a man becomes progressive about is the activities of his own wife."

THE "TRAITOR STATE"

1914. Perhaps at no time has a man with a gun had more of an impact on history. On June 28 of that year, a Serbian nationalist shot and killed Archduke Franz Ferdinand of Austria in the city of Sarajevo, Bosnia. The assassination set off what has become known as the "powder keg of Europe." World War I, which pitted the Allies (Britain, France, Italy, and Russia) against the Central Powers (Germany, Austria-Hungary, and Turkey), was the bloodiest conflict Western civilization had yet seen, as industrialization had turned the battlefield into a slaughterhouse.

World War I created deep divisions among Americans, especially in Wisconsin. Most wanted nothing to do with the war. Some, sympathetic to Britain and France, urged American entry on the side of the Allies. Others adamantly opposed US involvement. Antiwar sentiment was especially strong among the state's German population. In Wisconsin, some Germans raised money for German war relief, and a few even returned to Germany to fight. Most German Americans were loyal to America first, but simply wanted to avoid having to fight their cousins in the Old Country. Criticism of Germany in the press, in their view, was the result of British propaganda. Other groups in Wisconsin also opposed involvement. Socialists advocated international cooperation, and saw the war as the logical result of capitalism. Some progressives opposed joining the war, Robert La Follette foremost among them. La Follette, like many Midwestern politicians, was an isolationist who believed the United States should not become involved in the affairs of other nations. He believed that the European war was none of America's concern, and feared that the war would distract Americans from the task of political reform. Preparations for war would put government money in the hands of corporate interests, he argued, and allow corporations to regain dominance of the political system, ruining years of progressive reform.

American economic ties to the Allies, and German attempts to cut those ties through submarine warfare, forced the United States into the war in April 1917. World War I showed progressivism at its best and at its worst. The federal government successfully mobilized nearly five million men to fight, and channeled the nation's enormous economy into the war effort—all within a matter of months. Progressives in Washington also tried to regulate public opinion, however. A flood of propaganda emanated from Washington, suggesting that anyone who opposed the war was disloyal. Congress passed several laws to compel support for the war—laws that violated some of America's most cherished civil liberties. Antiwar speech was outlawed, for example. In Wisconsin, the federal government issued 92 indictments for "disloyal" utterances, such as expressing support for Germany, criticizing the Allies, and insulting the flag. Such violations of civil liberties alarmed and angered La Follette. "The citizen and his representative in Congress in time of war must maintain his right of free speech," he said:

> More than in times of peace, it is necessary that the channels for free public discussion of governmental policies shall be open and unclogged. I believe, Mr. President, that I am now touching upon the most important question in this country today.... I am contending for this right because the exercise of it is necessary to the welfare, to the existence of this Government, to the successful conduct of this war, and to a peace which shall be enduring and for the best interests of this country.... Any man who seeks to set a limit upon those rights, whether in war or peace, aims a blow at the most vital part of our Government.

The harassment continued nonetheless. Victor Berger found that the postal service would not deliver his socialist

Railroad Heritage

East Troy Electric Railroad Museum
2002 Church Street, East Troy, WI 53120
(262) 642-3263
www.easttroyrr.org
At the turn of the twentieth century, many Wisconsin cities built electric train systems to transport people through the ever-more-crowded streets or to connect cities. Most urban rail systems were phased out after World War II. The museum provides rides on trains used by the Milwaukee Electric Railway & Light Company. Dinner trains are also available, by reservation only.

Fennimore Historical Railroad Museum
610 Lincoln Avenue, Fennimore, WI
(608) 822-6144
www.fennimore.com/railmuseum/
This Fennimore museum is home to "The Dinky," a rare narrow-gauge train that ran in the area during the late nineteenth and early twentieth centuries.

Mid-Continent Railway Museum
E8948 Diamond Hill Road, PO Box 358
North Freedom, WI 53951
(800) 930-1385
www.mcrwy.com
The museum's collection of train engines and cars is impressive, but the highlight of the museum is a seven-mile train ride through the scenic Baraboo Range.

National Railroad Museum
2285 South Broadway, Green Bay, WI 54304-4832
(920) 437-7623
www.nationalrrmuseum.org
The museum collection contains many interesting railroad specimens, including the world's largest steam locomotive and General Dwight D. Eisenhower's command train used during World War II.

newspaper on the grounds that it was disloyal, then stopped delivering his mail altogether. Berger was eventually hauled into federal court on trumped-up charges of conspiracy (the government claimed his opposition to war was akin to counseling draft evasion) and sentenced to twenty years in prison.

Government harassment set an example for citizens. Whipped up by propaganda warning of potential spies and saboteurs, hysteria gripped the nation. So-called superpatriots attacked people whose loyalty was in question. Perhaps no group suffered more than German Americans. Individual Germans were subjected to demeaning acts like flag kissing ceremonies to prove their loyalty, or they were threatened with violence. In Outagamie County, a mob broke into the farm house of John Deml and demanded he buy war bonds. He refused. "Then a man shouted, 'Get the rope!'" recalled Deml. "The first I knew was when the rope was about my neck and around my body under my arms. Someone then gave a sharp jerk at the rope and forced me to my knees and hands; at the same time some of them jumped on my back, and while bent over someone struck me in the face." Superpatriots denigrated German culture, a sentiment that was taken to ridiculous extremes. Sauerkraut became "liberty cabbage," for example; German measles even became "liberty measles."

German Americans found it expedient to shed all vestiges of their ethnic heritage. Hundreds Anglicized their names; Schmidt easily became Smith, for example. In Milwaukee, more than 200 people legally changed their names during the first four months of the war alone. Organizations followed suit. The Germania Bank of Milwaukee became the National Bank of Commerce. Milwaukee's elite Deutscher Klub, which occupied Alexander Mitchell's former mansion on Wisconsin Avenue, was renamed the Wisconsin Club. Many of Milwaukee's great German cultural organizations faded away. World War I had killed the German Athens. All of this occurred despite the fact that confirmed cases of espionage or sabotage involving German Americans were virtually nonexistent. That an ethnic group as large, powerful, and respected as the Germans could be so thoroughly demonized so swiftly is a testament to the depth of the anti-German hysteria of World War I.

The political visibility of La Follette, as well as the state's German population and socialist contingent, led many fellow Americans to cast a suspicious eye on the Badger State. Some had taken to calling it the "Traitor State." Wisconsin was anything but disloyal, of course. Its factories equipped the soldiers and its farms fed them. It also contributed its fair share to the ranks of the armed forces. Overall 122,215 Wisconsinites served in World War I, of whom 3,932 died. Wisconsin men served with particular valor in the 32nd Infantry Division, a unit composed of National Guard troops from Wisconsin and Michigan. Wisconsin's National Guard troops began their training amid the sandstone bluffs of Juneau County at the Wisconsin Military Reservation near Camp Douglas. The 32nd Division conducted more extensive training in Texas, and then shipped out to France. In May 1918, the 32nd Division arrived at the front lines in Alsace—the first US troops to occupy German soil. In the Aisne-Marne Offensive of July and August, the French nicknamed the division "*Les Terribles*" because of the tenacity with which they pushed back the Germans. The 32nd also participated in the Meuse-Argonne Offensive of September through November. Because the 32nd had advanced in every engagement, they adopted an insignia of a red arrow piercing a horizontal line and became known as the "Red Arrow" division. State Highway 32, which runs north–south through the pastoral countryside of eastern Wisconsin, is designated the 32nd Division Memorial Highway. It was the first of many veterans' memorial highways in the Badger State.

On November 11, 1918, Germany capitulated to the Allies. World War I was finally over, but it left the world dramatically changed. The war had killed 10 million people and left 20 million wounded. Wisconsin was greatly changed as well. Its once large and proud German-American community emerged from the war a mere shadow of its former self. As La Follette had predicted, the war had also largely destroyed progressivism as a force in national politics. In Wisconsin, Fighting Bob tried to keep the embers of the progressive torch burning, but the "laboratory of democracy" had effectively been closed.

7

BETWEEN THE WARS

For Americans, the contrast between the 1920s and 1930s could not have been greater. The "Roaring Twenties" was a time of unprecedented prosperity, and signaled the emergence of a new, modern society. The stock market crash of October 1929 changed all that. The crash and the resulting Great Depression was the worst financial calamity in American history. Many who had prospered in the 1920s found themselves homeless and hungry in the 1930s. Wisconsinites, like other Americans, tried to cope with the roller coaster of the two decades. But in tackling these challenges they often bucked the national trends and developed innovative solutions to the problems they faced. Between the wars, Wisconsin liked to march to the beat of a different drummer.

HANGOVER OF HYSTERIA
The hysteria of World War I lingered on into the postwar years. The war was over, but peace did not bring an end to social and political conflict. In the immediate aftermath of the war, the economy sunk into a brief but deep depression. Bitter labor strikes broke out across the nation, and labor radicalism increased, including a series of terrorist bombings. Adding to these tensions was the Russian Revolution and creation of the Soviet Union—the world's first communist state. The Soviets announced their intentions to export their revolution to other countries, and indeed European communist movements gained in strength. Many Americans feared that Soviet communism might spread to the United States as well. The atmosphere of hysteria turned legitimate concern about communism into irrational fear, leading to an episode known as the Red Scare. Violations of civil liberties continued into the postwar era.

Billy Mitchell

William "Billy" Mitchell was born in Nice, France in December 1879, son of Milwaukee's John L. Mitchell (who later served as US senator from Wisconsin) and grandson of railroad baron Alexander Mitchell. In 1898, Mitchell left college to fight in the 1st Wisconsin Infantry Regiment during the Spanish-American War. He made the army his career, serving in the Signal Corps, where he began to fly airplanes. During World War I, Mitchell was the first American to fly over enemy territory in a combat situation, and he quickly rose to command all US air forces in Europe. In 1918 he commanded an attack by 1,500 planes on the German positions near St. Mihel. He entered the war a lieutenant colonel and was a brigadier general when it was over, and received numerous decorations to boot.

It was after the war that Mitchell gained his greatest notoriety. He began to argue that air forces would eventually make traditional land and sea forces obsolete. To prove his point, Mitchell had airplanes attack several captured German battleships in Chesapeake Bay in 1921 and again in 1923. The ships were sunk. Mitchell's theories did not sit well with many army and navy traditionalists, however. In addition, Mitchell was very outspoken about his views, and his abrasive personality only made matters worse. After continued criticism of his superiors, Mitchell was demoted and eventually court-martialed in 1926. He resigned his commission, but spent the rest of his life promoting his views on air power. He died in 1936. Billy Mitchell is today recognized as a pioneer in air power theory. After his death, Congress awarded him a special Medal of Honor. Later wars would vindicate Mitchell's ideas, but only partially. Air power played a crucial role in World War II and Vietnam, but while air power could create incredible destruction, its ultimate effect is still hotly debated. Traditional ground and sea forces have not yet been rendered obsolete.

Mitchell grew up near Milwaukee on the family estate known as Meadowmere, located in present-day West Allis near the intersection of 57th and Hayes Streets. The best-known memorial to the famous general is Milwaukee's General Mitchell International Airport, which is Wisconsin's most important. Located in the airport terminal building is the Mitchell Gallery of Flight, a small museum dedicated to the memory of Mitchell and Wisconsin's aviation history in general. The gallery contains exhibits of original and reproduction Mitchell artifacts, including the insignia from the general's World War I Spad aircraft, ceremonial swords, and various decorations, including his 1940 special medal from Congress. The museum honors other Wisconsin aviation notables, including Milwaukee's Lance Sijan (killed in Vietnam and awarded the Congressional Medal of Honor), astronaut and Milwaukee native Jim Lovell, and World War II fighter ace Richard I. Bong (see Chapter 8). It also traces the history of Mitchell Field from a small landing strip in the early part of the twentieth century to the modern international facility it is today.

William "Billy" Mitchell posing next to an airplane wearing flight gear. Circa 1916.

Wisconsin was spared from radical bombings and bitter strikes. In the midst of the Red Scare, Wisconsin's conservative socialists only saw their vote totals increase. German Americans, feeling abandoned by both of the major parties, voted for the socialists in record numbers. In Milwaukee, socialist Daniel Hoan was elected mayor in 1916, and held that job for more than two decades. Indeed, socialists would hold the mayor's office in Wisconsin's largest city until 1960. Milwaukee's voters understood that the city's "sewer socialists" were a far cry from the communist revolutionaries of the Soviet Union. However, Victor Berger's travails during the postwar years suggest that the rest of America did not. In 1918, Berger ran for Congress from the fifth district. Bolstered by angry German voters, he won. But when Berger arrived in Washington to take his seat, Congress refused to admit him. Milwaukee voters were outraged, and when another election was held, Berger won that one too. Congress again refused to seat the socialist. As the wartime hysteria faded, Berger finally gained acceptance. Elected for a third time in 1922, Berger was finally able to claim his rightful seat in Congress.

The revitalized career of Robert La Follette also showed Wisconsin's maverick political tradition. During World War I, La Follette was perhaps the most hated man in America. Many of his best friends had abandoned him because of his antiwar views. The Wisconsin State Legislature even passed a resolution denouncing him. Once the war was over, Americans were in a much more conservative mood, and progressivism had fallen out of favor with the voters. Up for re-election in 1922, La Follette's political career seemed doomed, but Fighting Bob battled back. German Americans, who had never really backed La Follette before, now voted for him. As the wartime hysteria waned, many of his criticisms of the war seemed validated. President Wilson justified American entry into the war claiming it would make the world "safe for democracy," but in the war's aftermath democracy only seemed endangered—at home and abroad. In the postwar peace negotiations, Wilson advocated vigorous American engagement in world affairs, including American membership in a new international organization called the League of Nations, but the war had soured Americans on foreign involvement. Isolationist sentiment grew, especially in Midwestern states, including Wisconsin. Long an isolationist, La Follette was a leading member of a Senate faction known as the "Irreconcilables" who fought successfully to keep America out of the League of Nations. By 1922, La Follette seemed more like a prophet than a pariah to many voters. That year he was re-elected to the Senate overwhelmingly—one of the most remarkable comebacks in Wisconsin political history.

Wisconsin progressives tried to keep the "laboratory of democracy" open for business. In 1920, progressive Republican James J. Blaine was elected governor. Blaine and a progressive coalition in the state legislature continued to set the agenda in Wisconsin politics, although stalwarts blocked any major reforms. Ever the political warrior, La Follette tried to reignite the embers of progressivism nationally. In 1924, he ran for president as an independent candidate. He was 69 years old. Still filled with fire and determination, Fighting Bob lashed out at both Democrats and Republicans for giving up the cause of progressive reform. In stark contrast to the nation's conservative mood, La Follette spoke passionately about his reform agenda, which included disarmament, public ownership of the railroads, and protecting workers' rights. On election day, La Follette received 16 percent of the popular vote, the second-highest total for a third-party candidacy in the twentieth century, but he won only one state—Wisconsin. The grueling campaign proved to be Fighting Bob's last hurrah. Robert M. La Follette died in Washington on June 18, 1925. After an elaborate funeral at the State Capitol, he was buried in Forest Hill Cemetery in Madison. His 30-year-old son, Robert M. La Follette, Jr. easily won the special election to fill the vacant seat. With La Follette's death, Wisconsin politics began to follow national trends—for a time. In 1928, stalwart Republican Walter Kohler, heir to the Sheboygan plumbing fortune, was elected governor.

The hysteria of World War I and the Red Scare had some long-lasting implications. Due to fears of radicalism and a mass influx of war refugees, European immigration was restricted for the first time in American history. In a state as multi-ethnic as Wisconsin, immigration restriction had a profound effect. Without reinforcements from

Business Heritage

Eisner Museum of Advertising and Design

208 North Water Street, Milwaukee, WI 53202

(414) 847-3290

www.eisnermuseum.org

A program of the Milwaukee Institute of Art and Design, the Eisner museum features multimedia exhibitions of advertisement techniques through the ages, with emphasis on Wisconsin companies.

Harley-Davidson Museum

www.h-dmuseum.com

Currently under development, the Harley-Davidson Museum will become one of Milwaukee's premier tourist attractions. Tours of Harley-Davidson's powertrain factory in Wauwatosa are also available. Call (877) 883-1450 for tour information.

Kohler Design Center

101 Upper Road, Kohler, WI 53044

(920) 457-3699

www.kohlerdesigncenter.com

The main purpose of the Kohler Design Center is to showcase the company's products, but the center devotes considerable space to the company's history. On display are Kohler sinks, bathtubs, toilets, and engines from the late nineteenth century to the present, as well as examples of the farm implements the company originally produced. Entrance to the design center is free and open to everyone. Kohler factory tours are also available from the center. To tour the factory, visitors must be fourteen years old and wear closed-toe shoes. Reservations are required.

Paper Discovery Center

PO Box 9050, Appleton, WI 54911

(920) 749-3040 x103

www.paperdiscoverycenter.org

The museum explores the process of papermaking, as well as its history. The facility includes the Atlas Mill, an 1874 building that was one of the first used by Kimberly-Clark. Also included is the Paper Industry International Hall of Fame, which pays homage to innovators in the evolution of the industry.

Wisconsin Automotive Museum

147 North Rural Street, Hartford, WI 53027

(262) 673-7999

www.wisconsinautomuseum.com

The Wisconsin Automotive Museum features the products of the Kissel Motor Car Company, which manufactured cars in Hartford from 1906 until the late 1930s, when the company became a victim of the Great Depression.

abroad, the vitality of the Badger State's many ethnic communities began to wane. Old World languages and customs succumbed to the pressures of assimilation, with only traces left behind. Another symptom of anti-immigrant feeling was the revival of the Ku Klux Klan. The Klan emerged in the South after the Civil War to terrorize former slaves and suppress their attempts at freedom. Reborn in 1915, the Klan gained a national following in the 1920s. The Klan appealed to working-class Protestants and the rural poor who felt frustration with a changing world, and dedicated itself to protecting "traditional values." In addition to terrorizing blacks, the new Klan also targeted Catholics and Jews, whom they viewed as "un-American." The Klan was not as powerful in Wisconsin as it was in some Midwestern states, but it certainly made its presence felt. Wisconsin's first klavern was organized in Milwaukee in 1920. Madison also saw considerable Klan activity, including among university students and the police. Many rural communities in the Cutover were also Klan strongholds. Oddly, some Germans were attracted to the movement as a way to show their "Americanism." The Klan held large rallies in Milwaukee and other cities. It also faced vociferous opposition, however. Catholics and progressives, powerful forces in the Badger State, abhorred its ideology. After someone tried to shoot a Klansman at a rally in Boscobel in 1924, Governor Blaine pardoned the gunman.

"A Beerless Milwaukee"

Perhaps the most famous legacy of the World War I hysteria was the 18th Amendment to the Constitution, prohibiting the manufacture and sale of alcohol in the United States. Prohibition had long been the goal of many reformers, and the war provided them with the opportunity to make their dream a reality. Traditional concerns about alcohol's effects—vice, crime, political corruption—were now combined with the virulent anti-German sentiment of the period. Prohibitionists castigated Milwaukee as "Schlitzville-on-the-Lake," manufacturing "Kaiser brew" that corrupted the morals of the nation's fighting men and wasted foodstuffs needed to feed soldiers and starving refugees. "The worst of all our German enemies," claimed one wartime prohibitionist, "are Pabst, Schlitz, Blatz, and Miller." The 18th Amendment was ratified in 1919, and the following year America officially became dry.

"A beerless Milwaukee," complained one anti-prohibition newspaper, "is like a beanless Boston—it can't be done." Clearly, it would have to take some getting used to. Prohibition did not just affect the cultural habits of Wisconsin residents, but also the state's economy. Home to nationally known breweries Miller, Pabst, and Schlitz, Wisconsin faced devastating consequences for halting beer production, including lost tax revenues and scores of unemployed workers. Milwaukee's breweries got by as best they could. The breweries switched to production of numerous malt-related products, including malt syrup and non-alcoholic "near beer." Pabst produced a non-alcoholic beer it called "Pablo." Miller introduced "Vivo" and Schlitz made "Famo." The brewing companies also diversified their operations, producing such items as soft drinks and cereal products. Pabst also went into the cheese business. Schlitz attempted to enter the chocolate business, and changed its familiar slogan to "the *name* that made Milwaukee famous." Many smaller breweries went out of business. Taverns and saloons converted themselves into drug stores or other kinds of retail establishments, or just closed their doors.

Many Americans refused to give up their beer and other alcoholic beverages. Illegal booze was smuggled in from Canada and other foreign countries. Some took to making their own "moonshine." Home beer and wine making became common. Magazines advertised such brewing and distilling accoutrements as bottles, corks, and bottle caps. The malted syrup produced by Wisconsin's ex-brewing companies was frequently used for making homemade beer. When legal taverns closed, illegal "speakeasies" or "blind pigs" emerged to serve a thirsty clientele. Wisconsin was notorious for violations of prohibition. Many speakeasies operated openly, with little fear of public approbation or police raids. In Madison, University of Wisconsin students made frequent trips to the nearby Greenbush section of the city for booze. "The Bush" was home to an Italian woman known as the "Queen of the Bootleggers" who catered

Georgia O'Keeffe

Georgia O'Keeffe was one of the most important painters of the twentieth century. She was born on a farm near Sun Prairie in 1887. She showed artistic abilities as a child and her parents nurtured those talents. She took private lessons from a Sun Prairie watercolor artist named Sarah Mann, and excelled in her classes at Madison High School. In high school, her art teacher had the students examine the intricate forms of a flower.

After graduation from high school in 1905, O'Keeffe pursued a career as a professional artist—an unusual choice for a woman of that time. She enrolled at the Art Institute of Chicago. She soon left for New York City, and took classes at the Art Students League, and later at the University of Virginia. O'Keeffe supported herself by teaching, but she became disillusioned with artistic conventions of the day—so much so that she stopped painting for a time. "I began to realize that a lot of people had done this same kind of painting before I came along," she once said. "I didn't think I could do it any better." However, her work had come to the attention of Chicago photographer Alfred Stieglitz, who convinced her to resume painting. They later married.

When she returned to the art world, she developed her own distinctive style. Her paintings expressed a great deal of emotion, using soft yet rich colors and gently rounded exaggerated forms. In the 1920s, she became noted for painting close-ups of flowers; many saw these works as expressions of raw female sexuality. She spent much of the 1920s in New York, but by the 1930s had settled in New Mexico, where she began to paint the landscape of the Southwest in her distinctive style. She continued to paint until the 1960s, although art historians sometimes claim that her work lost its innovative edge after Stieglitz's death in 1946. She died in Santa Fe, New Mexico in 1986 at the age of 98.

specifically to campus fraternities. According to one federal report, only 20 of 71 counties could be considered "dry" in 1929. Anecdotal evidence suggests that liquor flowed virtually everywhere. Wisconsin was "one of the wettest states west of the Alleghenies," according to one newspaper report. Prohibition-era Milwaukee, as well as the rest of the state, was not nearly as "beerless" as many had feared.

When alcoholic beverages could not be obtained legally, mobsters moved in to meet the demand. Organized crime was nothing new to America in the 1920s, but Prohibition made it exceptionally profitable. Nearby Chicago became notorious for its gangland violence. During the 1920s, that city experienced more than 500 gang-related murders. The most famous of the Chicago gangsters was Alphonse Capone. A native of Brooklyn, New York, Capone arrived in Chicago in 1919, and by 1922 dominated the Windy City's liquor trade, gambling establishments, and prostitution outlets. To maintain his position, Capone bribed public officials and killed members of rival gangs, as in the infamous St. Valentine's Day Massacre of 1929. But even gangsters need to get away from it all now and then. One of Capone's many retreats was located in northern Wisconsin near Couderay. "The Hideout," as it is known today, was an island of modern opulence in the remote Wisconsin Cutover, complete with spiral staircases, the finest furniture, and a stunning chandelier. Located in an area without electricity, it had its own state-of-the-art generators. The grounds also included a machine-gun tower, manned whenever Capone was visiting. The "cottage" lies on the shores of Cranberry Lake, which Capone is said to have used to smuggle liquor from Canada by plane, as well as to dispose of business rivals.

Contrary to popular belief, per capita alcohol consumption decreased during the 1920s. Drinking had been cut down, but at what price? A law designed to uphold the nation's morality had instead turned America into a land of criminals. Prohibition became a hot political topic, with "Wets" favoring repeal of the 18th Amendment and "Drys" for maintaining the law. In Wisconsin, the Wets were clearly in the majority. Badger State voters approved a 1926 referendum calling for the revision of prohibition laws to allow the production of beer with reduced alcohol content. In 1929, voters repealed the state's liquor control laws

Overhead view of bar and crowd in Fauerbach Brewing Co. tavern at 651 Williamson Street, celebrating the end of Prohibition. April 7, 1933.

altogether. These actions were purely symbolic; alcohol could not legally flow again until the federal government changed its liquor laws. Prohibition finally ended in 1933, with the passage of the 21st Amendment to the Constitution, which simply revoked the 18th.

WISCONSIN IN THE "ROARING TWENTIES"

Klansmen and prohibitionists tried to cope with the unsettled world of the 1920s by returning to traditional values and morals. At the same time, there were many others who looked to the past with a sense of distaste and disillusion. After the traumas of the World War I years, many Americans made a conscious break with the past. For others, social and cultural change just seemed to happen naturally. During the 1920s, older values and morals began to give way to "modern" attitudes.

Key to understanding American life in the 1920s is the buoyant postwar economy. After a brief depression at the beginning of the decade, the economy took off to unprecedented heights. Financially, Americans had never had it so good. Workers saw their wages go up and their hours go down. The eight-hour workday had become the standard in many industries during the decade. Prosperity also stimulated the development of a national consumer culture. Countless products flooded the national marketplace, including many manufactured in Wisconsin. Kimberly-Clark introduced Kleenex to the market in 1924. Household appliances such as washing machines and refrigerators also became common. Kohler marketed an "Electric Sink," forerunner of the modern dishwasher, in 1926. To purchase big ticket items, retailers developed the "installment plan"—put some money down and pay the remainder in installments, or as one critic charged: "A dollar today and a dollar forever."

No product in the 1920s was more revolutionary than the automobile. The internal combustion engine was nothing new to the 1920s—automobiles had been around since the late nineteenth century—but they were prohibitively expensive for the ordinary consumer. Henry Ford pioneered the mass production of cars in his Michigan assembly plant, particularly his Model T, introduced in 1908. With the return of prosperity after World War I, automobile ownership rose dramatically. It shortened travel times and freed people from the schedules of the railroads and urban transit. It helped to diminish rural isolation for farmers, and helped to bring urban dwellers into the countryside. It altered the dating habits of the young. Life in American would never be the same.

Modern automobile tourism was born in the 1920s. Perhaps no region of Wisconsin was more greatly transformed by the automobile than the Cutover regions of the north. With the decline of lumber, many tried their hand at farming the region, but with the exception of a few hearty crops such as cranberries and potatoes, the land proved too cold and infertile to sustain agriculture. As the great northern forests began to grow back, northern

Caswell Block, Milwaukee, Wis.

Caswell Block commercial district in Milwaukee. Pedestrians on the sidewalks and streets, among automobiles and streetcars. Circa 1924.

communities turned to tourism. The automobile provided a fast and efficient link between the Northwoods and Milwaukee, Minneapolis, and Chicago. Prosperity provided disposable income, and the eight-hour workday the leisure time needed to make that "weekend getaway." Campgrounds and resorts cropped up across the north. Thousands of city dwellers also purchased vacation homes. In some parts of northern Wisconsin today, summer cottages outnumber dwellings occupied year round by the local inhabitants. Many enjoyed the north's hunting, fishing, and boating opportunities. Northern Wisconsin became a haven for those city dwellers who wanted to get away from the stresses of modern life. Perhaps unwittingly,

Al Capone had started a trend. Winter sports made Northwoods tourism a year-round moneymaker. Indeed, the snowmobile was invented in Vilas County in the 1920s.

The production of automobiles was also big business. The industry employed thousands of people, generated millions of dollars, and stimulated numerous other industries, such as steel, rubber, and oil. Although Detroit became the center of the American automobile industry, Wisconsin made important contributions too. Beginning in 1902, Thomas B. Jeffrey began to manufacture an automobile in a Kenosha bicycle plant that he called a "Rambler." In 1916, Charles W. Nash left General Motors in Detroit and bought Jeffrey's company. By the 1920s, Nash Motors was among the top automakers in the country. (In 1954, Nash merged his company with several other smaller ones to form the American Motors Corporation, which was later bought out by Chrysler). The Kissel Motor Company was founded in Hartford, Wisconsin in 1906. The "Kissel Kar" was a popular model in the 1920s. Wisconsin is perhaps more famous for producing motorcycles. In 1903, William S. Harley and Arthur Davidson began to make motorcycles in a Milwaukee plant. By the 1920s, Harley-Davidson was America's largest manufacturer of motorcycles. Harley motorcycles acquired the nickname "Hog" in the 1920s after a racing team carried its mascot, a pig, on their victory laps.

The 1920s was the first time Americans enjoyed a mass, national popular culture. National radio broadcasting networks began to emerge, allowing Americans to hear the same programs from coast to coast. Hollywood became the center of the American movie industry. One of the most famous entertainment figures in the 1920s was Harry Houdini. Born Erich Weiss in Hungary in 1874, Houdini and his family moved to Appleton, Wisconsin, where his father, a rabbi, served a local congregation. He spent much of his boyhood in Appleton, and he sometimes claimed to have been born there—although he is also reputed to have said that the greatest escape of his career was the one he made from Appleton! He eventually landed in New York City, where he began performing and adopted his famous stage name. Houdini became noted as a magician and an escape artist—perhaps the greatest of all time—and by the 1920s he was an international celebrity. In the 1920s,

Houdini starred in several silent films and enjoyed debunking spiritualists. He died unexpectedly on October 31, 1926 of a ruptured appendix.

Sports also became an integral part of American popular culture. Wisconsin did not yet have a major league baseball team, but the state played a significant role in the development of professional football. In 1919, Curly Lambeau and George Calhoun founded a team in Green Bay. The Indian Packing Company, Lambeau's employer, donated $500 for uniforms, and Lambeau gratefully named his team the "Packers." In 1921, the Packers joined with such teams as the Canton Bulldogs (Ohio), the Muncie Flyers (Indiana), and the Decatur Staleys (Illinois) in the American Professional Football Association, the forerunner of the National Football League. Over time, teams folded or moved to big cities (the Staleys moved to Chicago and changed their name to the Bears), but the Packers never left Green Bay. In all, the Packers have won fourteen league titles, including three Super Bowls. Green Bay is the smallest city to have a national sports franchise today, and the Packers are the only publicly owned team. No trip to Green Bay is complete without a visit to the storied "frozen tundra" of Lambeau Field and the Packer Hall of Fame.

The 1920s also brought some important social trends. For one, women finally received the vote. On June 10, 1919, Wisconsin became the first state to ratify a constitutional amendment providing women with suffrage. By August 1920, enough states had ratified the measure for it to become the 19th Amendment. Urbanization also accelerated during the 1920s. In fact, the decade marked an important demographic turning point in Wisconsin history. In the 1920 census, 47.3 percent of Wisconsinites lived in urban areas. By 1930, that figure rose to 52.9 percent—the first time that city mice outnumbered country mice in the Badger State's history. The ethnic makeup of some Wisconsin cities began to change as well. With immigration from Europe effectively cut off, Mexican American migrants, primarily from south Texas, came up to Wisconsin in increasing numbers. Some immigrants from Mexico, which was not affected by the restrictive immigration laws of the 1920s, came too. Many came as migrant farm laborers, arriving in the summer and

Sports Heritage

Green Bay Packer Hall of Fame
1265 Lombardi Avenue, Green Bay, WI 54307
www.packers.com/hall_of_fame/
The Packer Hall of Fame, located inside Lambeau Field, tells the story of America's most famous football club, from Curly Lambeau to Brett Favre and all the years in between.

National Freshwater Fishing Hall of Fame
PO Box 690, 10360 Hall of Fame Drive
Hayward, WI 54843
(715) 634-4440.
www.freshwater-fishing.org
Sportsmen (and women) will enjoy this museum, which contains a seemingly endless assortment of fishing accoutrements such as lures, reels, rods, and outboard motors, as well as a great variety of stuffed fish. Commemorated in the museum are fishing record holders and noted fishermen, including television personality Babe Winkelman and baseball great Ted Williams. The grounds contain larger-than-life fiberglass fish, including a giant muskellunge with an observation deck in its mouth. The museum's title is a bit misleading since it also contains exhibits on saltwater fishing.

Snowmobile Hall of Fame
8481 West Highway 70, PO Box 720
St. Germain, WI 54558
(715) 542-4488
www.snowmobilehalloffame.com
The snowmobile has helped make northern Wisconsin a year-round tourist destination. The museum displays many different kinds of snowmobiles, and pays tribute to those who hold snowmobiling records.

leaving in the fall. Some stayed permanently, seeking factory jobs. By 1930, Milwaukee had a Mexican population of nearly 2,000.

African Americans also came to the Badger State in increasing numbers. World War I began a mass movement of African Americans from the segregated South to the cities of the North. In 1910, Milwaukee's black population stood at a mere 980. By 1920 the figure had increased to 2,229, and had jumped to 7,501 by 1930. An African-American neighborhood known as "Bronzeville" or the "Core" grew up just west of the Milwaukee River, in an area running northwest from the corner of Third and State Streets. Racine and Beloit also saw substantial African-American migration. Most came as unskilled laborers, though skilled artisans, ministers, and businessmen also arrived. Racial discrimination kept black and Mexican workers from all but the lowest-paying jobs, and most landlords refused to sell or rent to them, forcing them into the most dilapidated sections of cities. Despite its hardships, Wisconsin offered a chance at a better life.

The Great Depression

The Great Depression that struck in October 1929 was the worst economic calamity the United States has ever seen. Wisconsin, like the rest of the nation, suffered tremendously. By 1932, one in five people in Milwaukee was on county relief, and the nationwide unemployment rate reached 25 percent. Scores of men, women, and children were forced from their homes. Bread lines were long and soup kitchens were crowded. Compounding the poor agricultural economy was a severe drought. Wisconsin did not experience the Dust Bowl conditions experienced in the Great Plains; nevertheless, it was the worst drought in the state's history, adding further misery to already hard-pressed farmers. In the desperate days of the Depression some turned to crime. Bank robbers like Bonnie and Clyde become folk heroes in the eyes of some. During the 1930s, Wisconsin was visited by a gang of bank robbers led by John Dillinger—the most notorious outlaw in the Midwest. In 1934, Dillinger, Lester Gillis (a.k.a. "Baby Face Nelson"), and several others sought refuge in the wilds of northern Wisconsin. That April, the Federal Bureau of Investigation (FBI) surrounded Dillinger's gang at the Little Bohemia Inn in Vilas County. Three agents were killed in the shootout that followed, but Dillinger and his gang managed to escape.

The president, Republican Herbert Hoover, tried to reassure Americans that the economy would soon right itself, promising that prosperity was "just around the corner." But he resisted using the federal government to combat the depression, believing that public welfare was the responsibility of the states. Americans grew increasingly angry with Hoover, and in 1932, New York's Democratic governor Franklin Roosevelt easily defeated Hoover for the presidency. Roosevelt implemented a bold plan of government action to combat the Depression that he called the "New Deal." The Emergency Banking Act arrested the high rate of bank failures, and the Federal Deposit Insurance Corporation safeguarded bank deposits. The Social Security Act provided pensions to elderly Americans and others who could not work. The Rural Electrification Administration helped bring electricity to thousands of farmers, including many in Wisconsin. The federal government grew in size and power during the Depression.

The work of one New Deal program, the Civilian Conservation Corps (CCC), can still be seen on the Wisconsin landscape today. The CCC was a military-style work force that performed civil engineering duties related to the conservation of the natural environment. The organization employed young men and war veterans (both considered unstable political elements), organized them into work companies, and sent them into the countryside. CCC camps cropped up across Wisconsin. In the southwestern part of the state, the CCC combated soil erosion. In the north, efforts focused on reforestation and fighting forest fires. CCC workers built trails and campsites in state forests and parks, as well as in the national forests of northern Wisconsin. In all, there were 54 CCC camps in the Badger State engaged in at least 182 different projects. One of the most accessible CCC sites today is Camp Madison, which is now the University of Wisconsin Arboretum. Camp Taylor Lake in southeastern Bayfield County was one of the few camps designated specifically for World War I veterans. (The ruins of the camp are still evident at the junction of Pioneer and Sunset Roads.) If visitors to Wisconsin's forests and parks look carefully, they may well see historical markers and other evidence of CCC activities.

The New Deal also had a significant impact on the

American labor movement. The 1935 Wagner Act firmly established the right of workers to form unions. As a result, union membership increased dramatically, especially among unskilled workers. Labor tested its newfound muscle during the Depression and won several important strikes, most notably the 1937 "Sit-Down Strike" against General Motors in Flint, Michigan. The growth of labor's power did not go unchallenged, however, and the unions did not win all their battles. The bitter strike at Kohler in 1934 was Wisconsin's worst Depression-era labor conflict. Kohler employees had long complained of poor treatment and unsafe working conditions, and the American Federation of Labor (AFL) attempted to organize the plant. On July 27, pro-union workers walked off the job and paraded through the streets of Kohler—the company village that grew up around the plant—with slingshots and clubs. Some vandalized company property. Police attacked the strikers with tear gas and firearms. "Such things as have happened tonight are not possible," wrote a shocked *Milwaukee Journal* reporter, "flaming bitterness such as this, blazing of guns such as this, charging of armed men such as this." Two workers were killed and forty wounded in the melee, and the National Guard had to be called in to restore order. The episode made many people worry about keeping social order and peace in the desperate days of the Depression.

There was also unrest in the Wisconsin countryside. When depression hit, Badger State farm prices fell by more than 50 percent, hurting an already lagging segment of the economy. In some cases, prices sagged so low that it cost more to grow crops than could be made selling them. Many farmers believed that withholding farm products from the market would increase prices. Wisconsin's dairy farmers were hard hit, especially those who produced milk for cheese and butter. By 1933, some dairy farmers were willing to take desperate action. The Wisconsin Cooperative Milk Pool organized three "Milk Strikes" that year, pledging to withhold milk from the market until the price went up. Dairy farmers blocked trucks and trains bringing milk to market and dumped milk alongside highways and railroad tracks. The first strike occurred in February, and was confined mainly to eastern Wisconsin, but by November the strikes had spread statewide. The National Guard and local

Edna Ferber, Come and Get It

Appleton native Edna Ferber was one of the most celebrated women writers of the 1920s and 1930s. Before becoming a novelist Ferber was a newspaper reporter, first with the Appleton Post-Crescent *and then the* Milwaukee Journal. *She received the Pulitzer Prize in 1924 for her novel* So Big. *Many of her novels became Broadway plays, or were made into films, from* Cimarron *(book 1929, film 1931) to* Giant *(book 1952, film 1956). Her 1935 novel* Come and Get It *focused on the meteoric rise of the lumber and paper industries in Wisconsin in the late nineteenth and early twentieth centuries. Near the conclusion of the novel, Ferber depicted the impact of the Great Depression on the fictionalized Fox Valley city of Butte des Morts:*

There had been a tremendous fall of snow on New Year's Day. But the great mechanical snow-scraper and shovel had cleared the Butte des Morts streets so quickly that an old-fashioned sleigh ride was almost impossible. The roads had to be kept clear for

automobiles, of course. Besides, a sleigh ride in the streets of
Butte des Morts was now as much of a novelty as an automobile
had been twenty years before. A group of mill men, the holiday
heavy on their hands, stood at the curb, staring and spitting,
fascinated by the ingenuity of the mechanical shovel. Its giant
arm and capacious maw reached, clutched, stuffed, disgorged.
Before the Butte des Morts City Council had invested in the big
snow shovel it would have taken a hundred men twenty-four
hours to do the work this giant accomplished in an hour.

"Some spoon."

"I'll say."

The men at the curb eyed the robot and into their admiring
gaze there began to creep a vague doubt. New Year's holiday. In
good times the day shifts and the night shifts went on just the
same, holiday or no holiday, as inevitably as the sun and the
moon swung around. But now almost any excuse to lay the men
off. Almost sheepishly they looked at their own idle hands.
Scoop-clank-thud said the great iron workman, taunting
them....

Butte des Morts... was having its bad times, but here was
an industry that went on. Not full force, of course. And even the
serious, prideful paper makers were not such good fellows
anymore. A good many of them had lost their homes. They held
meetings and talked about unemployment insurance, old-age
pensions, hours, wages. You saw some of the older fellows
sitting on benches in Hewitt Park or on the Glasgow Library
grounds that sloped down to the water, staring with bewildered
eyes out across the Fox River to the mills on the opposite shore.
Their hands, too, were inert on their knees. Sometimes you saw
the younger mill workers—men on half time—wheeling baby
buggies. Strong young men with set sullen faces whirling their
1932 babies in rather rickety perambulators that had done duty
before, through the streets and parks of the lovely little
Wisconsin town. They pushed the gocarts and buggies with
unnecessary force over the grassy slopes and quiet paths, as
though trying to use unspent strength. A racy gleam developed
in the babies' eyes. The wind whistled past their ears. When their
mothers took them out for their airing, walking with gentle,
strolling step, they wondered at the yells of baffled rage and
impatience emitted by their speed-crazed offspring, accustomed
now to swifter travel on their outings.

police used tear gas and billy clubs to break up the strikes, and violent clashes also broke out between pro-strike and anti-strike farmers. Some strikers took to vandalizing dairies, and in at least eight cases, bombed cheese factories. Two strikers were killed in the clashes of that year. The violence eroded support for the strikes in the eyes of many, and President Roosevelt's Agricultural Adjustment Act of 1933 began a system of crop subsidies to prop up farm prices.

Indeed, the severity of the Great Depression led some to flirt with radical political ideologies. In the eyes of a few, the Depression showed the inherent weaknesses in capitalism and in response they turned to communism. Milwaukee's conservative socialists increasingly found competition from the rise of militant communists who looked to the Soviet Union as a model. Others turned to fascism, a radical right-wing ideology that emerged in Europe after World War I. Fascists believed that democracy was weak and ineffective, and that only a strong, charismatic dictator could hold society together. Fascist governments emerged first in Italy, and then in Germany under Nazi leader Adolf Hitler, who took power in 1933. Hitler extinguished the fragile German democracy and rearmed his country in defiance of the World War I peace settlement. Preying on fears of communism, Hitler also appealed to racism, blaming Germany's Jews for all the nation's problems. Fascism reared its ugly head in Wisconsin too, most notably in the emergence of the German-American Bund. Based in New York, the Bund was composed mostly of German immigrants who had come to America after World War I. The Bund established "Camp Hindenburg" near Grafton, at which they held rallies that featured members dressed in "storm trooper" uniforms, the singing of Nazi songs, and displays of the Nazi swastika. The Bund also ran a youth program, and harassed the state's Jews and communists. It should be noted that most Americans maintained an adherence to capitalism and democracy, but the Great Depression tested Americans' faith in their system more vigorously than it had ever been tested before.

THE LA FOLLETTE BROTHERS

During the Depression, Wisconsin re-opened the "laboratory of democracy." Although progressivism had become a political dirty word in most of the United States, it never quite died in Wisconsin. Robert M. La Follette, Jr. still represented Wisconsin in the US Senate, and his younger brother Philip also commanded a great following among progressive Republicans. After the Great Depression struck, Wisconsin dusted off its political heritage and the La Follettes continued to be on the cutting edge of political developments. One of them, like his father, had presidential ambitions only to have them blocked by a Roosevelt.

The Depression cost Governor Walter Kohler his job and catapulted Philip F. La Follette into the office in 1930. He was just 33 years old when elected. Of the two La Follette brothers, Phil was considered to have the political gifts of his father—a flair for oratory and boundless energy on the campaign trail. Phil also had vision. He argued that government had an obligation not just to regulate the economy but to take an active role in finding solutions to the Depression. He wanted broad powers to regulate banks and utilities. He also envisioned a reorganization of government that placed responsibility for devising legislation in the hands of the governor and not the legislature. Such a system, he argued, provided more expedient solutions to problems than the protracted deliberations of the assembly and senate. Many interpreted it as simply a grab for power. In the end, La Follette lacked a progressive majority in the legislature, and conservatives (Democrats and Republicans alike) killed most of his proposals. One important victory was America's first unemployment compensation law, passed in 1931, though financing it proved difficult. The architect of the bill was University of Wisconsin professor John R. Commons, who helped previous progressive governors. The Wisconsin Idea was still alive.

Wisconsin's Depression-era voters were in a fickle mood, however. Stalwarts rebounded, and Walter Kohler defeated Philip La Follette in the Republican primary for governor in 1932. The La Follette brothers then backed Franklin Roosevelt for president, and reluctantly supported Democrat Albert G. Schmedeman for governor. It became clear to the La Follettes that they were no longer welcome in Wisconsin's increasingly conservative Republican Party. The state's Democrats were even more conservative than the Republicans—so much so that when dealing with Wisconsin, President Roosevelt preferred to work with progressive Republicans rather than with members of his own party. Again following in their father's footsteps, the La Follette brothers decided to form their own party, naturally calling it the Progressive Party. In 1934, Phil ran for governor and his brother Bob ran for reelection to the US Senate on the Progressive ticket. Both won, as did a substantial number of Progressive state senators and assemblymen. Progressives also took seven of Wisconsin's ten congressional seats, leaving three Democrats and—for the first time since 1854—no Republicans at all. In 1936, the Progressives finally had a majority in the legislature. Governor Phil rammed through the legislature a broad series of bills that have been called the "Little New Deal," including a state labor relations board, a power development authority, an agricultural authority, and much more. Many, including some Progressive Party members, complained that the governor's tactics were dictatorial, but La Follette justified them on the grounds that he represented the will of the people.

Phil La Follette was not interested merely in a "Little New Deal" or simply implementing programs created in Washington. He wanted to be president. La Follette was openly critical of Roosevelt, arguing that the president was not going far enough with the New Deal, yet also complaining about its "centralizing" tendencies. Phil believed that he had a broader vision than Roosevelt, and the political skill to carry out that vision. In the recession of 1938, La Follette saw a chance to unseat the president. He organized the National Progressives of America, a new national political party meant to provide an alternative to Roosevelt's Democrats. Challenging Roosevelt proved to be an ill-advised and catastrophic blunder. Noting how charismatic dictators like Hitler had created a spirit of national unity in their countries, La Follette got carried away with the theater of politics, believing that he could use such tactics to preserve democratic capitalism in America. His party's symbol also seemed inspired by Nazi

Germany—a red flag with a black X inside a white circle. It was meant to symbolize a marked ballot, but it bore a striking resemblance to the Nazi swastika. Some critics even called it a "circumcised swastika." Though La Follette was clearly not a Nazi, his 1938 campaign frightened more voters than it inspired. The National Progressives went nowhere, and La Follette was resoundingly defeated in the governor's race in 1938. The victor was Julius Heil, a conservative Republican businessman from Milwaukee who, interestingly enough, had been born in Germany.

The Progressives remained Wisconsin's second strongest political party into the 1940s. In 1942, Orland Loomis took the governorship back from the Republicans, but died before taking office. The lieutenant governor, Republican Walter S. Goodland, got the job instead. The Progressive Party would never again be a force in Wisconsin politics. But by Goodland's time in office, the Great Depression was over. Despite all the depression-fighting programs enacted during the 1930s—at the state and federal levels—what finally ended the Great Depression was World War II. That war would be an important turning point for the history of the world, the United States, and also for Wisconsin.

8

World War II and Beyond

On September 1, 1939, Nazi Germany invaded Poland and ignited World War II in Europe. Meanwhile, Japan was expanding its holdings in the Far East. The world was once again in flames, but most Americans hoped to stay out of it. Isolationist sentiment was especially strong in Wisconsin, where bitter memories of World War I were still fresh in many people's minds. But the Japanese attack on Pearl Harbor on December 7, 1941 forever ended the illusion that the oceans could protect America from problems overseas. America rose to the challenge and, along with its allies, defeated Germany and Japan, emerging as the greatest power on earth. The nation then faced another crisis—the potential spread of communism from the Soviet Union. But in confronting their enemies abroad, Americans were forced to confront their own shortcomings, especially when it came to race relations. The social and political forces unleashed by World War II and the Cold War hit Wisconsin like a tornado, leaving its people and their culture greatly changed. Those forces continue to shape the lives of Wisconsinites, and all Americans.

Wisconsin and World War II
World War II put Wisconsin back to work. Government defense contracts reawakened the slumbering economy, ending more than a decade of depression. No country could match America's colossal economic output. The wartime demands for farm products revived Wisconsin's agricultural economy. The Badger State led the nation in wartime production of dairy products and canned vegetables, producing fully 46 percent of the nation's cheese in 1942. To meet the wartime demand for rope, Wisconsin farmers devoted 32,000 acres to hemp production by 1943.

Agricultural production was so important to the war effort that many young farmers received draft exemptions, though deferments grew increasingly scarce was the war dragged on. Teenage boys and girls were recruited for farm labor. Migrant Mexican farm labor, which had all but disappeared during the depression, was renewed with vigor. The federal government relocated small numbers of Japanese Americans, forcibly removed from their homes on the West Coast due to exaggerated fears about their loyalty, to Wisconsin for agricultural work. German prisoners of war were another source of farm labor in wartime Wisconsin. German POWs reported being treated rather well in Wisconsin, and a handful returned to settle permanently after the war.

Wisconsin industry also made valuable contributions to the war effort. Wisconsin's metalworking and heavy machinery industries were essential to wage modern war. The Harnischfeger Company produced cranes and excavating equipment for the military. Harley-Davidson produced 90,000 motorcycles for military use. Nash Motors built aircraft engines at its Kenosha plant. Wisconsin shipbuilders produced landing craft, minesweepers, and other kinds of boats for the navy. Kimberly-Clark not only produced paper products, but made anti-aircraft gun mounts and artillery fuses as well—a far cry from Kleenex. By May 1944, the Milwaukee area alone had received nearly $2.3 billion in military contracts. Roughly 37 percent of Milwaukee's war contracts involved ordnance materials, and another 30 percent was devoted to aircraft parts. To supply the troops with the vast amounts of artillery shells they would need, the federal government established the Badger Ordnance Works along the Wisconsin River between Baraboo and Sauk City. The vast complex employed 7,500 workers, housed in temporary quarters across the road. As in agriculture, labor shortages plagued Wisconsin's wartime industries. African Americans continued to come north; Milwaukee's black population had surpassed the 10,000 mark by 1945. Despite a federal law that forbade defense industries from discrimination based on race, African-American war workers usually received the lowest-paying jobs with few opportunities for advancement. Women also entered the workforce in large

Must-See Sites: USS Cobia

One of the most unique chapters in Wisconsin's World War II history is that of the Manitowoc submarines. As American involvement in the war drew closer, the US Navy sought to increase its submarine fleet. The Electric Boat Company of New London, Connecticut, the navy's usual builder of submarines, could not keep up with the increased demand. The Manitowoc Shipbuilding Company, which had gained a reputation for quality in the industry, landed a navy contract to build submarines in 1940. The first "fresh water submarine," the USS *Peto*, was launched in June 1941. Once accepted for service, the subs went through Chicago and the Illinois River to the Mississippi, where they were floated on barges to New Orleans and into the Gulf of Mexico. From there, they passed through the Panama Canal and into the Pacific Ocean. In all, Manitowoc produced 17 submarines, which were responsible for sinking 130 Japanese ships.

The USS *Cobia* is moored in the Manitowoc River at the Wisconsin Maritime Museum. Although she was not made in Manitowoc, she is the same kind of submarine made there during World War II. Museum visitors can take a guided tour of the *Cobia*, which sank 13 Japanese ships and 20,000 tons of shipping during World War II while losing only one man. The boat represents the some of the highest engineering achievements of the day and is a tribute to the skills of Manitowoc's shipbuilders. On their tour of the boat, visitors can see for themselves the cramped quarters for the crew of 80 sailors, many of whom slept alongside the torpedoes. The museum contains several exhibits about submarine warfare and the people who built these deadly machines.

numbers, not just in service industries but also in heavy manufacturing. Women too were paid less, and when the war was over they were expected to leave their jobs to make room for returning veterans.

Wisconsin supplied soldiers and sailors as well. In all, 16 million Americans served in World War II—the largest military force the nation has ever assembled. A total of

332,200 Wisconsinites saw military service in World War II, a figure that represents roughly 10 percent of the state's 1940 population. Unlike World War I, which had largely been confined to Europe, World War II was truly global in scope. Wisconsin's fighting men served in all corners of the world, from the steaming jungles of the South Pacific to the snowy battlefields of Europe. Women also served, though not in combat roles. Nearly 10,000 of Wisconsin's daughters answered the nation's call to duty. The Badger State was the home of several World War II notables. General Douglas MacArthur, the son of Wisconsin Civil War hero Arthur MacArthur, was born in Milwaukee in 1880. An "army brat" and West Point graduate, MacArthur commanded US Army troops in the Pacific during World War II and was military governor of occupied Japan after the war. MacArthur Square in downtown Milwaukee is named in his honor. Admiral Marc A. Mitscher, credited with breaking Japanese naval power at the Battle of Leyte Gulf in 1944, was born in Hillsboro in Vernon County. Richard I. Bong, a native of Poplar, was a fighter pilot in the Pacific who downed 40 Japanese aircraft—more than any other pilot in US history— earning him the nickname "Ace of Aces." Bong was killed in 1945 serving as a test pilot for America's earliest jet aircraft. Bong, MacArthur, and thirteen other Wisconsinites received the Medal of Honor during World War II.

The 32nd "Red Arrow" Division, composed of Wisconsin and Michigan men, once again saw action. Activated in 1940, the 32nd Division took part in war games in Louisiana, and after Pearl Harbor was sent to Australia to check Japanese advances in the South Pacific. In 1942, the Red Arrow Division was deployed to New Guinea and engaged the Japanese at Buna—one of America's first land battles in the Pacific Theater. The soldiers were ill-prepared for jungle warfare. Malaria and other diseases took a huge toll on the troops, but the Japanese had been stopped. From Buna, the 32nd fought its way along the northern coast of New Guinea, and took part in the 1944 invasion of the Philippines, where it fought until war's end. Overall, the 32nd Division logged more combat hours than any other division in the US Army, and after the war spent time on occupation duty in Japan before finally returning home.

General Douglas MacArthur congratulates Richard I. Bong, World War II "Ace of Aces" from Poplar, Wisconsin, after awarding him the Congressional Medal of Honor at an airstrip on Leyte Island, Philippines. December 12, 1944.

Nazi Germany surrendered in May 1945, and the atomic bombings of Hiroshima and Nagasaki in August forced the Japanese to capitulate as well. World War II officially ended on September 2, 1945. All told, roughly 60 million people died in the war—more than in any other conflict in world history. Hitler's twisted racial policies alone killed nearly 12 million people, including 6 million Jews. The United States was spared the scope of the death and destruction experienced in other lands. In all, more than 400,000 Americans died in the war, including 8,410 from Wisconsin.

POLITICAL REALIGNMENT

Postwar Wisconsin politics saw an important and dramatic realignment of party loyalties. Since the Civil War, Wisconsin had effectively been a one-party state, with the Republicans dominating. Only rarely did the Democrats mount a serious challenge. During the Great Depression, the La Follette brothers led the progressive Republicans out of the party and into a new Progressive Party, which instituted many important government reforms. But by World War II, the mood of the voters had grown more conservative and Wisconsin's progressives could no longer maintain their third-party movement. In 1946, the Progressive Party officially disbanded. Progressives were divided on what to do next.

Remembering the conservative nature of Wisconsin's Democratic Party, many older progressives opted to return to the Republicans, in hopes of moderating the party's increasingly conservative temper. But those Progressives who went back to the Republicans found it rough going. The old "loyal" Republicans were still mad at them for dividing the party in the first place. Many stalwarts were simply glad to be rid of the progressives, and given the conservative postwar mood, many saw them as a potentially disruptive force at just the time when their ideas were current with the voters. The plight of Senator Robert M. La Follette, Jr. symbolizes the dilemma of the Progressive-turned-Republican. La Follette was up for reelection in 1946. In the Republican primary La Follette faced an unknown Appleton judge named Joseph R. McCarthy. La Follette did not campaign enthusiastically, and spent very little time in Wisconsin. McCarthy proved to be a vigorous and capable campaigner, alleviating the doubts of many party regulars. In the end, La Follette lost in a close election. The US Senate seat that had been occupied by a La Follette for 40 years now went to McCarthy. The La Follette spell on the Wisconsin voter had been broken. The election also sent a strong signal to ex-Progressives that the Republican Party was hostile territory.

Meanwhile, the Democrats were undergoing an immense transformation of their own. Elements of Wisconsin's Democratic Party wanted to move away from its conservative traditions and align it with the liberal philosophies of the national party. Daniel Hoan, the long-time socialist mayor of Milwaukee, abandoned third-party politics and led many ex-socialists to the Democrats. Angered by the pro-business policies of the Republicans, Wisconsin's labor unions threw their weight behind the Democrats as well. This gave the liberal Democrats a strong base in Milwaukee, but to compete for statewide offices they had to gain support in other parts of the state. Led by State Senator Robert Tehan, the Democrats actively courted ex-Progressives, gaining footholds in Dane County and in northwestern Wisconsin, where progressivism remained strong. An army of young progressives, in particular, gave the Wisconsin Democrats a vigor they had not had in years. Democrats began to build a statewide organization, and fielded candidates across the Badger State, including in strongly Republican districts where Democrats rarely appeared on the ballot.

Another factor in the growth of Wisconsin's Democrats was Joseph McCarthy, who became one of the most controversial figures in American history. McCarthy rose to national prominence because of the Cold War, an immense international struggle that broke out after World War II between the United States and the Soviet Union. Though allied against Nazi Germany, the Americans and the Soviets had antagonistic political systems (democratic capitalism vs. communism) and were deeply suspicious of each other. After World War II, the Soviet Union established communist satellite states in Poland and other Eastern European countries, renewing fears that the Soviets would seek world domination. The United States

Must-See Sites:
EAA AirVenture Museum

One of the most important developments in human history was the achievement of powered flight. The Wright Brothers' brief flight at Kitty Hawk, North Carolina in 1903 dramatically changed the way we view the world. The Experimental Aircraft Association (EAA), based in Oshkosh, has kept alive the pioneering spirit of the Wright Brothers and other aviation innovators.

The museum collection includes some of the most unusual airplanes in the world, including the Aerocar, which doubled as an airplane and an automobile. (Its wings could be folded in for highway driving.) Also in the collection is the Voyager, the first plane to make a non-stop unrefueled flight around the world. The "Eagle Hanger" is dedicated to World War II aircraft. The Pioneer Airport located nearby is a re-creation of a typical airport during the early days of aviation. The museum offers rides in vintage planes from the airport's grass runway. Visitors can ride in a variety of aircraft, including a 1929 Ford Tri-Motor, a reproduction of Charles Lindbergh's Spirit of St. Louis, and a Bell 47 helicopter—the type used in the Korean War and made famous on the television program *M*A*S*H*.

The EAA was founded in Milwaukee in 1953 by people who enjoyed building their own airplanes. That year the EAA held its first "fly-in" air show in Milwaukee, attracting a mere 50 planes. Today the EAA AirVenture Oshkosh is arguably the most important air show in the world. Each July, Whitman Field in Oshkosh becomes the world's busiest airport, attracting the most modern civilian and military aircraft on the planet. Many fly their home-built airplanes to Oshkosh as well. Indeed, air show participants occasionally crash in the Wisconsin countryside on their way to Oshkosh, so travelers might be well advised to keep an eye to the sky in July!

EAA AirVenture Museum
PO Box 3065, Oshkosh, WI 54903
(920) 426-4818
museum.eaa.org

pledged to contain the spread of communism, keeping soldiers overseas, forming alliances with other nations, and sending military and economic aid to countries fighting communist movements. As in the Red Scare after World War I, many Americans also feared communist subversion at home. Historians today fiercely debate the extent to which domestic communism threatened American democracy, but clearly it was more of a threat after the Second World War than it was after the First. In the desperate years of the Great Depression some Americans were converted to communism, and communists had wormed their way into liberal organizations like labor unions and even government positions. The Soviets also had a network of spies in the United States, the most notable case being that of Julius and Ethel Rosenberg, convicted of passing atomic secrets to Russia. A series of events in the late 1940s escalated Cold War tensions, including the communist victory in the Chinese Civil War and the Soviet detonation of their own atom bomb. As 1950 dawned, Cold War tensions had reached a fever pitch.

Enter Joe McCarthy. The senator faced reelection in 1952 and had little to show for his years in Washington. Following the lead of California Republican Richard M. Nixon and others in Washington, McCarthy seized upon the communism issue. In a speech in Wheeling, West Virginia in February 1950, the senator claimed to have a list of known communists in the US State Department, though he never turned over a list, and the number of people he claimed were on it kept changing. These were the most sensational charges yet, and they earned McCarthy headlines and notoriety. Then came the Korean War. In June 1950, communist North Korea attacked capitalist South Korea, and the United States—following its policy of containment—sent combat troops to that country. (These forces, incidentally, were commanded by Wisconsin's own Douglas MacArthur until his dismissal for insubordination in 1951.) Some saw the conflict in Korea as a prelude to World War III. As the climate of fear rose, McCarthy's charges of domestic communism and the Democratic Party's alleged complicity with it grew ever more sensational. He charged that Democrats and communists were involved in "a conspiracy so immense and an infamy so black as to dwarf any previous venture in the history of man." McCarthy held hearings in which he accused people of communist sympathies, and then badgered them when they tried to defend themselves. Though McCarthy offered little proof for his charges, he tapped into a well of anxiety and apprehension in Cold War America, and became the most feared politician in the nation.

McCarthy's rise to power was quick, but so was his downfall. In 1954, he began investigating communism in the US Army, but failed to realize that the public mood had changed. The Korean War was over and the Rosenbergs had been executed. Republican Dwight D. Eisenhower was elected president in 1952, a career army man and World War II hero who did not take kindly to McCarthy's allegations against the army. The Army–McCarthy Hearings were also broadcast on the new medium of television, bringing McCarthy and his bullying tactics into people's own living rooms. McCarthy's accusations now brought only scorn and contempt, and led to a Senate censure in 1954. He died in 1957. Joseph McCarthy still elicits strong feelings. Some view him as a brave crusader for democracy who was destroyed by his subversive enemies. Others see him as an opportunist and a demagogue who posed a greater threat to American democracy than did the communists. His hometown of Appleton is strangely silent about the legacy of its most famous citizen. McCarthy's grave is located in St. Mary's Cemetery along the Fox River. A bust of McCarthy was unveiled in the lobby of the Outagamie County Courthouse in 1959, but it proved so controversial that it was taken down and donated to the Outagamie County Historical Society in 2001. Appleton, like the rest of America, has yet to come to terms with Joseph McCarthy.

McCarthy also proved to be a rallying cry for Wisconsin Democrats. To replace McCarthy, the Democrats nominated William Proxmire, a transplant from Illinois who had run unsuccessfully for governor three times. This time, Proxmire won. The following year, an ex-Republican progressive named Gaylord Nelson won the governor's office for the Democrats. By the mid-1960s, the Democrats would control half of Wisconsin's congressional seats, and by the 1970s a majority of them. They would dominate the state's US

During the first day of the Army-McCarthy Hearings, Senator Joseph R. McCarthy holds both hands over the microphones while speaking with counsel Roy Cohn. April 22, 1954.

Senate seats as well. After a century of minority status, Wisconsin Democrats could finally rival the Republicans. With a revived and competitive Democratic Party, Wisconsin politics finally mirrored the rest of America. Badger State Democrats and Republicans have essentially been evenly matched ever since.

POSTWAR DEMOGRAPHIC TRENDS

After World War II, Wisconsin's population underwent some important changes. For one, the trend toward urbanization continued. In fact, much of Wisconsin's growth occurred in suburban areas surrounding its cities.

World War II brought prosperity back to America, but after the war there was a severe housing shortage. During the years of depression and war little new housing had been built. To complicate matters further, America experienced a "baby boom" after the war, increasing pressure on the housing market. Postwar prosperity allowed many to purchase new homes, as did government programs such as the Federal Housing Authority (a New Deal initiative) and the G.I. Bill of Rights (a benefit package for World War II veterans). The development of controlled-access freeways made the commute from suburb to city much easier. President Eisenhower signed the Interstate Highway Act in 1956, providing federal money for expressway construction. Wisconsin's first segment of the system, a seven-mile stretch of Interstate 94 in Waukesha County, opened in 1958. Housing developments grew up like corn in the fields surrounding Wisconsin's cities, especially around Milwaukee and Madison. The village of Menomonee Falls west of Milwaukee, for example, saw its population rise from 1,469 in 1940 to 18,276 in 1960.

The ethno-cultural makeup of Wisconsin's population has always been in flux, and the post–World War II years were no exception. African Americans continued to come to Wisconsin in substantial numbers. By 1960, Milwaukee had a black population of 62,000, two-thirds of whom had been born outside the state. African Americans continued to come from Southern states, as well as from Chicago and other Northern cities. The new arrivals expanded the "Core"—the section of Milwaukee to which blacks had been confined—to encompass much of the old German neighborhood on the city's north side, moving into older houses abandoned by whites. Racine, Beloit, and Madison also saw substantial black migration. By 2000, Wisconsin's African-American population had increased to 304,460, comprising 5.7 percent of the state's population. Mexican-American migration from Texas, as well as immigration from Mexico itself, also increased. In the decades immediately following World War II, farm work remained the most common economic activity for Wisconsin's Mexican population, but as time went on Mexicans became increasingly urban. Many sections of Milwaukee's south side became Mexican in character. As one south side priest said in 1980: "My funerals are all Polish. My weddings and baptisms are all Latino." After World War II, other Spanish-speaking groups (classified by the Census Bureau as Hispanic or Latino) moved into Wisconsin, most notably Puerto Ricans, who concentrated in Milwaukee. According to the 2000 census, Wisconsin was home to 192,921 Latinos, of whom 126,719 were Mexican in ethnicity.

The Vietnam War also shaped Wisconsin's ethnic makeup. Following its policy to contain the spread of communism, the United States backed the anti-communist government of South Vietnam, which was waging war against communist guerrillas inside the country supported by communist North Vietnam. South Vietnam proved unable to quell a communist guerrilla movement, however, and by the mid-1960s the United States sent in its own combat troops. More than 500,000 Americans were in Southeast Asia by 1968. The war was not confined to Vietnam. Communist movements emerged in neighboring Laos and Cambodia, and North Vietnam spirited troops and supplies into South Vietnam through remote regions of these two countries. In Laos, the United States recruited a secret army of Hmong—an ethnic minority in the highlands of Southeast Asia. The Hmong interdicted communist supply routes, battled Laotian communists, and aided downed American airmen. Ultimately, the communists prevailed in Laos in 1975 (as well as in Vietnam and Cambodia), and the Hmong were forced to flee the country, often under gunfire and, according to some reports, even chemical weapons.

After the war, thousands of Hmong refugees came to Wisconsin, usually sponsored by church groups. The Hmong faced tremendous problems assimilating to American life. In Laos, many were farmers of rice and opium who practiced small-scale "slash and burn" agriculture—moving from place to place when the soils gave out—much as Native Americans in Wisconsin had done centuries before. America was a radically different place. In Wisconsin, the Hmong suddenly found themselves in the modern world—automobiles and airplanes, radio and television, shopping malls and a monetary economy. Then there was the shock of moving from the tropics to Wisconsin's harsh winters. Some

Hmong have equated their life in America as having moved "from the mountain to the moon." The Hmong have struggled to make adjustments to life in America while keeping as much of their culture alive as they can. The Hmong are particularly noted for their needlework. At craft fairs across Wisconsin today, travelers can purchase a *pa ndau* (story quilt) that describes Hmong history and culture. Today more than 40,000 Hmong live in Wisconsin, behind only California and neighboring Minnesota in numbers. The Hmong are the largest Asian ethnic group in Wisconsin, but not the only one. Since the reform of immigration laws in 1965, Wisconsin has seen the arrival of people from several Asian nations, including China, Japan, India, Korea, the Philippines, and Vietnam.

WISCONSIN AND THE CIVIL RIGHTS MOVEMENT

World War II also proved to be a turning point in American race relations. Fighting against Hitler's virulent racism forced Americans to confront racial inequality in their own country. Even after the abolition of slavery in 1865, African Americans had been systematically denied an equal place in American society. While no Southern-style system of formal race segregation existed in the North, an informal one certainly did. Blacks were not the only group to suffer from race prejudice. In Wisconsin, Native Americans and Mexicans faced similar plights. Civil rights activism was nothing new to postwar America. The National Association for the Advancement of Colored People (NAACP), the leading civil rights organization in the nation, was founded during the Progressive Era. But after the horrifying events of World War II, the issue of racism in America could no longer be ignored. The struggle for racial equality was one of the most important issues in postwar Wisconsin society and politics.

In the 1950s and early 1960s, civil rights activities focused on the South, where most African Americans lived. Dr. Martin Luther King, Jr. led a crusade to end segregation and win back voting rights for blacks through nonviolent direct action. Young black college students staged "sit-ins" at segregated facilities. Northern cities such as Milwaukee were little better than the South, however. Milwaukee's African Americans lived within very strict social, economic, and geographic boundaries. By 1960, black Milwaukee was still confined to the north side of town. Landlords refused to rent to blacks outside of the Core, and restrictive housing covenants and the scheming of real-estate agents kept them from purchasing homes outside of it. Segregated housing meant segregated schools, with Core schools getting less attention from the school board. Continued job discrimination kept most African Americans at the low end of income scales. There were tensions with police. Many blacks felt that the Milwaukee police department was more of an occupying force than a force for their protection. Inspired by events in the South and driven by circumstances at home, civil rights activists in Milwaukee intensified their work. By 1963, the NAACP, the Urban League, and the Congress of Racial Equality all had active chapters in Milwaukee. In response to the growing pressure for civil rights reform, city officials counseled patience and urged a gradual "step by step" approach to improving the city's race relations. It was a formula for disaster. Milwaukee's first organized civil rights protests occurred in August 1963 after a member of a community relations commission made a number of remarks offensive to African Americans. It galvanized Milwaukee's civil rights community.

By 1964, civil rights activists focused on school desegregation, organizing several boycotts of public schools and picketing the homes of school board members. The NAACP also sued the Milwaukee public schools. Although the NAACP eventually won the case, it remained tied up in the courts for years, delaying meaningful school desegregation. America was making progress on civil rights, such as the Civil Rights Act of 1964 and the Voting Rights Act of 1965, but that progress was slow and incomplete. In 1967, racial tensions in Milwaukee exploded. In July, an altercation between African Americans and police sparked eight days of disturbances on Milwaukee's north side, resulting in the deployment of 4,800 National Guard troops. Three people died. In August, marchers began to protest the city's steadfast refusal to pass an open housing law. On August 28, more than 200 members of the NAACP's Youth League, joined by a white Roman Catholic priest named James E. Groppi, marched from the

Father James Groppi with young civil rights activists. They have all joined hands and are singing. Circa 1968.

north side to the south side. They crossed the 16th Street Bridge, dubbed the "longest bridge in the world" since it connected "Poland and Africa." They continued south to Lincoln Avenue, and then east to Kosciuszko Park. There they met a crowd of 8,000 angry whites, some of whom shouted slogans like "we want slaves" and "white power." A march along the same route the next day was met by 13,000 whites who threw rocks at the marchers and burned Groppi in effigy. The violent confrontations were a tremendous shock for Wisconsinites, who like to view themselves as progressive and tolerant. Marches continued for 200 straight days, and an open housing ordinance was finally passed in 1968.

The African-American struggle for civil rights awakened Americans to the troubles of other minority groups. In 1966, migrant Mexican farm workers marched from Wautoma to Madison to protest economic exploitation. The 1960s also stirred activism among the state's Native Americans. By the mid-twentieth century, Indian life was under severe stress. Indian reservations, to which Native Americans had been confined a century earlier, were among the poorest places in the United States. After World War II, reformers in the Bureau of Indian Affairs claimed that the reservations were holding Indians back from success and advocated a policy of "termination," whereby tribal status would be revoked and Native Americans would become ordinary citizens. One of the first tribes targeted for termination was the Menominee, whose lumber mill made them among the most prosperous in the nation. Fearing economic dislocation and the erosion of their traditional culture, the Menominee resisted, but termination came anyway. In 1961, the Menominee Reservation ceased to exist, and the lands became Menominee County. All tribally owned property was transferred to a private corporation, Menominee Enterprises. Although well intended, termination was a disaster. Menominee County was the smallest and poorest in the state. Federal support was withdrawn, but the county had too small of a tax base to support basic services like police and fire protection. The county's only hospital was forced to close, and land was sold to non-Indians for cash. By 1970, tribal members began lobbying Washington to reverse termination, and in 1973 the Menominee won back their tribal status.

The Native American civil rights movement, like that for African Americans, also had a militant stage. The American Indian Movement (AIM), formed in Minneapolis in 1968, began to occupy abandoned properties they believed had been illegally seized from Native Americans, such as the 1969 occupation of Alcatraz Island in California. AIM members seized a Milwaukee Coast Guard station in 1971. Wisconsin's most dramatic confrontation occurred near Gresham in 1975. On New Year's Day, armed militants of the Menominee Warrior Society occupied the abandoned Alexian Brothers novitiate near the Menominee Reservation with the hope of turning it into a tribal hospital. "We are prepared to die," claimed the warriors. Local police and the National Guard surrounded the facility. Joining the militants were Milwaukee civil rights activist James Groppi and actor Marlon Brando, a champion of Indian rights. Some angry nearby residents took pot shots at the novitiate. "It was a little like Disneyland at the beginning," Brando said of his participation. "And then when we were up on the roof and the bullets started to fly all around us, then there was a certain kind of reality." Many Menominee leaders did not support such violent and confrontational tactics, and the occupation caused deep divisions among tribal leaders. The occupation ended after 34 days with several militants jailed.

Native Americans found much more success in pursuing their treaty rights. In nineteenth-century treaties, Indians often retained off-reservation economic rights that the government subsequently failed to honor. In the 1837 and 1842 land cession treaties, the Ojibwe were granted off-reservation fishing rights, but Wisconsin officials prevented the Indians from exercising those rights, sometimes arresting Ojibwe "violators" who fished off the reservations without a license. In response, the tribe took a very American approach—they went to court. In 1983, the courts affirmed the Ojibwe's rights to fish in lakes off their reservations outside of the state's usual procedures. Fearful that Indians' "special" rights would ruin the region's tourist economy, some whites protested. During the late 1980s and early 1990s many tense confrontations occurred on the docks at northern Wisconsin lakes, especially in Oneida and Vilas Counties. Some even attacked the Native Americans with rocks and firearms, and police had to be called in to keep the peace. Indian legal savvy has also led to the proliferation of gambling casinos. Indian reservations fall under the jurisdiction of the federal government, where state powers are limited. Native Americans, in Wisconsin and other states, used their unique legal status to open gaming facilities. Tribes saw gaming as a way to raise revenue, employ members, and lessen dependence on federal assistance. During the 1980s, federal, state, and tribal officials negotiated a framework for Indian gaming in Wisconsin. Today, the Badger State contains sixteen Indian gaming facilities in all portions of the state, employing Indians and non-Indians alike.

Aldo Leopold

Aldo Leopold is recognized today as one of the founders of the modern environmental movement. A native of Iowa, Leopold received a Master's degree in forestry from Yale and entered the US Forest Service, where he served for nineteen years. Among the locations Leopold worked was the Forest Products Laboratory at the University of Wisconsin in Madison. In 1933, he became a professor of game management and agriculture at the university. Leopold began to view the environment as a living organism, and grew concerned that the activities of man were killing it. He believed that humans had to live with, not in opposition to, nature.

In 1935 he purchased a farm along the Wisconsin River, and began to restore the natural prairie environment. He spent many days living in an old chicken coop known as "The Shack," communing with nature and getting away from what he called "too much modernity." He died in 1948 fighting a grass fire. A year later, a collection of his essays was published entitled *A Sand County Almanac*—today a classic of environmental theory. The Aldo Leopold Foundation, based in Baraboo, is dedicated to the memory and ideals of Leopold. The foundation offers tours of Leopold's farm, including the shack he occupied and the lands he began to preserve. Reservations are required for the farm tours.

Leopold is not the only Wisconsin environmentalist of note. John Muir, founder of the Sierra Club, spent his boyhood on a farm in Marquette County during the 1850s, and US Senator Gaylord Nelson is credited with being the founder of Earth Day in 1970.

Aldo Leopold Foundation
PO Box 77, Baraboo, WI 53913
(608) 355-0279
www.aldoleopold.org

MADISON AND THE SIXTIES

One of the most colorful and controversial episodes in Wisconsin history involves the student movement in Madison during the 1960s and early 1970s. The University of Wisconsin was one of the largest universities in the nation, attracting students from all parts of the United States and around the world. As a meeting place of peoples and ideas, Madison was a particularly fertile ground for social and political activism. During the 1960s, the university's students and faculty blended East Coast intellectual trends with Wisconsin's own progressive traditions to create an exceptionally animated discourse about politics and society. Madison was, as one student activist phrased it, where "New York meets Oshkosh." Wisconsinites outside of Madison did not always appreciate the city's intellectual prominence, and frequently referred to it derisively as the "People's Republic of Madison" or "64 square miles surrounded by reality." But like it or not, Madison played a prominent role in the drama that was "The Sixties."

By the 1960s, many young baby boomers, then reaching the nation's colleges and universities, began to reject the middle-class values and lifestyles of their parents. Society had grown too conformist and bureaucratized, they believed, and the political system was unresponsive to the needs of ordinary people. They wanted an end to the constant threat of nuclear war with the Soviet Union. Activist students were also deeply disturbed by the state of race relations in the United States. It was the Vietnam War that turned a handful of student protesters into a mass movement. Activists saw the war not as a necessary step to halt the spread of communism, but rather as an example of aggressive American imperialism. The draft, and the prospect of having to fight in a war they did not agree with, also galvanized many college students against the war.

Madison was on the leading edge of student unrest. Madison's first significant antiwar rally took place on the steps of the Memorial Union in October 1963. With the introduction of US combat troops to Vietnam in 1965, protests grew larger and more frequent. Following the example set by Martin Luther King, Jr., early protests were nonviolent but confrontational. Students held mass rallies and staged sit-ins. A few young men publicly burned their draft cards. Each new deployment of US troops to Vietnam only increased the numbers of protesters in the streets. By 1967, Madison's protest rallies often involved thousands. The most frequent gathering place for rallies on the campus was the Library Mall. From there, students would typically march up State Street to the State Capitol, or to a campus location associated with the war. As protests grew larger and more confrontational, law enforcement became more aggressive in its attempts to quash them. In October 1967, students staged a sit-in at the university's Commerce (now Ingraham) Hall to stop the Dow Chemical Company, the producer of the incendiary napalm bomb, from recruiting engineers on campus. Police forcibly cleared the building with billy clubs swinging. A riot then broke out on the campus, at which police expended copious amounts of tear gas; scores of students and policemen ended up in local hospitals. By 1968, Madison's antiwar movement had expanded beyond the campus, and included local housewives, business people, religious leaders, and even veterans of the Vietnam War.

In addition to opposing the nation's political system, the country's youth also began to rebel against society's cultural conventions. Intertwined with political protest was the "counterculture." Young people known as "hippies" began to grow their hair long, wear tattered jeans, and flout sexual mores. The use of illegal drugs such as marijuana and LSD was also common. Once again, Madison was on the forefront of cultural change in the 1960s. Counter-cultural communities emerged, especially along West Mifflin Street, a few blocks from the campus. The area became known as "Miffland," and residents declared it a "liberated zone" from the rest of society. In the heart of the neighborhood was the Mifflin Street Co-op, where a portrait of Vietnamese leader Ho Chi Minh hung in the front window. In May 1969, the denizens of Miffland planned to hold an end-of-the-semester block party, but the city refused to issue the required permit. The students decided to hold the party anyway, and police responded with force. During the Mifflin Street disturbances the local alderman, a student activist named Paul Soglin, was arrested and given an involuntary haircut by the police. Officers treated several other students to what became known as a "Soglin cut." Interestingly, Soglin was elected mayor of Madison in 1973, thanks to the support of 18- to 21-year-old voters recently enfranchised by the 26th Amendment. Discouraged by city police and university officials, the "Mifflin Street Block Party" has become an annual—albeit unofficial—event on the social calendar of University of Wisconsin students.

Henry Aaron

The Green Bay Packers dominate Wisconsin's professional sports scene, but they are not the only team to bring a major league sports title to the Badger State. The Milwaukee Bucks won the National Basketball Association championship in 1971, and the Milwaukee Braves won baseball's World Series in 1957. The key player for the Braves' championship team that year was right fielder Henry "Hank" Aaron.

Hank Aaron was born in Mobile, Alabama on February 5, 1934. As a teenager he landed a job hauling ice, and at the age of 15 played for the Mobile Black Bears, a semi-professional team. Scouts recognized his talents instantly and young Hank began to work his way up through the ranks of professional baseball. At age 18 he signed a contract with the Indianapolis Clowns of the Negro American League, and a year later the Boston Braves—which shortly thereafter moved to Milwaukee—signed him and placed him in their minor league system. He played for the Braves' farm team in Eau Claire, Wisconsin and then moved to the club in Jacksonville, Florida. He was one of the first black players to play on integrated teams in the South and despite receiving several death threats won Most Valuable Player honors. On Opening Day 1954, Aaron made his debut with the Milwaukee Braves—one of the first African Americans to play in the big leagues. In his first year he hit a respectable .280 and batted in 13 home runs. He was just getting started.

Over the next two decades, Aaron rewrote the baseball record book and made the Braves a National League powerhouse. The Braves defeated the New York Yankees in the 1957 World Series. The Braves and Yankees met again the following year, but this time New York prevailed. In 1965 the Braves moved to Atlanta—causing considerable heartache in Milwaukee—and Aaron went with them. In Atlanta on April 8, 1974 he hit home run number 715, surpassing Babe Ruth's longstanding record. Aaron returned to Milwaukee in 1975 to play with the new Milwaukee Brewers, where he finished off his illustrious career the following year. In all, "Hammering Hank" hit 755 home runs, most of them playing for Milwaukee—and all of them without the assistance of steroids. Aaron is still fondly remembered in the Badger State. Milwaukee County Stadium, the scene of many Aaron triumphs, has since been replaced with Miller Park. In the parking lot of Miller Park, a plaque marks the spot where Aaron's last home run fell. Winding its way through the heart of Milwaukee near Miller Park is the Henry Aaron State Trail, named in honor Wisconsin's greatest baseball legend.

By 1969, some in the student protest movement abandoned nonviolence. Battles between police and students in the streets of Madison increased in frequency and intensity. Protesters also took to smashing shop windows and other forms of vandalism. Some even began firebombing locations around Madison associated with the military, such as the university's ROTC facilities in the Old Red Gym. The Wisconsin National Guard was twice called to campus to quell disturbances; first during the black student strike of 1969, and then again in 1970 when students protested the US invasion of Cambodia. The sight of armed soldiers in the streets, the smashed glass and burned-out buildings, and the ever-present smell of tear gas wafting through the air, led many observers to describe Madison as a "war zone." For some, it was. A fringe of revolutionary extremists declared their intention to wage war against the US government. In August 1970, a small cell of radicals known as the New Year's Gang exploded a bomb next to the Army Mathematics Research Center, located in the east wing of Sterling Hall on the university campus. The blast left a gaping hole in the side of the building, and was heard 30 miles away. It also killed a late-working researcher. Three of the four bombers were captured and sent to prison; one was never apprehended. It was the most destructive act of domestic terrorism in American history until the 1995 Oklahoma City bombing.

The Sterling Hall bombing profoundly affected Madison and the rest of the nation. It forced Americans to face the realities of violent political confrontation, and led to a retreat from violence on the part of both protesters and police. Some have credited the bombing with effectively ending America's student movement altogether, though the gradual reduction of American troops in Vietnam after 1970 also contributed to the decline in protest activities. By the time the United States finally pulled out of Vietnam in 1973, Madison's student movement was a shadow of its former self. Though Madison remained a center of social and political activism long afterward, the city became a much more tranquil place. The University of Wisconsin campus has changed in many ways since the 1960s, but some parts of the campus look much the same today as they did during the heyday of the student movement. Campus landmarks, including the Library Mall, Memorial Union, and the Old Red Gym, remain. Sterling Hall and adjacent buildings still bear the scars of the 1970 bombing. West Mifflin Street appears much as it did in the '60s.

In the years that followed, Americans would continue to debate the meaning of the 1960s, and whether or not the antiwar movement and counterculture were positive steps toward a more free and just society, or a dangerous step away from traditional values. The experiences of that decade shaped the worldview of the baby-boom generation, and greatly influenced the nation's social, political, and foreign-policy discussions. Baby boomers still fight bitterly about those days, and probably always will. The 1960s were among the most turbulent years in American history, and Madison was at the center of the political, social, and intellectual forces that shaped those eventful and unsettling times.

To the Twenty-First Century

Life in Wisconsin has grown considerably more relaxed since the 1960s, but not many in the Badger State complain. The last decades of the twentieth century saw few dramatic events, but important social trends continued to shape Wisconsin life, such as suburban sprawl and urban poverty. Immigration remains an important part of Wisconsin's story. Since 1970, most immigrants to the United States have come from developing countries in Africa, Asia, and Latin America, a trend clearly seen in Wisconsin. By 2004, for example, 12 percent of the population of Barron, a small city in northwestern Wisconsin, was composed of immigrants from the African nation of Somalia, attracted to the area by meatpacking jobs. The most significant increases have come from Latinos, who are today America's largest ethnic minority. As in earlier periods, immigration remains a controversial topic. In 2006, Representative F. James Sensenbrenner of Wisconsin co-sponsored a bill in Congress to tighten the nation's immigration laws, including a crackdown on illegal immigration. The proposal set off protests across the United States, especially among Latinos, who felt such a crackdown could lead to discrimination against all Spanish-speaking peoples. Sensenbrenner's home state was no exception. In May of that year, anywhere from 15,000 (police estimate) to 70,000 (organizer estimate) participated in the "Day without Immigrants" march in Milwaukee to demonstrate the resolve and growing strength of the state's immigrant population. As the twenty-first century began, immigration was not nearly the force in Wisconsin life than it was a century before, but was nonetheless an important one. In the Badger State today, 7.3 percent of residents speak a language other than English at home.

Politically, Wisconsin remains equally divided between Democrats and Republicans. The state has lost congressional representation and electoral votes as Sunbelt states have grown at faster rates, but in some ways Wisconsin remains at the center of American politics. At the dawn of the twenty-first century, Wisconsin and other Midwestern states emerged as key swing states in national elections. Though reduced in number, Wisconsin's electoral votes are highly coveted by both major parties. Wisconsin does not have nearly the electoral prominence of New Hampshire or neighboring Iowa, but travelers to the Badger State in presidential election years might well see candidates on the campaign trail. Wisconsin's tradition of political reform lives on. During the 1990s, Governor Tommy Thompson (a Republican) gained notoriety for his efforts to reform welfare programs, and US Senator Russ Feingold (a Democrat) emerged as one of the nation's most important voices for campaign finance reform and civil liberties protections. A major corruption scandal in Madison broke in 2002, however, and led to convictions for some of the state's most powerful elected leaders— Democrats and Republicans alike—tarnishing Wisconsin's reputation for squeaky-clean politics. The extent to which the legacy of La Follette survives in twenty-first-century Wisconsin is open to question.

Agriculture remains a vital part of Wisconsin's economy, but it has undergone some substantial changes. Wisconsin retains the nickname "America's Dairyland," but the title has not gone unchallenged. California has surpassed the Badger State in the production of butter, milk, and even cheese. One of the most important and controversial changes to Wisconsin agriculture has been the decline in the number of family-owned farms. The number of dairy farms, for example, decreased from roughly 64,000 in 1970 to just 22,600 in 1998. Family farms have had increasing difficulty competing with large agribusinesses, which have bought up and consolidated many farms. Such businesses have a tremendous advantage over the family farmer in the ability to purchase the equipment and new technologies necessary to stay competitive. In fact, many family farms have gone bankrupt. One can drive through Wisconsin's rich country-side today and encounter a farm foreclosure auction. Many see the rise of agribusiness and the decline of family farms as an inevitable market development. Others see tragedy in the loss of a way of life that has characterized life in the Badger State since territorial times. Wisconsin made a name for itself in agriculture, but the number of state residents actually engaged in the practice of it is dwindling.

Wisconsin's industrial economy has also undergone important changes. For one, business mergers and takeovers have meant that many Wisconsin companies are now controlled by outsiders. Milwaukee's Miller Brewing Company, for example, was for many years a subsidiary of the Philip Morris Companies, and in 2002 was purchased by South African Breweries, forming a conglomerate known as SABMiller. The years after 1970 saw a decline in the heavy industries that had characterized life in Wisconsin cities for so long. The Cold War stimulated the aerospace and computer industries, which developed primarily in the Sunbelt states. Foreign competition cut into the markets of the automobile and heavy-machinery industries. Complaining of high taxes and unionized workers, many companies moved factories out of Wisconsin, sending jobs to the Sunbelt states or overseas. In the recession of the early 1980s, Wisconsin's unemployment rate reached 11.7 percent, the highest since the Great Depression. Some localities had even higher rates. Wisconsin and other states in the Midwest and Northeast have become known as the "Rust Belt" due to the decline of traditional heavy industry. Wisconsin's economy was better balanced and diversified than many of its neighbors—no single industry or company was dominant—and was able to weather the economic transition relatively well. As any traveler to Wisconsin today will note, manufacturing

Les Paul

One of the most influential figures in popular music after World War II was Wisconsin native Les Paul. Born Lester Polfus in Waukesha in 1915, Paul's interest in music came early. He learned to play harmonica at the age of eight—inspired by a local ditch digger—but soon switched to guitar. As a boy, he frequently rode his bicycle to see performers in local taverns. He began performing as well (often in a sailor suit), adopting the name "Rhubarb Red." He left high school to pursue a career in music, performing in cites such as St. Louis, Chicago, and New York. He was a versatile guitarist, gaining respect in the genres of country and jazz music. In 1937 he received national exposure while playing for bandleader Fred Waring. He then moved to California, where he played with the likes of Nat King Cole and Bing Crosby during the 1940s.

It was in the 1950s that Paul made his greatest contributions to popular music. He was a pioneer in the development of the solid-body electric guitar. In 1952, Gibson—one of the world's foremost guitar manufacturers—introduced its line of Les Paul guitars. Paul was also a pioneer in music recording technology. One of his most important innovations was the concept of "multi-tracking"—overlaying multiple recordings to create a deeper, richer sound. In 1949 he married Mary Ford, and together the couple recorded some of the most popular songs of the 1950s, including "How High the Moon," "Vaya con Dios," and "Mockin' Bird Hill." The couple divorced in 1963.

Les Paul's innovations came at the dawn of rock & roll music, which dominated popular music and youth culture after World War II. His recording techniques made this musical revolution possible, and Les Paul guitars remain popular with rock, jazz, and country artists today.

remains an integral part of the Wisconsin economy, but the Badger State is an active participant in the technological revolution as well. In 1998, for example, researchers at the University of Wisconsin developed the first human stem-cell lines, which many experts believe will revolutionize medicine.

One of Wisconsin's fastest-growing industries after World War II was tourism. The Badger State receives few international tourists, but has become an important regional travel destination, earning Wisconsin the nickname "playground of the Midwest." After World War II, Wisconsin Dells evolved into a massive Midwestern amusement center. Tourists have been attracted to the mystical scenery of the Dells since the nineteenth century, but beginning with Tommy Bartlett's water shows in the 1950s, a whole host of water parks, wax museums, and other gaudy attractions grew up around the area's sandstone canyons. Wisconsin Dells today boasts of being the "waterpark capital of the world." Door County, with its waterfront vistas and cool lake breezes, has been called the "Cape Cod of the Midwest," though thankfully it has avoided much of Cape Cod's commercialization. Wisconsin's reputation as a paradise for outdoor enthusiasts has only grown since World War II. Every year, sport fishing attracts thousands to the Northwoods, as well as lake port cities. Hunting remains important too. The state's annual gun deer-hunting season in November has taken on the equivalence of a holiday in Wisconsin culture. Thousands leave their jobs and families to sit in the cold woods hoping for a shot at a prize buck. Travelers should note that a leisurely walk though the forest in the late autumn without blaze orange can be dangerous. Driving along Wisconsin roads in November, travelers are likely to see cars and trucks streaming towards Milwaukee and other cities with two items strapped to the top—a dead deer and a Christmas tree.

Historic sites, museums, and other "cultural resources" also attract thousands of tourists to the Badger State. Wisconsin's long and illustrious history—from the Ice Age to the Space Age—has become an important part of the state's economy, generating millions of dollars annually. Increasingly, the state's future is tied to preserving its past.

Wisconsin's history is more than a mere market commodity, of course. It lies at the heart of Wisconsin life and culture. The traveler to Wisconsin who eats a bratwurst, tours a cheese factory, buys a *pa ndau*, or enjoys the quiet solitude of a Northwoods lake is partaking in activities deeply rooted in the state's history. Wisconsin might seem like an ordinary Midwestern state, but for travelers armed with an appreciation of the past, it becomes an extraordinary place.

Chronology of Major Events

10,000 BCE First human beings arrive in present-day Wisconsin
8000 BCE   Archaic phase of Native American development begins
500 BCE   Woodland phase of Native American development begins
800–1200   Effigy mound culture in southern Wisconsin
1000   Oneota and Middle Mississippian cultures begin in southern Wisconsin
c. 1600   Ojibwe Indians begin to enter present-day Wisconsin
1609   Samuel de Champlain founds Quebec
1621–23   French explorer Étienne Brûlé is believed to have explored the Lake Superior shoreline, including present-day Wisconsin

1634   Jean Nicolet believed to have landed at Green Bay

c. 1640   Potawatomie and other Indian tribes from the east move into Wisconsin seeking refuge from Iroquois attacks
1654   Groseilliers travels along the western shore of Lake Michigan
1659–60   Groseilliers–Radisson expedition in northern Wisconsin
1660s   Nicolas Perrot explores Wisconsin
1665   Father Allouez begins preaching at Chequamegon Bay
1671   Father Allouez founds St. Francis Xavier mission at De Pere
1673   Marquette–Joliet expedition passes through Wisconsin

1684   French establish Fort La Baye at Green Bay

1712–33   Mesquakie Wars in Wisconsin
1716   Battle of Butte des Morts
1754–63   French and Indian War in North America, a.k.a. Seven Years War; Wisconsin becomes British territory
1763   Pontiac's Rebellion in Great Lakes region
1775–83   American Revolution. Wisconsin becomes US territory
1812–15   War of 1812
1814   Battle of Prairie du Chien
1816   US Army establishes Forts Crawford and Howard
1820s–30s   Lead rush in southwestern Wisconsin
1825   Treaty of Prairie du Chien
1827   Winnebago War; Fort Winnebago established
1829–42   Native American land cessions
1831   Land surveying in Wisconsin begins
1832   Black Hawk War
1833   Milwaukee founded
1836   Wisconsin Territory created
1838   Territorial capital moved to Madison

The capitol building in Madison © Jeff Oien

1839   Freistadt, Wisconsin's first German settlement, is founded

1848   Statehood achieved on May 29

1851   Wisconsin's first railroad opens

1854   Joshua Glover incident in Racine and Milwaukee

1854   Republican Party founded in Ripon

1859   Presidential candidate Abraham Lincoln makes campaign swing through Wisconsin

1860   Sinking of *Lady Elgin*

1861–65   Civil War

1862   Port Washington draft riots

1871   Peshtigo Fire kills 1,200 to 1,500

1872   William Dempster Hoard founds the Wisconsin Dairyman's Association

1886   Bay View Massacre in Milwaukee

1890   Stephen Babcock develops butterfat test

1891   Ex-Congressman Robert La Follette claims that Senator Philetus Sawyer tried to bribe him, starting his career as political insurgent

1897   Robert La Follette gives his "Menace of the Machine" speech

1900   Robert La Follette elected governor

1906   Robert La Follette elected US senator from Wisconsin

1910   Peninsula State Park established

1910   Milwaukee reformer Francis E. McGovern elected governor

1911   Wisconsin passes America's first workers' compensation law, as well as numerous other progressive reforms

1912   Robert La Follette runs unsuccessfully for president

1912   Wisconsin voters reject women's suffrage in referendum

1916   Socialist Daniel Hoan elected mayor of Milwaukee

1917–18   United States involvement in World War I

1919   Green Bay Packers football team founded

1924   Robert La Follette again runs unsuccessfully for president

1925   Death of Robert La Follette; his son, Robert, Jr., elected to US Senate

1929–41   Great Depression ravages Wisconsin

1930   Philip La Follette, son of Robert La Follette, Sr., elected governor

1932   Philip La Follette defeated for reelection

1933   Milk strikes

1934   Kohler strike erupts in violence

1934   La Follette brothers found Progressive Party; Philip elected governor, Robert, Jr. returned to Senate, and Progressive majority in state legislature

1938	Philip La Follette forms National Progressives of America, but his presidential bid fails
1941–45	United States involvement in World War II
1946	Progressive Party disbands
1946	Appleton Republican Joseph McCarthy defeats Robert La Follette, Jr. for US Senate seat
1950	McCarthy speech in Wheeling, West Virginia, beginning his rise to prominence
1954	McCarthy censured by US Senate
1957	Death of McCarthy; Democrat William Proxmire elected to his US Senate seat
1958	Wisconsin's first stretch of interstate highway opens
1958	Democrat Gaylord Nelson elected governor
1961	Termination of tribal status for the Menominee Indians
1967–68	Open housing marches in Milwaukee
1970	Bombing of Sterling Hall on University of Wisconsin campus
1973	Menominee tribal status restored
1975	Siege at Alexian Brothers novitiate near Gresham
1980–90s	Treaty rights confrontations in northern Wisconsin
1998	Researchers at the University of Wisconsin isolate the first human stem-cell lines
2002	Political corruption scandal in Madison begins, leading to convictions of several elected state officials
2006	Immigrant rights marches in Milwaukee

Special Events

Birkebeiner (ski race), Hayward, February
Cranberry Festival, Warrens, August
Ethnic festivals (numerous), Milwaukee, Summer
Experimental Aircraft Association Fly-in, Oshkosh, July
Fish Days, Port Washington, July
Lake Superior Big Top Chautauqua, Bayfield,
      June–September
Lumberjack World Championships, Hayward, July
Prairie du Chien Rendezvous, Prairie du Chien, June
Summerfest, Milwaukee, July
Syttende Mai (Norwegian Constitution Day), Stoughton,
      May
Tobacco Heritage Days, Edgerton, July
Wisconsin State Fair, West Allis, August
World Championship Snowmobile Derby, Eagle River,
      January
World Dairy Expo, Madison, September

Cultural Highlights

ART AND ARCHITECTURE

Aaron Bohrod (1907–1992) Painter, born in Chicago and served as artist-in-residence at the University of Wisconsin. Bohrod was a major force in the *Trompe-l'oeil* ("trick the eye") movement after World War II. The art gallery at the University of Wisconsin–Fox Valley campus is named in his honor.

John Steuart Curry (1897–1946) Painter, born in Kansas and served as artist-in-residence at the University of Wisconsin. Curry was one of most notable Midwestern regionalist painters of the twentieth century.

Georgia O'Keeffe (1887–1986). See page 167.

Frank Lloyd Wright (1867–1959). See page 152.

FILM AND STAGE

Don Ameche (1908–1993) Actor, born in Kenosha. His films include *The Three Musketeers*, *Heaven Can Wait*, and *Cocoon*.

Willem Dafoe (b. 1955) Actor, born in Appleton. His films include *Platoon*, *The Last Temptation of Christ*, and *Mississippi Burning*.

Chris Farley (1964–1997) Actor, born in Madison. He was a regular on the TV series *Saturday Night Live*.

Heather Graham (b. 1970) Actress, born in Milwaukee. Her films include *Boogie Nights* and *Even Cowgirls Get the Blues*.

Harry Houdini (1874–1926) Magician, born Erich Weiss and raised in Appleton. The History Museum at the Castle in Appleton contains Houdini-related exhibits, and has developed a Houdini walking tour of the downtown area.

Alfred Lunt (1893–1977) Actor, born in Milwaukee. Lunt and his wife, Lynne Fontaine, were Broadway notables who maintained a retreat called Ten Chimneys at Genessee Depot outside Milwaukee. Today Ten Chimneys is a museum.

Fred MacMurray (1908–1991) Actor, raised in Beaver Dam. His films include *Double Indemnity* and *The Absent-Minded Professor*. Also star of television program *My Three Sons*.

Fredric March (1897–1975) Actor, born in Racine. His films include *The Best Years of Our Lives* and *Inherit the Wind*. A theater at his alma mater, the University of Wisconsin, is named in his honor.

Spencer Tracy (1900–1967) Actor, born in Milwaukee. His films include *Boys' Town*, *Thirty Seconds Over Tokyo*, and *Guess Who's Coming to Dinner*.

Orson Welles (1916–1985) Actor and producer, born in Kenosha. His films include *Citizen Kane*, considered by many critics to be the greatest film ever made. He is also noted for 1938 radio broadcast of *War of the Worlds*, which was so realistic that it convinced many listeners, unnerved by the Great Depression and the rise of Nazi Germany, that an invasion from outer space was actually underway.

Gene Wilder (b. 1935) Actor and producer, born Jerome Silberman in Milwaukee. His films include *Willy Wonka and the Chocolate Factory*, *Blazing Saddles*, and *Young Frankenstein*.

LITERATURE

Edna Ferber (1885–1968). See page 178.

Zona Gale (1874–1938) Writer, born in Portage. Gale wrote often about small-town life with an eye toward social criticism.

Hamlin Garland (1860–1940) Writer, born in West Salem. Garland is best known for his portrayals of Gilded Age farm life in the Midwest. The Garland homestead in West Salem is today a museum.

Sterling North (1906–1974). Writer, born in Edgerton, North became a popular author of books for children, most notably *Rascal* (1963). North's boyhood home in Edgerton is now a museum dedicated to his life.

Frederick Jackson Turner (1861–1932) Historian, born in Portage. Turner is best known for his "frontier thesis," which states that it was the rigors of frontier life that produced a distinctive American culture.

Laura Ingalls Wilder (1867–1957) Writer, born near Pepin. Wilder is internationally famous for her historical fiction based on her childhood on the frontier. One of her books, *Little House in the Big Woods*, is set in Pepin. The Laura Ingalls Wilder Historical Museum is located in Pepin.

Thornton Wilder (1897–1975) Writer, born in Madison. His works include *The Bridge at San Luis Rey*, *Our Town*, and *The Skin of Our Teeth*.

MUSIC

BoDeans. Rock & roll group fomed in Waukesha in 1983, most noted for their 1993 hit "Closer to Free."

Chordettes. Vocal group formed in Sheboygan, most noted for their 1954 hit "Mr. Sandman."

Garbage. Rock & roll group formed in Madison in 1994. Band member Butch Vig of Viroqua is also a noted record producer, having worked with such bands as Nirvana and Smashing Pumpkins.

Woody Herman (1913–1987) Jazz musician, born in Milwaukee. He was the leader of one of the most popular big bands of the 1940s.

Al Jarreau (b. 1940) Jazz singer, born in Milwaukee. He has won six Grammy awards for his work including Best Jazz Vocal Performance.

Liberace (1919–1987) Pianist, born Wladziu Valentino Liberace in West Allis. Known for his outrageous dress, Liberace was a Las Vegas favorite.

Les Paul (b. 1915). See page 211.

Steve Miller Band. Rock & roll group formed in Madison in 1974, noted for numerous hit singles, including "Take the Money and Run," "Jungle Love," and "Fly Like an Eagle."

Violent Femmes. Rock & roll group formed in Milwaukee in 1980, noted for post-punk classics including "Blister in the Sun" and "Kiss Off."

Contact Information

Historic Madison
PO Box 2721
Madison, WI 53701
(608) 233-9394
danenet.wicip.org/hmi

Historic Milwaukee
828 North Broadway, Suite 110
Milwaukee, WI 53202
(414) 277-7795
www.historicmilwaukee.org

Milwaukee County Historical Society
910 North Old World Third Street
Milwaukee, WI 53203
(414) 273-8288
www.milwaukeecountyhistsoc.org

Wisconsin Department of Tourism
201 West Washington Avenue
PO Box 8690
Madison WI 5370
(800) 432-8747
www.travelwisconsin.com

Wisconsin Historical Society
816 State Street
Madison, WI 53706
(608) 264-6400
www.wisconsinhistory.org

Sources and Further Reading

BOOKS

Barker, Brett. *Exploring Civil War Wisconsin: A Survival Guide for Researchers*. Madison: Wisconsin Historical Society, 2003.

Bates, Tom. *Rads: The 1970 Bombing of the Army Math Research Center at the University of Wisconsin and Its Aftermath*. New York: HarperCollins, 1993.

Birmingham, Robert, and Leslie Eisenberg. *Indian Mounds of Wisconsin*. Madison: University of Wisconsin Press, 2000.

Blakely, Harold. *The 32nd Infantry Division in World War II*. Madison: 32nd Infantry Division History Commission, 1957.

Bogue, Margaret. *Fishing the Great Lakes: An Environmental History, 1783–1933*. Madison: University of Wisconsin Press, 2000.

Buhle, Paul. *History and the New Left: Madison, Wisconsin, 1950–1970*. Philadelphia: Temple University Press, 1990.

Campbell, James. *The Ghost Mountain Boys: Their Epic March and Terrifying Battle for New Guinea—The Forgotten War of the South Pacific*. New York: Crown, 2007.

Carver, Jonathan. *Travels Through the Interior Parts of North America* (1778). Available online though the American Journeys collection of the Wisconsin Historical Society at www.americanjourneys.org.

Christofferson, Bill. *The Man from Clear Lake: Earth Day Founder Gaylord Nelson*. Madison: University of Wisconsin Press, 2004.

Conzen, Kathleen. *Immigrant Milwaukee, 1836–1860: Accommodation and Community in a Frontier City*. Cambridge, MA: Harvard University Press, 1976.

Cooper, John M., Jr. *Pivotal Decades: The United States, 1900–1920*. New York: Norton, 1992.

Current, Richard N. *Wisconsin: A History*. Champaign: University of Illinois Press, 2001.

Ferber, Edna. *Come and Get It*. Madison: Prairie Oak Press, 1988.

Gjerde, Jon. *From Peasants to Farmers: The Migration from Balestrand, Norway to the Upper Midwest*. New York: Cambridge University Press, 1985.

Gough, Robert. *Farming the Cutover: A Social History of Northern Wisconsin, 1900–1940*. Lawrence: University Press of Kansas, 1997.

Gurda, John. *The Making of Milwaukee*. Milwaukee: Milwaukee County Historical Society, 1999.

Holmes, Fred L. *Old World Wisconsin: Around Europe in the Badger State*. Eau Claire: E.M. Hale, 1944.

Hurley, Alfred. *Billy Mitchell: Crusader for Air Power*. Bloomington: University of Indiana Press, 1975.

Jensen, Joan. *Calling This Place Home: Women on the Wisconsin Frontier, 1850–1925*. St. Paul: Minnesota Historical Society Press, 2006.

Kinzie, Juliette. *Wau Bun: The "Early Day" in the Northwest* (1857). Available online through the American Memory collection of the Library of Congress at memory.loc.gov/ammem/index.html.

Klement, Frank. *Wisconsin in the Civil War: The Home Front and the Battle Front, 1861–1865*. Madison: Wisconsin Historical Society, 1997.

La Follette, Robert. *La Follette's Autobiography: A Personal Narrative of Personal Experiences*. Madison: Robert M. La Follette, 1913.

Leary, James P. *Wisconsin Folklore*. Madison: University of Wisconsin Press, 1999.

Leopold, Aldo. *A Sand County Almanac: And Sketches Here and There*. New York: Oxford University Press, 1987.

Loew, Patti. *Indian Nations of Wisconsin: Histories of Endurance and Renewal*. Madison: Wisconsin Historical Society, 2001.

Lurie, Nancy O. *Wisconsin Indians*. Rev. ed. Madison: Wisconsin Historical Society, 2002.

Madaus, Howard Michael and Richard H. Zeitlin. *The Flags of the Iron Brigade*. Madison: Wisconsin Veterans Museum, 1995.

Manchester, William. *American Caesar: Douglas MacArthur, 1880–1964*. Boston: Little, Brown, 1978.

Maraniss, David. *They Marched into Sunlight: War and Peace in Vietnam and America, October 1967*. New York: Simon and Schuster, 2004.

McBride, Genevieve, ed. *Women's Wisconsin: From Native Matriarchies to the New Millennium*. Madison: Wisconsin Historical Society, 2005.

McBride, Sarah. *History Just Ahead: A Guide to Wisconsin's Historical Markers*. Madison: Wisconsin Historical Society, 1999.

Nesbit, Robert C. *Wisconsin: A History*. Revised by William S. Thompson. Madison: University of Wisconsin Press, 2004.

Nolan, Alan. *The Iron Brigade: A Military History*. Bloomington: Indiana University Press, 1994.

Oshinsky, David. *A Conspiracy So Immense: The World of Joe McCarthy*. 2nd ed. New York: Oxford University Press, 2005.

Ostergren, Robert, and Thomas Vale, eds. *Wisconsin Land and Life*. Madison: University of Wisconsin Press, 1997.

Paul, Barbara D., and Paul Justus. *Wisconsin History: An Annotated Bibliography*. Westport, CT: Greenwood Press, 1999.

Rosebrough, Amy, and Bobby Malone. *Water Panthers, Bears, and Thunderbirds: Exploring Wisconsin's Effigy Mounds*. Madison: Wisconsin Historical Society, 2003.

Roush, James. *The 32nd Division: "Les Terribles."* Paducah, KY: Turner Publishing Company, 1992.

Sasgen, Peter. *Red Scorpion: The War Patrols of the USS Rasher*. New York: Pocket Star Books, 1995.

Schoolcraft, Henry R. *Personal Memoirs of a Residence of Thirty Years with the Indian Tribes on the American Frontiers* (1851). Available online through the American Memory collection of the Library of Congress at memory.loc.gov/ammem/index.html.

Thelen, David P. *The New Citizenship: The Origins of Progressivism in Wisconsin, 1885–1900*. Columbia: University of Missouri Press, 1972.

———. *Robert M. La Follette and the Insurgent Spirit*. Madison: University of Wisconsin Press, 1984.

Thwaites, Reuben Gold, ed. *The Jesuit Relations and Allied Documents*, Vol. LIX, 1899. Available online through Creighton University at puffin.creighton.edu/jesuit/relations.

Trask, Kerry. *Black Hawk: The Battle for the Heart of America*. New York: Henry Holt, 2005.

————. *Fire Within; A Civil War Narrative from Wisconsin.* Kent, OH: Kent State University Press, 1995.

Trotter, Joe William. *Black Milwaukee: The Making of an Industrial Proletariat, 1915–45.* Urbana: University of Illinois Press, 1985.

Unger, Nancy. *Fighting Bob La Follette: The Righteous Reformer.* Chapel Hill: University of North Carolina Press, 2000.

Waller, Douglas. *A Question of Loyalty: Gen. Billy Mitchell and the Court-Martial That Gripped the Nation.* New York: HarperCollins, 2004.

Weisberger, Bernard. *La Follettes of Wisconsin: Love and Politics in Progressive America.* Madison: University of Wisconsin Press, 1994.

Wilder, Laura Ingalls. *Little House in the Big Woods.* New York: Harper Trophy, 1981.

Wisconsin Cartographers' Guild. *Wisconsin's Past and Present: A Historical Atlas.* Madison: University of Wisconsin Press, 1998.

Wisconsin Historical Society. *Collections of the State Historical Society of Wisconsin*, 20 vols. Madison: Wisconsin Historical Society, 1888–1931.

Wisconsin Historical Society. *The History of Wisconsin.* 5 vols. Madison: Wisconsin Historical Society, 1973-1990.

Woodward, David, et. al., eds. *Cultural Map of Wisconsin: A Cartographic Portrait of the State.* Madison: University of Wisconsin Press, 1996.

Wyman, Mark. *Wisconsin Frontier.* Bloomington: University of Indiana Press, 1998.

Zaniewski, Kazimierz, and Carol Rosen. *The Atlas of Ethnic Diversity in Wisconsin.* Madison: University of Wisconsin Press, 1999.

Zeitlin, Richard H. *Old Abe the War Eagle.* Madison: Wisconsin Historical Society, 1986.

DOCUMENTARY FILMS

Burns, Ken and Lynn Novick. *Frank Lloyd Wright.* Alexandria, VA: PBS Home Video, 1997.

Derks, Mik and David Hestad. *Wisconsin WW II Stories.* Madison: Wisconsin Public Television, 2004.

Erickson, Dave. *The Rush for Grey Gold.* Spring Green, WI:

Ootek Productions and Wisconsin Public Television, 1998.

Hermann, Edward and Phyllis Berg-Pigorsch. *The Germans Are Coming*. Madison: Wisconsin Public Television and Deutsche Welle, 1991.

Sabol, Steve. *The Complete History of the Green Bay Packers*. New York: NFL Films, 2003.

Silber, Glenn, and Barry Alexander Brown. *An American Ism: Joe McCarthy*. Madison: First Run Films, 1987.

————. *The War at Home*. Madison: First Run Features Home Video, 2003.

WEBSITES

American Journeys (Wisconsin Historical Society).
www.americanjourneys.org

Dictionary of Wisconsin History
(Wisconsin Historical Society).
www.wisconsinhistory.org/dictionary/

Mississippi Valley Archaeology Center (UW–La Crosse).
www.uwlax.edu/MVAC/

National Register of Historic Places—Wisconsin.
www.nationalregisterofhistoricplaces.com/WI/state.html

Pioneering the Upper Midwest: Books from Michigan, Minnesota, and Wisconsin
(American Memory, Library of Congress).
www.memory.loc.gov/ammem/umhtml/umhome.html

State of Wisconsin Collection
(University of Wisconsin Digital Collections).
www.digicoll.library.wisc.edu/WI/

Turning Points in Wisconsin History
(Wisconsin Historical Society).
www.wisconsinhistory.org/turningpoints/

Wisconsin Electronic Reader
(University of Wisconsin Libraries).
www.library.wisc.edu/etext/WIReader/Contents.html

Wisconsin History Day by Day. **www.wishistory.com**

Wisconsin Local Histories Network. **www.wlhn.org**

Wisconsin Pioneer Experience
(University of Wisconsin Digital Collections).
**www.digicoll.library.wisc.edu/WI/subcollections/
wipionexpAbout.shtml**

Wisconsin Public Land Survey Records:
Original Field Notes and Plat Maps.
www.digicoll.library.wisc.edu/SurveyNotes/

Wisconsin's French Connections. **www.uwgb.edu/wisfrench/**

Wisconsin Stories (Wisconsin Public Television).
www.wisconsinstories.org

Index of Place Names